The Earliest Inhabitants

The Earliest Inhabitants

The Dynamics of the Jamaican Taíno

Edited by

Lesley-Gail Atkinson

The University of the West Indies Press
Mona • St Augustine • Cave Hill • Global • Five Islands

University of the West Indies Press
1A Aqueduct Flats   Mona
Kingston 7   Jamaica
www.uwipress.com

© 2006 by Lesley-Gail Atkinson

All rights reserved. Published 2006. Reprinted 2025

10 09 08 07 06   5 4 3 2 1

CATALOGUING IN PUBLICATION DATA

Earliest inhabitants: the dynamics of the Jamaican Taíno / edited by
Lesley-Gail Atkinson
p. cm.
Includes bibliographic references.

ISBN: 978-976-640-149-8 (976-640-149-7)

1. Taino Indians – Jamaica – Antiquities. 2. Indians of the West Indies – Jamaica – Antiquities. 3. Taino Indians – Jamaica – Ethnobotany. 4. Excavations (Archaeology) – Jamaica. 5. Indian pottery – Jamaica. 6. Jamaica – History. I. Atkinson, Lesley-Gail.

F1875.E37 2006   972.92

Cover illustration: Anna Ruth Henriques, *Cocoa Zemi* (2006).
Reproduced with kind permission of the artist.

Book and cover design by Robert Harris.
E-mail: roberth@cwjamaica.com

Set in AdobeCaslon 10.5/14.5 x 27
Printed in the United States of America.

This book is dedicated to two men who have
influenced my life tremendously.

In loving memory of my
grandfather, Ernest Aaron Adair,
for loving me unconditionally, and for teaching me
the significance of laughter. In my heart you'll always
be "my favourite guy"!

and

Dr James W. Lee, founder and past president
of the Archaeological Society of Jamaica,
for your decades of contribution to
Jamaican archaeology, and for your
initiative and extensive research, which laid the
foundations for Jamaican prehistoric archaeology.

Thank you!

Contents

List of Illustrations / ix

List of Tables / xii

Preface / xiii

Acknowledgements / xv

Introduction / 1

Section 1 Assessment and Excavation of Taíno Sites

1   The Development of Jamaican Prehistory / 13
William F. Keegan and *Lesley-Gail Atkinson*

2   The Taíno Settlement of the Kingston Area / 34
Philip Allsworth-Jones, Gerald Lalor, George Lechler, Simon F. Mitchell, Esther Z. Rodriques and *Mitko Vutchkov*

3   The Pre-Columbian Site of Chancery Hall, St Andrew / 47
Philip Allsworth-Jones, Anthony Gouldwell, George Lechler, Simon F. Mitchell, Selvenious Walters, Jane Webster and *Robert Young*

4   Excavations at Green Castle, St Mary / 69
Philip Allsworth-Jones and *Kit Wesler*

5   The Impact of Land-Based Development on Taíno Archaeology in Jamaica / 75
Andrea Richards

Section 2 Taíno Exploitation of Natural Resources

6   Notes on the Natural History of Jamaica / 89
Wendy A. Lee

7	The Exploitation and Transformation of Jamaica's Natural Vegetation / 97 *Lesley-Gail Atkinson*	
8	Early Arawak Subsistence Strategies: The Rodney's House Site of Jamaica / 113 *Sylvia Scudder*	

Section 3 Analysis of Taíno Archaeological Data

9	Petrography and Source of Some Arawak Rock Artefacts from Jamaica / 131 *M. John Roobol* and *James W. Lee*
10	Jamaican Taíno Pottery / 146 *Norma Rodney-Harrack*
11	Jamaican Redware / 153 *James W. Lee*
12	Taíno Ceramics from Post-Contact Jamaica / 161 *Robyn P. Woodward*

Section 4 Taíno Art Forms

13	The Petroglyphs of Jamaica / 177 *James W. Lee*
14	*Zemís*, Trees and Symbolic Landscapes: Three Taíno Carvings from Jamaica / 187 *Nicholas Saunders* and *Dorrick Gray*

References / 199

Contributors / 214

Illustrations

A.1 Map of the sites mentioned in the text / 4–5
1.1 Irving Rouse's chronology of the series and subseries of cultures in the West Indies / 21
1.2 Ostionan pottery from Jamaica / 23
1.3 Chican pottery from Hispaniola / 23
1.4 Jamaican Meillacan boat-shaped vessel / 24
1.5 Meillacan pottery from Haiti / 24
1.6 Local styles in the Ostionan, Meillacan and Chican subseries / 25
2.1 Taíno sites in the Kingston area / 35
2.2 Histograms of the major elements in the pottery samples compared with the levels in the soils from the Kingston area / 43
3.1 Taíno skulls *in situ* / 48
3.2 Earthenware pot containing infant remains / 48
3.3 Beads associated with the skull / 49
3.4 JNHT excavations at Chancery Hall / 52
3.5 Stratigraphy of Chancery Hall / 56
4.1 Location of Green Castle / 70
4.2 Green Castle contour map / 71
4.3 Burial 1 / 73
4.4 Burial 2 / 73
5.1 Road cutting through Taíno site at Barbican, Hanover / 80
5.2 Road cutting through a portion of the Toby Abbott Taíno site / 81
5.3 Chancery Hall Taíno site, St Andrew / 83
5.4 Long Mountain prior to development / 84
5.5 Construction activity at the Long Mountain site / 84
6.1 Jamaican *hutia* or coney / 95

6.2	Hawksbill turtle / 95	
7.1	Fernández de Oviedo's illustration of Taínan *caney* / 101	
7.2	Dugout canoe from Black River, St Elizabeth / 102	
7.3	William Keegan explaining the use of the wild cane / 103	
7.4	Two-notched net sinkers / 104	
7.5	Four-notched net sinkers / 104	
7.6	The annatto plant / 104	
7.7	Members of the Paradise Park 2001 excavations measuring the *Ceiba* tree / 112	
9.1	Simplified geological map of Jamaica showing parishes / 134	
10.1	Redware, White Marl and Montego Bay styles / 147	
10.2	Normal boat-shaped vessel / 148	
10.3	Round vessel / 149	
10.4	Handled Taíno bowl / 150	
10.5	Handles, lugs and decorative motifs / 150	
10.6	Taíno bowl with hourglass-type handle / 151	
10.7	Laterally perforated handle / 151	
10.8	Ribbon decoration / 151	
10.9	Cross-hatch decoration / 152	
11.1	Map of Jamaican Redware sites / 154	
11.2	*Burén* rim profiles / 156	
11.3	Type I handles – plain "D" handles / 157	
11.4	Type II handles / 157	
11.5	Type III handles / 158	
11.6	Other handle variations / 158	
12.1	Map of St Ann's Bay, Jamaica / 162	
12.2	Distribution of New Seville and Taíno ceramics / 165	
12.3	Meillac ware: (a) boat-shaped vessel; (b) round bowl / 166	
12.4	Rim profiles / 167	
12.5	Decorated rim sherds / 167	
12.6	Spouted bowl / 168	
12.7	Taíno water bottle / 168	
12.8	New Seville ware bowls / 169	
12.9	New Seville ware: (a) pitcher; (b) pedestal cup / 170	
12.10	New Seville ware: (a) cup; (b) spout jug / 170	
12.11	New Seville ware: jug / 171	
12.12	New Seville pedestal cup / 171	
13.1	Map of cave art sites / 178	

13.2	Petroglyphs from Coventry and Cuckold Point / 180	
13.3	Petroglyphs from Gut River No. 1 / 180	
13.4	Petroglyphs from Reynold Bent, Milk River and near God's Well / 180	
13.5	Petroglyphs at Canoe Valley / 181	
13.6	Petroglyphs at Canoe Valley / 181	
13.7	Pictographs at Spot Valley / 183	
14.1	Anthropomorphic figure from Aboukir (detail) / 188	
14.2	Anthropomorphic figure from Aboukir / 188	
14.3	Bird figure from Aboukir (frontal view) / 189	
14.4	Bird figure from Aboukir / 189	
14.5	Carved wooden *zemí* of a bird standing on the back of a turtle or tortoise / 189	
14.6	Small ladle/spoon with anthropomorphic handle, from Aboukir / 190	
14.7	Small ladle/spoon with anthropomorphic handle, from Aboukir / 190	
14.8	Carved wooden *duho* stool, Dominican Republic / 192	

Tables

1.1	Midden Sites Reported by Robert Howard	/ 30
1.2	Cave Sites Reported by Robert Howard	/ 32
1.3	Cave Art Sites Reported by Robert Howard	/ 33
2.1	Shells Collected from Chancery Hall	/ 39
2.2	Neutron Activation Analysis of Pottery Samples	/ 42
2.3	Taíno Sites in the Kingston Area	/ 45
3.1	All Recovered Organic Materials	/ 60
3.2	Size Distribution of Charcoal Fragments	/ 60
3.3	Arthropod Remains	/ 61
3.4	All Bone	/ 63
3.5	Fish Bone	/ 64
3.6	Mammalian Bone	/ 65
5.1	Examples of Threats to Taíno Sites	/ 75
5.2	Recorded Number of Destroyed Taíno Sites in Jamaica by Parish	/ 76
6.1	Geologic Time and Corresponding Events in the Formation of the Island of Jamica	/ 90
6.2	Main Soil Types of Jamaica and Associated Landforms	/ 91
6.3	Total Number of Species	/ 94
6.4	Numbers of Endemic Species	/ 96
8.1	Significant Vertebrate and Crab Remains from the Rodney's House Site	/ 117
8.2	Faunal Comparisons	/ 123
8.3	Rodney's House Faunal List	/ 125
9.1	Lithology of Arawak Petaloid Celts from Jamaica	/ 135
9.2	Lithology of Petaloid Celts from Some Parishes of Jamaica	/ 142
13.1	New Petroglyph/Pictograph Sites, 1952–1985	/ 179
13.2	Jamaican Petroglyph Sites by Parish	/ 185

Preface

I HAVE ALWAYS been fascinated by prehistory. Even though I am a public archaeologist – and our research ranges from prehistoric settlements to World War II hangars – I have an unapologetic bias towards Taíno archaeology. I do not know if it is because my first dig was on a prehistoric site or because my maternal ancestors were Maroons, who are said to have integrated with the Taínos. Regardless of the reason, Taíno archaeology has become one of my special interests.

The idea for this publication originated in 1998, when I was an assistant curator in the Museums Division at the Institute of Jamaica. I had recently been assigned the project of refurbishing the Taíno Museum at White Marl, St Catherine. During my research for the museum, I uncovered a lot of data on Jamaican prehistory – much of it unpublished and unfortunately not accessible to the public at large. I felt that a book on Jamaican prehistory was long overdue.

Three years later, I was employed as an archaeologist at the Jamaica National Heritage Trust. As a consequence of my job, I faced constant complaints from Jamaicans, overseas archaeologists and enthusiasts about the inadequacy of publications on Jamaican archaeology. In addition, there were frequent questions as to whether there was any research being done on the island. I realized that the public was generally unaware. I knew that different projects were taking place, and I was allowed to participate in many of them, but that was mainly as a result of my job. I strongly believe that archaeology belongs to the public and not solely to archaeologists. The knowledge and the artefacts do not belong to the Jamaica National Heritage Trust or the Institute of Jamaica, but to the people of Jamaica. It is their heritage.

Jamaicans are very proud. Like a real Jamaican, I took my pride – and at times my embarrassment – and decided to undertake this ambitious project. I thought an edited volume would be ideal, as it would give various archaeologists an opportunity to discuss their research projects. I formulated a proposed structure for the text and contacted various people locally and overseas. I am happy to say that most of them liked the idea and were glad to contribute to the publication. The project took almost fifteen months to complete, and at times I felt my ambition almost outdid me. This volume does not pretend to be a comprehensive depiction of Jamaican prehistory, but it is a starting point, and it aims to fill some of the gaps in Jamaican archaeology.

Lesley-Gail Atkinson

Acknowledgements

I WOULD FIRST like to express my gratitude to all the contributors to this publication: Philip Allsworth-Jones, Dorrick Gray, William F. Keegan, Gerald Lalor, George Lechler, James W. Lee, Wendy A. Lee, Simon F. Mitchell, Andrea Richards, Norma Rodney-Harrack, M. John Roobol, Esther Z. Rodriques, Nicholas Saunders, Sylvia Scudder, Mitko Vutckhov, Selvenious Walters, Kit Wesler and Robyn Woodward. I would especially like to thank Philip Allsworth-Jones and my "left hand", Andrea Richards, who were tremendously supportive throughout the entire process. There are several people – Debra-Kay Palmer, Basil Reid, Betty Jo Stokes and Peter Harris – who were asked to contribute to the text but were unable to do so for various reasons; nevertheless, I would like to thank them for their support of the project.

The text includes six reprinted articles; therefore, permission had to be obtained from various organizations. I thank the Anthropological Research Papers, Arizona State University; La Fundación Arqueológica, Antropológica e Histórica de Puerto Rico; Antiquity; the Archaeological Museum of Aruba; and the Archaeological Society of Jamaica. I would like to specifically acknowledge Emily Lundberg, Arminda Ruiz, Raymondo Dijkhoff and Jay Haviser of the International Association of Caribbean Archaeology for their assistance. I am also grateful to the Institute of Jamaica, the Jamaica Bauxite Institute and the Archaeological Society of Jamaica for their permission to publish and reprint several photographs and illustrations.

Several people have been extremely helpful, providing insight, advice and assistance, in particular Ambassador Peter King, Verene A. Shepherd, James Robertson, Patrick Bryan, F. Roy Augier, Marlon Manborde and John Thaxter. Special thanks to the invaluable Karen Spence and the incredible Ainsley Henriques. In addition, I would like to thank Dayne Buddho, Lauris Codlin and Tyrone Barnett of the Institute of Jamaica for their assistance. I must acknowledge the support of my other "family", the staff of the Archaeology Division of the Jamaica National Heritage Trust, in particular Audene Brooks, Ann-Marie Howard-Brown, Rosemarie Whittaker, Colleen

McGeachy, Michelle Topping, Ava Tomlinson, Evelyn Thompson, Jasinth Williams and June Heath.

I am gratefully indebted to Linda Speth, Shivaun Hearne, Dionne Williams, Claudette Upton and the team at the University of the West Indies Press for their interest, patience and assistance throughout this project. A renowned Jamaican politician once said that "it takes cash to care"; funding is necessary for any publication, and this book is no exception. I would like to take this opportunity to thank my sponsors, the City of Kingston Cooperative Credit Union, the Shipping Association of Jamaica and Karen Adair. Without their contributions this publication would not have been a reality.

I wish to acknowledge my family for their encouragement and tolerance during this endeavour: my grandmother Dorothy Adair, my aunts Karen Adair and Millicent Lynch, my father, Lodric Atkinson, and my mother, Annette Adair-Hill. Finally, grateful thanks to my friends and special cheerleading squad – Tyrone Grandison, Andree Holness, Gifford Rankine, Cherena Forbes, Howard Dawkins, Susan Chung and Velmore Coke.

Introduction

In Jamaica, the indigenous population is still being referred to as the Arawaks, despite the adoption of the term *Taínos* to distinguish the native population of the Greater Antilles from the Arawaks of South America. Irving Rouse defines the Taínos as "the ethnic group that inhabited the Bahamian Archipelago, most of the Greater Antilles, and the northern part of the Lesser Antilles prior to and during the time of Columbus" (1992, 185).

According to Rouse, in Columbus's time the Taínos lacked an overall name. The people referred to themselves by the names of the localities in which they lived – for example, the Puerto Ricans called themselves *Borinquen*, their name for the island, and the Bahamians called themselves *Lucayo* (Rouse 1992, 5). This raises the question of what was the Taínan name for Jamaica. Traditionally Jamaicans have been taught that *Xaymaca* was the Taíno name given to the island, meaning "land abounding with springs", from which "Jamaica" – land of wood and water – was derived. However, D.J.R. Walker suggests *Yamaye* as the possible Taíno name for the island, based on information derived from Columbus's journal (1992, 236–37).

The Arawaks or Taínos

The term *Arawaks* has been, and still is, mistakenly used to denote the aborigines of the Greater Antilles and the Bahamas. The Arawaks were the ethnic group that lived in the northern part of the Guianas, which formerly extended onto the high land around the Orinoco delta (Rouse 1992, 173). According to John Peter Bennett, the Arawaks had names for themselves and their language, *Lokono* and *Loko* respectively (Bennett 1989, iv). For decades the terms *Arawak* and *Taíno* have been used interchangeably; however, they are two distinct ethnic groups.

It is not clear when the confusion occurred. However, one contributing factor was the attribution of the name of a language family to an ethnic group (Rouse 1987). The Taínan language is said to belong to the Arawakan language family tree. According to Rouse, linguists now believe that the Taíno, Island-Carib and Arawak languages diverged from the main line of Arawakan development at the same late date and that all three belong in the Maipuran subfamily (Rouse 1986, 120–23; Oliver 1989, 105).

Previously the Taínos were referred to as Island Arawaks; in fact, D.J.R. Walker still uses this term (1992). Rouse demonstrates that this is another source of the misnomer:

> Daniel G. Brinton (1871) preferred to call the group Island Arawak because it shared many linguistic and cultural traits with the Arawak Indians (also known as *Lokonos*), whose descendants still live in northeastern South America. His followers shortened the phrase to Arawak. That was a mistake. (1992, 5)

In the essay, "On the Meaning of the Term *Arawak*", Rouse (1972) argues that neither Columbus nor any of his counterparts came across the word *Arawak*: "These Indians in the Greater Antilles are now known as 'Arawaks', but they themselves did not use that name, nor did Columbus and his contemporaries ever come across it, as far as it is known." Rouse adds that *Arawak* does not appear in the literature until the exploration of the Guianas that began in the late 1500s, almost a century after the arrival of Columbus in the New World.

Centuries later, in 1894, Juan Lopez de Velasco noted the presence of people who called themselves Arawaks on the Guiana coast, southeastern Trinidad, and commented that a group of them had "intruded" into Trinidad. Sir Walter Raleigh confirmed these statements and in 1928 included the *Aruacos* in a list of five Indian "nations" that inhabited Trinidad (Jane 1988).

Ethnohistorians merged the groups of people who inhabited the Greater Antilles into one group – the Taíno – as they shared a single language and had the same culture (Rouse 1992, 5). *Taíno*, which means "good" or "noble", was chosen because several of its members spoke that word to Columbus to indicate that they were not Island Caribs (Alegría 1981). Andres Bernaldez explains:

> On the day when they came down the coast, there were many men and women together, on the shore near the water, wondering at the fleet and marvelling greatly at a thing so novel, and when a boat came to shore to have speech with them they said, "Taínon, Taínon," "good, good". (Jane 1988)

Since the 1980s the term *Taínos* has been accepted in Caribbean archaeology. In his article "Whom Did Columbus Discover in the West Indies?" Rouse (1987) suggested that the commonly used name *Arawak* be replaced with the name *Taínos* when discussing native West Indians at the time of contact.

It is important to note that throughout this volume, the reader will encounter the term *Arawaks* used to describe the Jamaican Taíno culture. These references are presented in their original context, as most of the literature assumed that the indigenous population of Jamaica was Arawak.

The Jamaican Taínos

It is believed that Jamaica was colonized after AD 600 by ancestors of the Taíno, the Ostionoid culture (Rouse 1992). At present, two of the earliest known sites on the island are Little River, St Ann, and Alligator Pond (Bottom Bay), Manchester, dated AD 650 ± 120 (Vanderwal 1968a) (see Figure A.1, nos. 89 and 4). These sites have been characterized as belonging to the Ostionan Ostionoid subseries (Rouse 1992) or, as it is called locally, Redware – a name reflecting its bright red ceramics. James W. Lee has published articles on the Redware culture in *Archaeology Jamaica* (see Lee 1980c, reprinted in this volume).

James Lee noticed that the Redware culture preferred coastal settlements and illustrated that all but two of the eleven Redware sites highlighted in 1980 were directly on the seashore (ibid.). The two exceptions were located about 1 km inland. Preliminary observations indicate that most of the present Redware sites are located at elevations of 0 to 15 m above sea level. These sites are also near the sea or a river source such as Alligator Pond, St Elizabeth, and Alloa, St Ann, suggesting a dependence on marine resources (Atkinson 2003, 8) (see Figure A.1, nos. 3 and 5). This reliance on the marine environment was highlighted at the Ostionan site at Paradise Park, Westmoreland (Keegan 2002). According to William Keegan (personal communication, 2001), the Ostionan deposit contains mostly sea turtles, freshwater turtles, large fish and shellfish (notably conch) from the seagrass environment. However, in Jamaica, traditional research on this cultural period has concentrated mainly on its ceramics and on comparisons with the Meillacan culture.

About three hundred years later another culture, categorized by Rouse (1992) as the Meillacan Ostionoid, settled on the island. The Meillacan culture, which is also referred to as the White Marl style after the largest Meillac site on the island, dated from AD 877 ± 95 to AD 1490 ± 120 (Silverberg, Vanderwal and Wing 1972). Traditionally, it was felt that the Ostionans were colonized by the Meillacans and absorbed into the latter cultural group, and the Ostionan period was believed to have ended around AD 900. However, recent archaeological investigations at the Sweetwater and Paradise sites at Paradise Park, Westmoreland (see Figure A.1, no. 119), and other sites across the island have indicated that the two groups possibly co-inhabited the island.

The settlement patterns of the Meillacans were more diverse than those of the Ostionans; they settled on the coast but also penetrated the interior as far

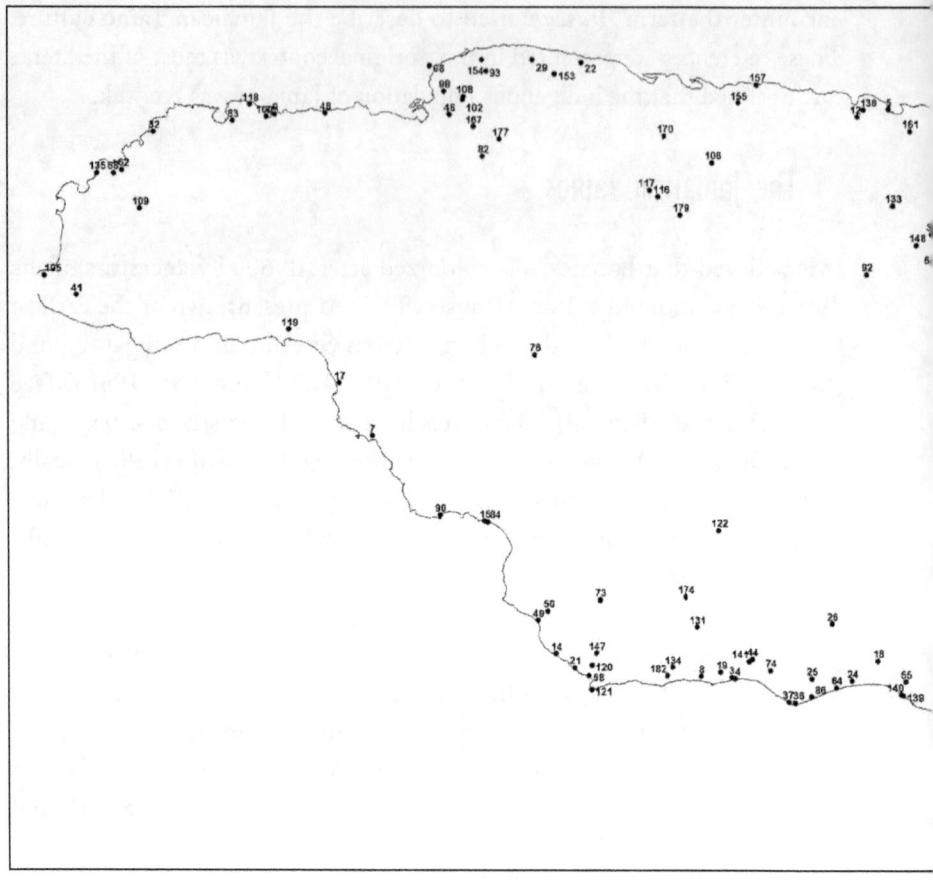

Figure A.1 Map of the sites mentioned in the text

1. Aboukir (Image Cave)
2. Alexandria
3. Alligator Pond (Alligator Pond River)
4. Alligator Pond (Bottom Bay)
5. Alloa
6. Armordale
7. Auchindown
8. Baalbec Cave
9. Barbican
10. Bellevue
11. Bellevue
12. Bengal
13. Beverly Hills
14. Billy Bay
15. Black River (Black River West)
16. Bloxblurgh
17. Bluefields
18. Bossue
19. Bull Savannah
20. Byndloss Mountain (Riverhead)
21. Calabash Bay
22. California
23. Cambridge Hill Cave
24. Canoe Valley
25. Canoe Valley Caves
26. Carpenter's Mountain
27. Caymanas Bay
28. Chancery Hall
29. Cinnamon Hill
30. Clitos Point
31. Coleraine
32. Cousins Cove
33. Coventry
34. Cranbrook
35. Creighton Hall
36. Cuckold Point
37. Cuckold Point Cave
38. Culloden
39. Dover
40. Downtown Kingston
41. Drummond
42. Dryland (Image Cave)
43. Duckenfield
44. Duff House
45. East Jackson Bay Cave
46. Fairfield (Fairfield View)
47. Ferry Hill
48. Flint River
49. Fort Charles
50. Fort Charles-Nembhard
51. Fort Haldane
52. Fort Nugent
53. Freetown
54. Friendship
55. God's Well
56. Great Goat Island
57. Great Goat Island Cave
58. Great Pedro Bay
59. (Great) Salt Pond
60. Green Castle
61. Green Hill
62. Green Island
63. Greenwich Park
64. Gut River # 1
65. Halberstadt
66. Harbour View
67. Harmony Hall
68. Haughton Hall
69. Holmes Bay
70. Hope
71. Hope Mine
72. Hope Tavern
73. Hounslow
74. Image Cave
75. Inverness
76. Ipswich
77. Iter Boreale
78. Ivor (Iver)
79. Jacks Hill
80. Jackson's Bay Cave
81. Jackson's Bay
82. Kempshot
83. Kew
84. Knapdale (Knapville)
85. Liberty Hill
86. Little Bay Cave
87. Little Miller's Bay
88. Llanrumney
89. Little River

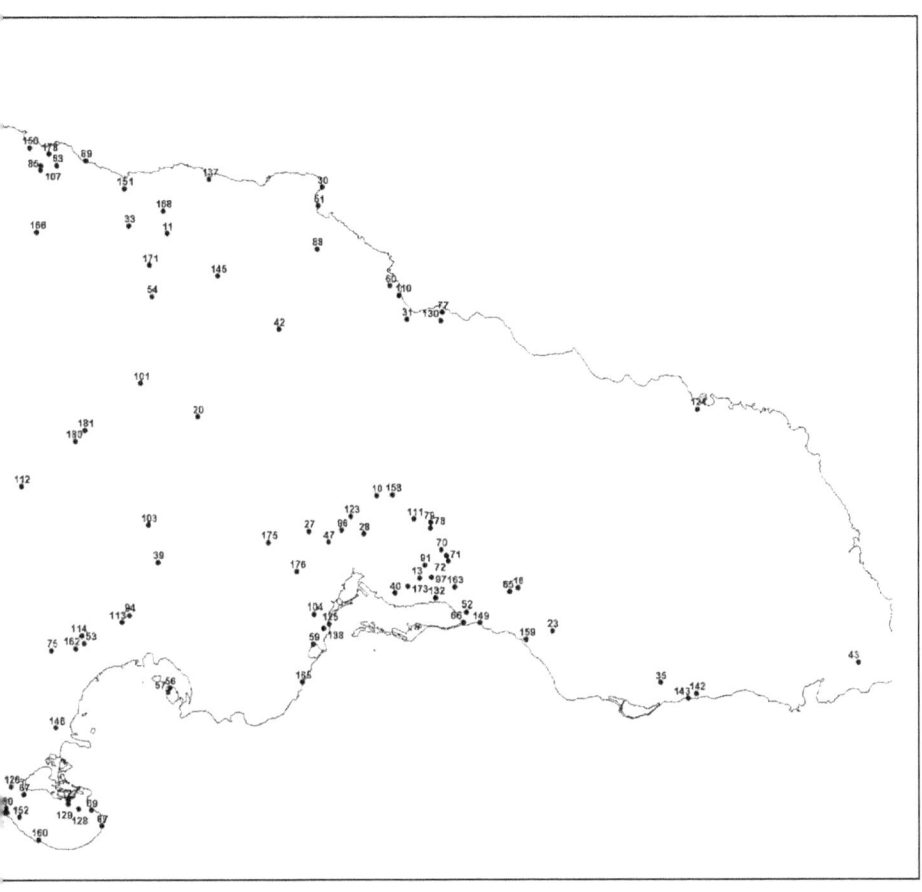

90. Long Acre Point	115. Orange Valley	137. Rio Nuevo	161. Tobolski
91. Long Mountain	116. Pantrepant East	138. Rodney's House	162. Toby Abbot
92. Mahogany Hill	117. Pantrepant West	139. Round Hill	163. Tower Hill (Dallas Castle)
93. Mammee Hill	118. Paradise	140. Round Hill B New Ridge	164. Treasure Beach
94. Marlie Mount	119. Paradise Park	141. Rowe's Corner	165. Two Sister's Cave
95. Milk River Spa	120. Parchment (Parchment Cave)	142. Rozelle	166. Tydenham
96. Molynes Mountain	121. Pedro	143. Rozelle Falls	167. Upper Retirement
97. Mona	122. Pepper	144. Runaway Bay	168. Upton
98. Montego Bay Point	123. Plantation Heights	145. Salisbury	169. Vere
99. Montego Bay		146. Salt River	170. Wales
100. Mosquito Cove	124. Port Antonio	147. Sandy Bank	171. Walkerswood
101. Mount Rosser	125. Port Henderson	148. Scarborough	172. Wallman Town
102. Mount Salem	126. Portland	149. Seven Mile Hill	173. Wareika Hill
103. Mountain River Cave	127. Portland Cave	150. Seville	174. Warminister
	128. Portland Ridge	151. Shaw	175. Waterloo
104. Naggo(s) Head	129. Portland Ridge Cave	152. Sommerville Cave	176. White Marl
105. Negril		153. Spot Valley	177. Williamsfield
106. New Forest	130. Prospect	154. Spotty Hill	178. Windsor
107. New Ground	131. Red Bank	155. Spring	179. Windsor Great Cave
108. New Market	132. Rennock Lodge	156. St Jean D'Acre	
109. Newfound River	133. Retreat (Little Nigger Ground)	157. Stewart Castle	180. Worthy Park # 1
110. Newry		158. Stony Hill	181. Worthy Park # 2
111. Norbrook	134. Reynold Bent	159. Sugar Loaf Hill	182. Yardley Chase (Lover's Leap)
112. Oakes	135. Rhodes Hall	160. Taylor's Hut Cave # 2	
113. Old Harbour	136. Rio Bueno		
114. Old Harbour Hill			

inland as Ipswich, St Elizabeth, the Worthy Park sites and Mount Rosser in St Catherine (see Figure A.1, nos. 76, 180, 181 and 101). They did not, however, settle in the interior mountain range. It is the general consensus among Jamaican archaeologists that Taíno sites have the best views. As their sites are generally panoramic – located overlooking the landscape – it is not known whether the purpose was defensive or aesthetic. The present research has illustrated that the Meillacans or White Marl culture were not as dependent on marine resources as the Ostionans. Although there is evidence that the Jamaican Redware culture cultivated cassava, it seems that the White Marl group was more dependent on agrarian resources.

The prehistoric culture that we call the Taíno developed about AD 1200. Samuel Wilson states that it is difficult to mark the "beginning" of the Taíno (1997b). Their society emerged as a continuation of the cultural development that had characterized Caribbean history for several thousand years. Wilson explains that the Taínos

> played the same ball game as their predecessors; their settlements were similar, although larger and more numerous; and their religious beliefs and rituals were related to those of their Saladoid and Archaic predecessors. In some cases, their pottery was different from Ostionoid ceramics in form, style, and decoration, but in other instances not. (ibid.)

In the past, the Jamaican Taíno were described as having sub-Taíno cultural traits (Lovén 1935); however, this terminology is no longer used. The term *Western Taínos* is now used by Rouse and other scholars to describe the Taíno culture of Jamaica, central Cuba, and the Bahamas (Rouse 1992, 17). The term is indicative of a culture less developed than that of the Classic Taínos of Hispaniola and Puerto Rico. Despite being characterized as less advanced, the Jamaican Taínos displayed certain similarities to the Classic Taínos, in terms of population density, agriculture and class system (Rouse 1948, 1992). Regardless of whether it is classified as Western or Classic Taíno, Jamaican cultural development was autonomous with respect to the other islands. This could be a result of its isolated southward location within the Greater Antilles (Walker 1992).

Jamaican prehistory is regarded as one of the least studied Caribbean disciplines. That is not necessarily the case; the fact is that published Jamaican archaeological research has not had sufficient international circulation. This has resulted in misconceptions about lack of scope, research activities and information on the Jamaican Taínos. These misconceptions are discussed and countered in Keegan and Atkinson's chapter in this volume. As early as 1897, J.E. Duerden published an excellent compilation on Jamaican prehistory, which included various sites and research on the island's Taíno artefacts.

The mid-1960s saw the creation of two important forums for archaeological publication in Jamaica. Geologist James W. Lee established the Archaeological Society of Jamaica (ASJ) in 1965. Since then, Lee and other ASJ members have conducted extensive research on Jamaica prehistory, which was frequently published in the society's newsletter *Archaeology Jamaica*. In 1967, the Institute of Jamaica began publishing *Jamaica Journal*, which has been an essential medium for promoting current archaeological research in Jamaica.

Factors Affecting Jamaican Taíno Research

In the past fifty years, Jamaican archaeology has undergone significant developments: the establishment of the Archaeology Division (Jamaica National Heritage Trust [JNHT]), the introduction of archaeology at the University of the West Indies in 1987, and improvements in the training of Jamaican archaeologists. The past decade has seen increased interest in Jamaican Taíno archaeology and promotion of it via international archaeological associations. Despite these advances, research in Jamaican prehistory is negatively affected by limited resources, a shortage of personnel, poor attitudes towards conservation, the improper monitoring of the island's archaeological resources, and the great evil – ignorance. These factors affect the investigation, recovery, and interpretation of Jamaica's prehistory, and its context within the island's archaeological development.

The lack of resources for archaeological investigations is a critical, even paralysing factor. It affects the training of staff, the acquisition of essential equipment and the comprehensive investigation of sites. Archaeological investigations are expensive and time-consuming, and this poses a problem for developers, the general public, administrators and even some personnel within the JNHT.

Manpower is a serious problem in Jamaica, despite its having the largest contingent of professional archaeologists in the English-speaking Caribbean. At present the severely short-handed staff at the Archaeology Division of the JNHT cannot cope with the needs of the island's archaeological resources – it is physically impossible. In addition, because of the various development projects taking place on the island, the JNHT is forced to conduct primarily watching briefs and rescue operations, leaving little room for academic investigations and long-term research.

Responsibility for the protection, preservation, promotion and study of Taíno sites and artefacts is shared among the JNHT, the National Environmental and Planning Agency and the University of the West Indies. However, there is limited collaboration between the JNHT and other government agencies such as the Department of Mines and Geology, the Ministry of Land and

Development and the National Works Agency. Better interaction and collaboration between the JNHT and these government agencies would bring about an improvement in both the circulation of information and the facilities and resources available.

More collaboration is essential given the island's increased pace of development. The threat of development on Taíno sites is a matter of concern that Andrea Richards addresses in this volume. Two examples are Seville, St Ann, and Rio Nuevo, St Mary (see Figure A.1, nos. 150 and 137), both important Taíno centres mentioned in the Spanish chronicles. These sites face destruction despite archaeologists' efforts, demonstrating the need for more controlled development and for the implementation of an archaeological policy.

In Jamaica, more attention needs to be paid to Taíno artefacts – their recovery, treatment, storage and research. Despite the presence of qualified archaeological conservators in the island, the importance of conservation is not completely appreciated. This is a problem not only for Taíno research but for Jamaican archaeology in general. At present, the focus is mainly on interventive conservation – treating artefacts chemically. But conservation, which is required for an artefact's physical welfare, should begin with the environment from which the artefact is recovered – meaning that conservators should frequently be present in the field. Conservation does not begin in the lab but on the first day the project is considered, so that danger to artefacts is minimized. Pottery, for example – the most abundant type of Taíno artefact recovered in Jamaica – is sometimes found to have been incompletely fired and thus requires special handling, particularly in the field. Because of the absence of conservators in the field, by the time an artefact enters the lab, the conservators can sometimes do nothing more than damage control. At the other end of the spectrum is storage of artefacts, which is also crucial to conservation. These are matters that preventive conservation addresses. Unfortunately, the preventive approach has not been widely implemented. Jamaican conservators are concerned that the focus on interventive methods results in a loss of information that can be gained from an artefact, because the interventive methods essentially constitute tampering with the artefact.

Another matter of concern is the monitoring of the material culture in the island. Over the years many people have acquired private collections of Taíno artefacts. In the absence of effective legislation prohibiting the collection of artefacts by private individuals, what is needed is an inventory of these private collections, so at least researchers can get a clear idea of what cultural material has been recovered from what areas across the island. Unfortunately, in Jamaica a substantial portion of the island's archaeological collections has been obtained from surface collections rather than controlled excavations, which means that provenance is not known for many artefacts in these collections. Knowledge of the provenance or context of an artefact or feature is critical in archaeology, as it makes possible identification of associated artefacts or features, establishment of the chronology of the stratum or site, and educated assumptions about the site's function.

Archaeology is renowned as an interdisciplinary subject. The Jamaican archaeological research establishment needs to embrace the various scientific techniques available in the island. At the University of the West Indies, the International Centre for Environmental and Nuclear Sciences offers analytic techniques such as neutron activation analysis (NAA), X-ray diffraction and X-ray fluorescence, which can help archaeological data reveal more information. However, the high cost of scientific analytical tools limits their application in Jamaican archaeological investigations. This is especially apparent in regard to radiocarbon (C^{14}) dating, as this method is only available overseas and is extremely expensive.

Publication of archaeological research is a serious matter. The JNHT, as the agency in charge of research and protection of the island's archaeological resources, needs to produce and encourage more publications, and to conduct its own research on Taíno archaeology. At present the research on Jamaican Taíno archaeology, with the exception of rescue archaeology, is being conducted by the University of the West Indies and overseas archaeologists. Jamaica's prehistory needs to be studied in relation to the developments taking place in the wider Caribbean and not as an isolated phenomenon.

It is difficult, in a developing country like Jamaica, to see the importance of the island's archaeological heritage when the country is burdened with debt and essential socioeconomic matters demand attention and action. In Jamaica the preservation of culture is not considered important outside of the possibility of economic gain. As we move into the twenty-first century, archaeologists, conservators and cultural resource personnel need to come together and address these issues.

This book, *The Earliest Inhabitants: The Dynamics of the Jamaican Taíno*, seeks to promote Jamaican Taínan archaeology and highlights the variety of the research conducted on the island's prehistoric sites and artefacts. The text consists of a compilation of fourteen papers – six reprinted articles (edited slightly for style and audience) that were deemed to be of archaeological significance, and the remaining articles are based on recent archaeological research. These fourteen chapters are subdivided into four thematic areas: Assessment and Excavations of Taíno Sites, Taíno Exploitation of the Natural Resources, Analysis of Taíno Archaeological Data, and Taíno Art Forms.

The four themes were selected in an effort to illustrate the diverse areas of research conducted in the island. The first section, Assessment and Excavations of Taíno Sites, looks at the various archaeological investigations across the island. Taíno Exploitation of the Natural Resources examines how the Taínos exploited the natural environment to fulfil their needs. The third section, Analysis of Taíno Archaeological Data, highlights research conducted on various artefacts. The final theme, Taíno Art Forms, focuses specifically on evidence of Taíno cave art, both *in situ* and mobiliary, and its impact on the interpretation of the Jamaican Taíno livelihood.

Section 1

Assessment and Excavation of Taíno Sites

THE FIRST FOUR hundred years of European occupation saw the growth of collections of prehistoric objects of curiosity such as the Carpenter's Mountain *zemís*. The first recorded archaeological investigations in Jamaica did not occur until the late nineteenth century. During the past century, a series of investigations have taken place across the island. Some archaeologists discredit many of these investigations because amateur or "avocational" archaeologists conducted them. Regardless, the works of these amateurs have contributed a lot of insight to Jamaican prehistory. The first chapter, "The Development of Jamaican Prehistory", provides a background, not only for the evolution of Jamaican Taínan archaeology but also for the overall development of Jamaican archaeological research. It highlights the various investigations and their significance, from the late nineteenth century to the present.

The remaining chapters in this section are based on research that took place during the past decade. The second article, "Taíno Settlement of the Kingston Area", reports on a survey of eighteen sites in Kingston. The authors examine the findings of two pilot studies, an examination of the molluscs recovered from Chancery Hall and the application of the neutron activation analysis of the pottery samples from the selected sites.

The Chancery Hall site is discussed in further detail in the three-part chapter "The Pre-Columbian Site of Chancery Hall", which chronicles the investigations of this Taíno site from its discovery by George Lechler to the post-excavation analysis of the material recovered.

The subject of the fourth chapter is the Green Castle, St Mary, excavations, a joint project between the University of the West Indies and Murray State University. The project directors, Philip Allsworth-Jones and Kit Wesler, describe progress and findings during the past three seasons.

Andrea Richards, in the final chapter in this section, "The Impact of Land-Based Development on Taíno Archaeology in Jamaica", examines the effect of development on prehistoric sites.

1 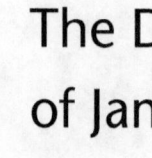 The Development of Jamaican Prehistory

WILLIAM F. KEEGAN

and

LESLEY-GAIL ATKINSON

ARCHAEOLOGY IN JAMAICA developed from prehistoric interests. The island has a long, rich history of archaeological investigations. On the one hand, foreign archaeologists have come to Jamaica with the goal of fitting the island's pre-Columbian past into the dominant frameworks of the time. Their studies have had the widest dissemination and are most frequently cited in synthetic studies (for example, Howard 1950, 1956, 1965). On the other hand, Jamaica has a tradition of research conducted by local, "avocational" archaeologists (that is, those lacking a professional degree in archaeology), whose work was less widely disseminated because their results were published primarily in *Archaeology Jamaica*, the newsletter of the Archaeology Society of Jamaica. Only those foreign archaeologists who have made a conscious effort to learn Jamaica's prehistory have made use of the extensive literature that is available.[1] As a result, Jamaican archaeology is often portrayed as a "black hole" and as lacking any prior systematic research.

But that characterization of Jamaican archaeology is false. The Institute of Jamaica, the Archaeological Society of Jamaica, the Jamaica National Heritage Trust and the University of the West Indies have sponsored and supported numerous projects, including both surveys and excavations. The results of these projects provide a rich database that is the equal to studies conducted on other islands in the West Indies. It is our goal in this chapter to broaden the distribution of information about Jamaica's past by drawing attention to research conducted on the island over the past century. We will pursue this objective by using a frame of reference for the history of West Indian archaeology introduced by Irving Rouse (1996). In this regard we will consider artefactual research, chronological order, culture-historical inquiry and sociocultural research, as these have been exemplified by investigations undertaken in Jamaica. The review that follows will provide a basic outline for the investigations of the past, as well as references to work that should heighten awareness of Jamaica's rich history among archaeologists working in the West Indies.

Frame of Reference

In writing a history of Jamaican archaeology, we need to acknowledge that Irving Rouse established the main framework and research agenda. Rouse's approach to culture history has dominated the field for more than sixty years (Rouse 1939, 1992). Rouse (1996) identified four levels of interpretation that developed in sequence. The first, called *artefactual research*, involved the discovery, description and identification of archaeological materials that were often removed to private collections and public museums. Such activities began in the eighteenth century and continue today, but they reached their acme in the early twentieth century.

Rouse reports that by the 1920s attention had shifted to the second level – organizing known assemblages in *chronological order*. Coincident with chronology is the spatial distribution of material remains. The third level, initiated in the 1950s, involves using material remains to define "cultures" which in turn define the "peoples" who are the subject of *culture-historical inquiry* (Rouse 1972, 1996). The fourth level, called *sociocultural research*, emerged in the 1970s. It involves a shift of attention from the peoples who produced the local cultures to the societies that used them (Rouse 1996).

Rouse's scheme provides a useful frame of reference for characterizing prehistoric archaeological investigations conducted in Jamaica over the past century. For this reason we will review past research within the structure of these four categories. However, it should be noted that classification schemes, including Rouse's characterization of stages of research, tend to emphasize similarities and disregard differences. In other words, these categories are fuzzy and porous. Some researchers were ahead of their time, while others have clung to the old ways of doing things. What is most important is that people recognize the breadth of research already conducted in Jamaica. Our review ends by highlighting the present research in the island.

Finally, Caribbean archaeology cannot outrun its past. Even on islands like Jamaica, where local historical goals have been pursued, the general tendency has been to lump all of the islands into one Caribbean/West Indian culture history. Yet self-awareness at a variety of different levels is important. According to Bob Marley, "If you know your history, then you will know where you're coming from." Jamaica needs to relish its past, but at the same time its archaeologists need to move toward using Jamaican prehistory to broaden our understanding of West Indian history.

Artefactual Research

An early interest in Native American archaeology can be traced to the eighteenth century. American archaeologists have dated the founding of their discipline to excavations conducted by Thomas Jefferson in 1780 on his property in Virginia (Thomas 1979). Yet Edward Long (1774) had already described prehistoric artefacts in Jamaica. These early forays into prehistoric archaeology certainly generated an interest in artefacts from the past, yet these remained isolated in the "curiosity cabinets" of the eighteenth and nineteenth centuries.

Jamaican Taíno artefacts, particularly the wooden *zemís* (representations of supernatural spirits), have been a subject of curiosity since the eighteenth century. George "Tony" Aarons (1994) has written about the discovery of Jamaican *zemís* before 1757. One of the most spectacular Jamaican discoveries was three wooden *zemís* from Carpenter's Mountain (Manchester) found in 1792. The Carpenter's Mountain *zemís* are individually referred to as the "Bird Man", the "Rain Deity" and the "Man with the Canopy". These *zemís* were presented to the British Museum in 1799 (ibid.).

It was not until the late nineteenth century that a more formal interest in the archaeology of the Americas developed. In the United States, the Smithsonian Institution was founded in 1846 with a gift from James Smithson of England, and in 1916 the George G. Heye Foundation in New York established a museum that is currently being transformed into the Museum of the American Indian. Moreover, the Field Museum in Chicago sponsored the Colombian Exposition in 1893–94. Among the attractions of that World's Fair was an exhibition of Native American encampments, presented as a kind of human zoo. Today we view this exploitation of native peoples as an unfortunate episode in the history of American anthropology.

What many people fail to realize is that Jamaica's history rivals that of its North American neighbour. Founded in 1879 by then Governor Sir Anthony Musgrave, the Institute of Jamaica is one of the oldest cultural heritage organizations in the Americas. The Institute of Jamaica played a formidable role in the development of Jamaican archaeology, being responsible for all archaeological expeditions, surveys and exhibitions from its inception up to the mid-1980s. In the 1890s, the Institute of Jamaica was pivotal in the emergence of two important figures in Jamaican archaeological research: J.E. Duerden and Frank Cundall. Cundall and Duerden both worked on the Institute of Jamaica staff and made significant contributions to the evidence of pre-Columbian peoples in Jamaica. The late nineteenth century witnessed a renewed interest in pre-Columbian peoples (Cundall 1894a, 1894b, 1895; Duerden 1895, 1897) perhaps in relation to the quatercentenary of Christopher Columbus's first voyage to the Americas. Frank Cundall's 1894 publication on Columbus (Cundall 1894c) is testimony to this interest.

Between 1879 and 1930 the primary focus of Jamaican archaeology was prehistoric sites, and more intensive archaeological investigations were carried out in the 1890s than at any other period in the nineteenth century. Lady Edith Blake, the wife of the then governor general, had an abiding interest in Jamaican archaeology. She published a paper on the Norbrook kitchen midden (Blake 1895) and amassed a collection of artefacts that eventually was purchased by the Heye Foundation, Museum of the American Indian. She also promoted her interests among the staff of the Institute of Jamaica, resulting in an exhibition of pre-Columbian artefacts at the Institute in 1895 and the publication of a pioneering book by Duerden in 1897. R.C. MacCormack's excavations in southern Vere and the Portland Ridge in Clarendon in 1897–98 ended the excavations for the nineteenth century.

The twentieth century was a crucial period for archaeological growth and development, beginning at the start of the century with J.F. Brennan's investigations at Knapdale, St Elizabeth (1901) and Cundall's research at Liberty Hill, St Ann (1902). In addition, archaeologists from the Museum for Volkepkunde, Berlin, investigated cave and open-air sites near Montego Bay, St James (Reichard 1904). Philip Sherlock and Frank Cundall both summarized the results of these studies in 1939.

The more general interest in the archaeology of the West Indies also continued into the early twentieth century. Jesse Walter Fewkes made an expedition to Puerto Rico in 1907 for the Smithsonian Institution and wrote about West Indian archaeology in general (Fewkes 1922). Theodoor De Booy, working for the Heye Foundation, visited the Bahamas, the Turks and Caicos Islands, Margarita Island off the north coast of Venezuela, St John, Trinidad, the US Virgin Islands and Jamaica. Under the sponsorship of American museums, Fewkes, De Booy and Herbert Kreiger (1931) all worked to bring Caribbean archaeology to light.

De Booy (1913) excavated a midden on the Retreat property in St Ann. The site is of special interest because it is about 10 km from the sea. The hill on which the site is located is 365 m above sea level. The hilltop is level, with a series of middens positioned below the hilltop. The pottery in the site was executed in the White Marl style, and there are a large number of handles that are typical of the unique Jamaican canteen. As De Booy noted, despite the similar use of incision and appliqué decorations, the pottery in Jamaica is considerably different from that found on neighbouring islands. Land snails (*Pleurodonte acuta*) were the dominant molluscs in the deposits, but marine taxa (*Arca*, *Strombus* and *Fasciolaria*) were also observed. A year later, G.C. Longley (1914) provided supplementary information to De Booy's Jamaican investigations.

The initial phase of archaeological investigation consisted of simple descriptions of site locations and artefacts from pre-Columbian sites. For example, Sven Lovén (1932) reported the discovery of projectile points ("stone dart points") from Old Harbour, St Catherine. Projectile points are not common in West Indian sites, and there is some question as to what these mean in terms of Jamaican archaeology (Harris 1991). Some effort was made to interpret how the native peoples of Jamaica might have lived by using the reports from the early Spanish chroniclers (Sherlock 1939); however, there was little attempt to determine the accuracy of the Spanish characterization of the Taíno. Moreover, because the Spanish tended to report that all of the peoples on these islands were the same, there has been a tendency among ethnohistorians to generalize as well. For example, religious beliefs recorded among the Macorix of central Hispaniola have been used to characterize Taíno religious beliefs on all of the islands (see Bourne 1906).

This phase of investigation had run out of steam by the 1930s. Lovén (1935) published an encyclopaedic summary of ethnohistoric reports and archaeological investigations, *The Origins of the Taínan Culture, West Indies*. By the time this synthesis was published, there seemed to be nothing new that could be learned from collecting the artefacts of Jamaica's prehistoric peoples. Thus, the 1930s saw a shift in interest toward Jamaica's Hispanic heritage (Aarons 1983b, 1984), epitomized by the work of Charles S. Cotter. After the 1940s, archaeological interest was focused on the historic sites, primarily Port Royal, Kingston and Sevilla la Nueva (New Seville), St Ann.

Chronological Order

Initial efforts to arrange the events of the past in historical order were based on the development of "relative" chronologies. One of the basic principles of archaeology is the *law of superposition*, which states that the deepest artefacts in a deposit generally are the oldest. In a midden (garbage heap), for instance, later deposits bury the first objects discarded. There is always the possibility that later activities can disturb the sequence (for example, when a burial pit is dug into existing deposits), but with careful attention to the integrity of strata, the observer can identify such disturbances. By developing sequences of artefacts, from the most deeply buried to those closest to the surface, it is possible to develop a "relative" chronology, with the oldest materials at the bottom and the youngest at the surface.

By 1950, Willard Libby had developed a technique for "absolute" dating, which enabled the calendar year in which an organic material died to be established, within an error range based on the accuracy of the technique. Yet radiocarbon dating of archaeological deposits in Jamaica has never been a priority. As a result, there are very few absolute dates for any of the sites. Instead, the tendency has been to cross-date material remains on the basis of similarities to previously dated artefact styles. Cross-dating is accomplished by matching artefacts from one site with those from other sites that have been radiocarbon-dated.

Over the past decade, scientists have recognized potential sources of error in radiocarbon dates. The method measures concentrations of carbon-14, an isotope of carbon-12 whose abundance in the atmosphere has varied through time. In addition, different living tissues contain different concentrations of C^{14}. Various correction factors are now applied to give corrected and calibrated radiocarbon dates, which are given as a mean date ± an error range (for example, one of the dates for the Sweetwater site at Paradise Park is calibrated AD 1430 ± 70).

The calibration of radiocarbon dates indicates that the age ranges given for Jamaican cultures may need revision. It should be remembered that radiocarbon dates are not really "absolute"; they come with an error range and are based on statistical probabilities. When atmospheric fluctuations in C^{14} are considered, the dates for Jamaican cultures are about a century younger than previous estimates, so some of the dates may need to be adjusted. For example, the AD 650 date, which is used for the beginning of the Little River style, should be revised to around AD 750. In addition, the early dates for the White Marl site (Silverberg, Vanderwal and Wing 1972) – AD 877 ± 95 and AD 934 ± 95 – would calibrate to around AD 1000–1020. These calibrated dates are more consistent with other dates from the site, which range from AD 1150 to AD 1350. We mention these modifications because it is often assumed that radiocarbon dating provides absolute dates for material, and such is not the case: radiocarbon dates indicate only a range of possibilities for the timing of past events (see Davis 1988).

Research in Jamaica is more characteristic of the culture-historical approach, in which the sequence of Redware to White Marl is viewed as an adequate rendering of the cultural sequence. Marion De Wolf in 1933 conducted excavations at three sites in the parish of St Ann: Little River, Little Nigger Ground Hill (Retreat) and Windsor. Twenty years later she highlighted her findings in a report on these excavations entitled "Excavations in

Jamaica" (De Wolf 1953). The Little River site revealed pottery of a characteristic red nature which had not previously been noted in Jamaica. De Wolf stated that the pottery resembled that of the Ostiones and Cuevas cultures of Puerto Rico (see Rouse 1986). This ceramic culture is locally referred to as Redware. Its discovery established that the island had three ceramic cultures.

In 1968, Ronald Vanderwal presented the results of his investigations of twenty-six sites across the island in his thesis "The Prehistory of Jamaica: A Ceramic Study". Vanderwal's research included radiocarbon dates of samples from Alligator Pond (renamed Bottom Bay), Manchester and Bengal, St Ann. The Alligator Pond site was dated AD 650 ± 120. It was not until thirty-five years after the De Wolf excavations that an associated date range was allocated to the Little River site, via cross-dating it with the Alligator Pond site. These data established the Redware culture, or the Little River complex, as the earliest period in the island's chronology. The Bengal sample was dated AD 1180 ± 100, and Vanderwal (1968a) suggests that the Fairfield Complex originated sometime before this date.

In the past seventy years, three main ceramic cultures have been identified, and radiocarbon dating has been used to establish their place in the island's chronology. The earliest is the Little River Style, dated AD 650 ± 120 (Howard 1950; De Wolf 1953; Tyndale-Biscoe 1962; Vanderwal 1968a). The second is the White Marl Style, dated AD 877 ± 95 to 1490 ± 120 (Howard 1950; Vanderwal 1968a; Silverberg, Vanderwal and Wing 1972). The third is the Montego Bay Style, or the Fairfield complex, dated AD 1180 ± 100 (Howard 1950; Tyndale-Biscoe 1962; Vanderwal 1968a, 1968b).

Culture-Historical Inquiry

From the 1930s until 1960, Yale University conducted a special programme in Caribbean Anthropology. Professor Cornelius Osgood supervised the archaeology component of this programme. The goal was to inventory archaeological sites on different islands and to catalogue and classify the material remains that were found. As part of the programme, Irving Rouse and Froelich Rainey conducted research in Haiti (Rainey 1941; Rouse 1939, 1941) and Puerto Rico (Rainey 1940; Rouse 1952); Osgood and Rouse investigated eastern Cuba (Osgood 1942; Rouse 1942); Marshall McKusick (1959) conducted field research in St Lucia; and Robert Howard (1950) investigated Jamaica.

Of this group, only Rouse would continue to work in the islands for his entire career. Rouse, who is considered the "doyen of Caribbean prehistory" has laboured for more than sixty years to delimit the time-space systematics of West Indian culture history (see Rouse 1939, 1972, 1992; Rouse and Allaire 1978). His system of classifying material remains came to dominate research in the West Indies. In fact, his methods are highly idiosyncratic, and there are no other regions on the planet where archaeologists today use his technique. For this reason, it is imperative that one understand his methods for classifying archaeological materials. It is essential to understand this system in Jamaica, as Robert Howard was strongly influenced by Rouse's methods, and Howard's framework for Jamaican culture history continues in use to the present.

Rouse's method starts with the artefacts and works up. The basic organization of the chart has *space* on the horizontal axis and *time* on the vertical axis (see Figure 1.1). Temporal positions are determined by stratigraphic relations (that is, superposition) with calendar years obtained by radiometric dating. Until recently, relatively few radiocarbon dates were available, so the tendency has been to cross-date assemblages. However, a number of problems have been observed, including the selective reporting of dates, the potential for misdating burials because older potsherds were mixed in the fill, the dating of potentially contaminated samples, and an over-reliance on mean dates to the exclusion of standard deviations (Davis 1988).

Space in the chart is organized by island, island group and water passage. The emphasis on water passages reflects the observation that archaeological complexes that face each other across passages are more similar than those on opposite ends of the same island (Watters and Rouse 1989). Names within the body of the chart distinguish pottery styles that are observed in different geographical areas. In the absence of pottery, other elements of material culture are substituted. Styles are defined on the basis of shared "modes", which are the basic elements of manufacture and decoration. These styles are then classified into hierarchical groupings based on shared modes. The highest order of grouping is *series* (ending in *-oid*), which Rouse equates with "peoples and cultures". They are distinguished "by comparing their ceramic styles and associated traits and grouping together peoples that resemble each other most closely in their styles and in other diagnostic traits" (Rouse 1992, 33). In the past two decades Rouse recognized the need for a mid-level classification to characterize smaller geographical units that share similar modes. Thus the concept of *subseries* (ending in *-an*), created by dividing series into smaller units, was introduced.

Robert Howard's research in Jamaica in 1947–48 initiated a new period of interest in Jamaican prehistory. He acknowledged the important contributions of C.B. Lewis, curator of the Science Museum of the Institute of Jamaica. Howard introduced Rouse's taxonomy and, in the process, established a new mindset for archaeological research on the island. Previous investigations had emphasized the description of artefacts that were unique and exotic. In contrast, the culture-historical approach focused on the mundane, everyday artefacts of life; this approach asked when and where particular forms of pottery

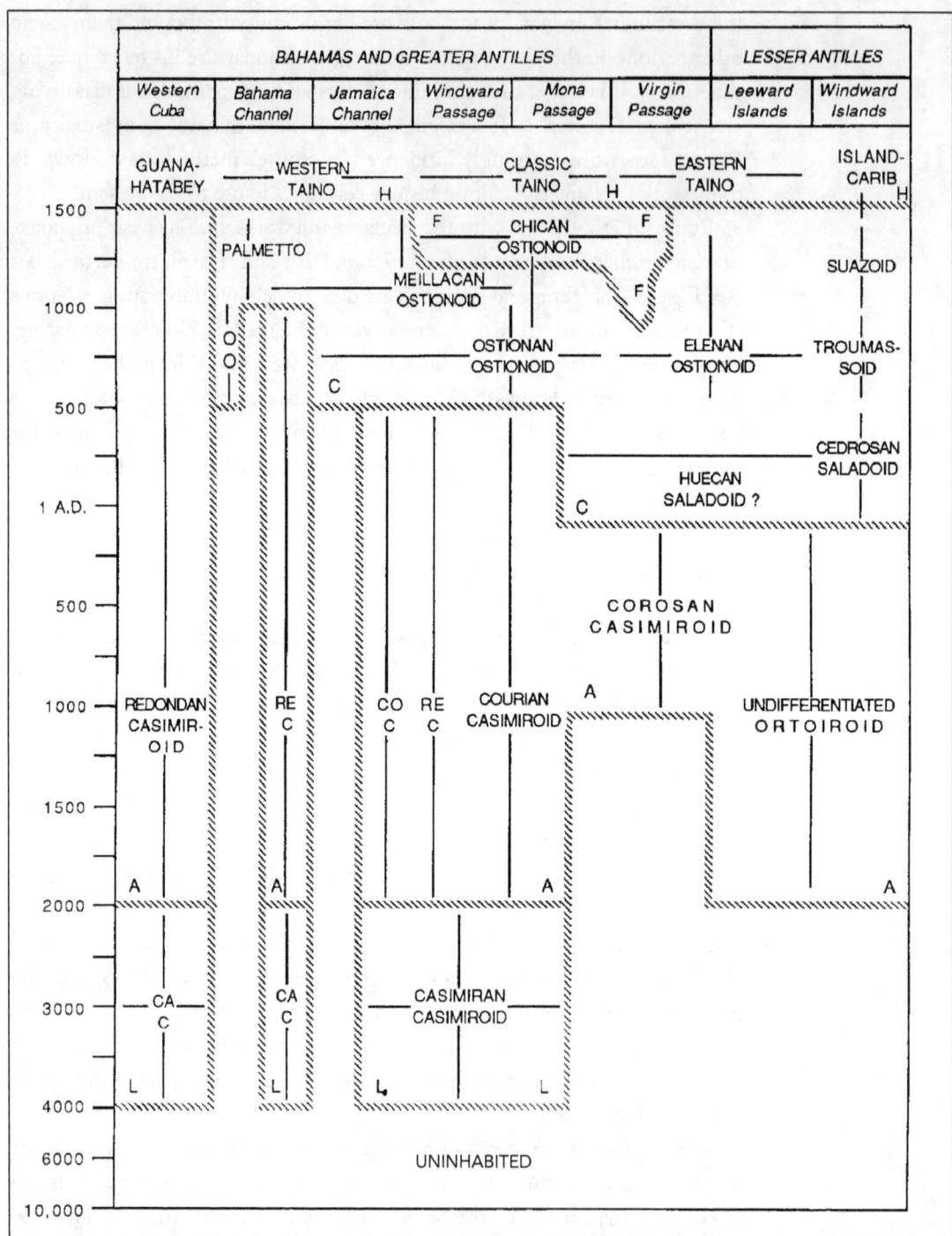

Figure 1.1 Irving Rouse's chronology of the series and subseries of cultures in the West Indies. Ages: A, Archaic; C, Ceramic; F, Formative; H, Historic; L, Lithic. The Bahama Channel area includes the Bahama Islands, the Turks and Caicos Islands and central Cuba; the Jamaica Channel area, Jamaica and southwestern Haiti; the Windward Passage area, eastern Cuba and the adjacent parts of Haiti; the Mona Passage area, the Dominican Republic and western Puerto Rico, and the Virgin Passage area, eastern Puerto Rico and the Virgin Islands. (Rouse 1992, Fig. 8.)

decoration and other artefacts were found. In essence, the change in emphasis reflected a shift from quality to quantity. On the one hand, the discovery of exotic artefacts is a rare occurrence akin to winning the lottery; on the other, archaeological sites are common in Jamaica, and new ones can be found with relatively little effort.

Howard's dissertation (1950) describes in detail archaeological investigations that had been conducted before 1950. In this regard it provides an important starting point for an inventory of archaeological sites and descriptions for material remains. He recorded seventy-five midden sites, twenty-seven cave sites, and nine rock art sites. His inventory and references to the original publications on these sites are reported in Tables 1.1–1.3 (see appendix). We include these tables to provide present and future researchers with the sources for research up to that date.

In his later publications Howard (1956, 1965) fitted Jamaican archaeology into the dominant classification scheme of the time. It is worth reiterating that his scheme was based on Rouse's taxonomy, which identified a single line of development for the islands. Other archaeologists identified every different pottery series as representing the migration of a new group of people into the West Indies (see Keegan 2000). In contrast, Rouse has always maintained that there was a single line of development, that each new pottery series developed from the previous series and that new immigrants were not responsible for the observed changes (Siegel 1996).

According to Rouse's scheme at the time, the first Ceramic Age peoples in the islands were the Saladoid (named for the Saladero site on the Orinoco River in Venezuela). They reached Puerto Rico about 400 BC but did not expand into Hispaniola, and there was no further movement to the west, until after AD 600. Rouse (1986) described the failure of pottery-making to expand westward at this time as evidence for a "frontier" at the Mona Passage. By AD 600 a new pottery series had developed, which Rouse called Ostionoid (named for the Punta Ostiones site in Puerto Rico). The Ostionoid peoples began a new phase of population movement, expanding into Hispaniola, Cuba, the Bahamas and Jamaica after AD 600. The Ostionoid series is distinguished by simple hemispherical and boat-shaped vessels, frequently decorated with red paint (see Figure 1.2). For this reason the pottery is often called Redware.

Rouse (1986) at one time concluded that the Ostionoid series then developed into the Meillacoid series (named for the Meillac site in Haiti), through the abandonment of red paint and the adoption of fine-line incised and appliqué decorations. The change occurred in central Hispaniola, and the new form of decoration spread to Cuba and Jamaica. Rouse views this transition as the spread of new ideas about decoration rather than the actual movement of

Figure 1.2 Ostionan pottery from Jamaica. (Florida Museum of Natural History Collection.)

peoples from Hispaniola to the west. Finally, the Chicoid series (named for the Boca Chica site in the southeastern Dominican Republic) developed out of the Meillacoid and spread west to eastern Cuba and east to Puerto Rico and the northern Lesser Antilles (Figure 1.3). Again, Rouse (ibid.) attributed the spread of these decorative modes to the movement of ideas and not the migration of peoples.

Figure 1.3 Chican pottery from Hispaniola. (Florida Museum of Natural History Collection.)

Howard (1965) recognized that Redware pottery was similar to the Ostionoid pottery described by Rouse. Jamaican Redware, however, is different from Ostionoid pottery found elsewhere in the Greater Antilles; for that reason he named the style after the Little River site (though many people continue to use the name Redware to describe this style). Howard noted that there was another kind of pottery decorated with incised designs and filleted rims that was very similar to the Meillacoid pottery from Hispaniola, and he called this style White Marl after the site at which it was first described. Howard (ibid.) recognized that the pottery from the Fairfield site near Montego Bay was similar to White Marl pottery, but that it was also quite distinctive. He therefore identified the Fairfield complex or the Montego Bay style, which characterized the pottery of northwestern Jamaica.[2]

Meillacoid vessels, including the White Marl style, typically are boat-shaped or hemispherical and turn inward at the shoulder, such that the opening (aperture) is smaller than the greatest diameter of the vessel (*casuela*) (Figure 1.4). Filleted rims are common and incised and appliqué decorations are located between the shoulder and the rim. Meillacan pottery from Jamaica is distinctive in that the distance between the shoulder and the rim is shorter than that observed on casuela vessels in Haiti (Figure 1.5). The Montego Bay style is also distinctive in that a wider fillet or separate band of clay (in addition to a filleted rim) is affixed at the rim and is decorated with deeply incised parallel lines on this band.

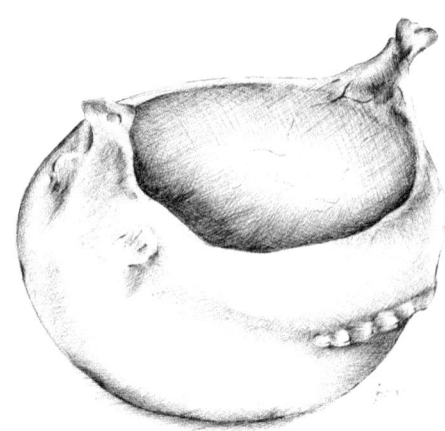

Figure 1.4 Jamaican Meillacan boat-shaped vessel. (Illustration by Joslyn Reid, Institute of Jamaica Collection.)

Figure 1.5 Meillacan pottery from Haiti. (Florida Museum of Natural History Collection.)

Descriptions of Jamaican Redware were based on pottery recovered during excavations at the Little River site in 1933 (De Wolf 1953). The Little River site was the first at which Redware pottery was identified, although since then a number of Redware sites have been discovered, primarily along the south coast. The Alligator Pond site is a good example (Silverberg, Vanderwal and Wing 1972). Howard (1950) reported the Little River style as being part of the Ostionoid series, and the White Marl and Montego Bay styles as part of the Meillacoid series.

Rouse has since modified his classification system to include subseries, apparently based on his belief that all of the late-period styles were derived from the Ostionoid series. According to the new scheme, there were Ostionan, Meillacan, and Chican subseries of the Ostionoid series (Figure 1.6). In accord with this revised scheme, Jamaican Redware fits in the Ostionan Ostionoid, and White Marl and Montego Bay styles are part of the Meillacan Ostionoid. The main problem with this classification is that new evidence from Haiti indicates that the Ostionan, Meillacan, and Chican subseries are probably separate traditions. Meillacan and Chican apparently developed from an early migration of people or the diffusion of pottery making to archaic groups in the eastern Dominican Republic around 350 BC. The Ostionan subseries did not reach Hispaniola until after AD 600 (Keegan 2003; Veloz Maggiolo and Ortega 1996). The classification system has not, as yet, been modified to account for these new developments.

These new data on the origins of the Ostionan and Meillacan subseries are especially important for Jamaican archaeology. It has been assumed, following Rouse, that the Redware peoples changed their style of decorating pottery and transformed themselves into the White Marl people. The new data suggest that there were two separate migrations to Jamaica. The first was by people

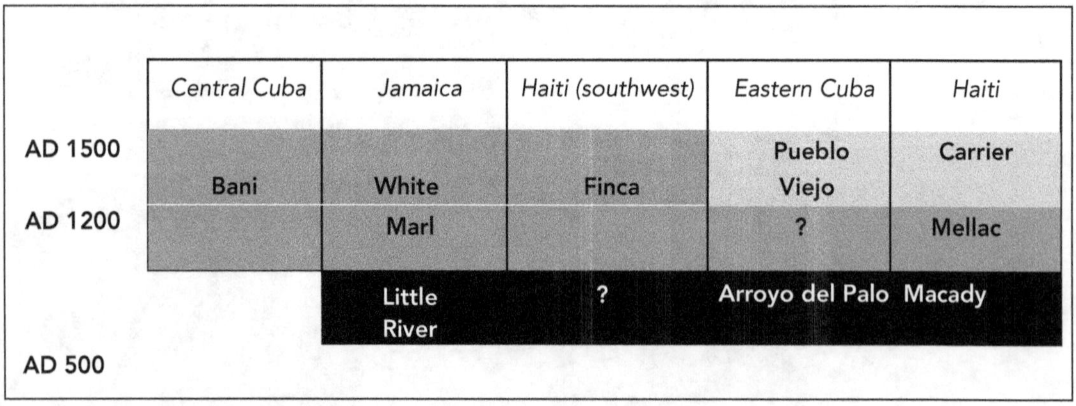

	Central Cuba	Jamaica	Haiti (southwest)	Eastern Cuba	Haiti
AD 1500				Pueblo Viejo	Carrier
	Bani	White Marl	Finca		
AD 1200				?	Mellac
		Little River	?	Arroyo del Palo	Macady
AD 500					

Figure 1.6 Local styles in the Ostionan (in black), Meillacan (in dark grey) and Chican (in light grey) subseries, Ostionoid series, for Cuba, Haiti and Jamaica. (Rouse 1992, fig. 14.)

making Ostionan (Redware) pottery, who arrived on the island after AD 700. The second was by people making Meillacan (White Marl) pottery, and they arrived around AD 1000. The questions that face us concern the interactions between these distinct cultures and the way in which the Meillacan peoples were able to displace the Ostionan peoples who arrived before them. Finally, we need to address why the people near Montego Bay developed a distinct style of pottery decoration. These and other questions concerning the lifeways of the first people on Jamaica are the subject of the next phase of research that began in the 1970s.

Sociocultural Research

The papers collected in this book reflect *sociocultural research*, the most recent phase of archaeological investigation as defined by Rouse. This research initially was sponsored by the Archaeological Society of Jamaica, and was published in the society's newsletter, *Archaeology Jamaica* (for example, see Wallace 1992). The ASJ began as an Archaeology Club, established by James Lee in 1965. Five years later, with outside support, Lee transformed the organization into the Archaeological Society of Jamaica. James Lee is a remarkable man. Not only did he devote substantial energy to identifying the prehistoric cultural resources of Jamaica, he also published reports on his investigations that provided a foundation for the future (see Lee 1991).

During the 1960s and 1970s the main excavation projects were conducted at White Marl (S-1) (Perrins 1981; Silverberg, Vanderwal and Wing 1972), Rodney's House (S-5) and Port Henderson (S-29) (Wilman 1978, 1979), all in St Catherine. Others were carried on at Bellevue (K-13), St Andrew (Medhurst 1976a, 1976b, 1977a, 1977b; Wing 1977); Cinnamon Hill (J-10), St James (Osborne and Lee 1976, 1977; Johnson 1976); and Upton (A-43), St Ann (Wilman 1983, 1984, 1992). Although most of the members of the ASJ have been avocational archaeologists, their investigations have always been of the highest quality. In addition to visiting newly discovered prehistoric sites and conducting an active programme of prospecting for new sites, a number of the members conducted excavations.

During the Lee administration the society focused primarily on the island's prehistory, which is evident in issues of *Archaeology Jamaica* from the period. Between 1965 and 1985, James Lee and the ASJ conducted intensive investigations, and subsequently published several articles, on Jamaican prehistoric artefacts, such as Taíno stone celts, pendants, grinding stones and net-sinkers (Lee 1978a; Roobol and Lee 1976, reprinted in this volume). Lee also published research on Taíno *buréns* or cassava griddles (Lee 1980a) and Jamaican *adornos*, which are clay heads that adorn the rims of pottery vessels

(Lee 1983b). Dr Lee made a concerted effort to bring Jamaican archaeology to the archaeological community at large, and his work has been widely disseminated.

In 1999, Lee handed over his collection to the University of the West Indies. This collection is currently being studied by the archaeological lab at the university's Mona campus under the direction of Dr Philip Allsworth-Jones. The research done by Lee and the ASJ has also greatly benefited the Jamaica National Heritage Trust, as Lee's site codes and mapping information have provided important data for the Jamaica National Heritage Trust's National Inventory of Sites and Monuments.

The past two decades have involved diversification and growth in Jamaican archaeology. During this period we have seen the beginnings of investigations of the Afro-Jamaican, Spanish and Jewish heritage – illustrating the island's multiethnic composition, encapsulated in the motto on the national coat of arms, "Out of Many, One People".

The Jamaica National Heritage Trust was actually established as the Jamaica National Trust Commission in 1958, under the administration of the Institute of Jamaica. In 1985, the commission was separated from the Institute of Jamaica and renamed the Jamaica National Heritage Trust. According to Roderick Ebanks, Technical Director of Archaeology at the Jamaica National Heritage Trust, the new and improved institution was responsible for "the legal protection and administration of all historical sites, ranging from small houses – Taíno sites to Plantations" (personal communication, 1997). For almost two decades the Archaeology Division of the Jamaica National Heritage Trust has been responsible for most of the investigations conducted on the island. Although its members are highly trained and would like to pursue more scholarly research, the limited resources available have afforded the opportunity for little more than rescue and salvage operations (see Richards, this volume).

When archaeology as a discipline was established at the University of the West Indies, the first lecturer was the Ghanaian Emmanuel Kofi Agorsah. "Dr Kofi", as he is affectionately called, was influential in diversifying Jamaican archaeological research. His special interest was in Afro-Jamaican and Maroon archaeology, which he brought to the forefront (Agorsah 1992, 1993, 1994). He also challenged traditional methods of classifying the past (Agorsah 1994).

Since his arrival in 1998, Philip Allsworth-Jones has contributed to Jamaican prehistoric research with his collaborative investigations at Chancery Hall, St Andrew, and Green Castle, St Mary (both reported in this volume).

During the past decade significant progress has been made. In 1992, there was the recovery of the Aboukir *zemís* – the most significant Taíno find in two hundred years (discussed by Saunders and Gray in this volume). Subsequently there has been renewed interest in Jamaican prehistory, as seen by Elizabeth Rega at Sommerville Cave, Clarendon, William "Bill" Keegan at Paradise Park, Westmoreland, and, recently, Betty "Jo" Stokes at Rio Nuevo, St Mary.

Conclusions

Archaeologists throughout the West Indies have begun to move beyond the simple classification of pottery decorations to ask questions about where ancient people lived, what they ate, what types of trade they engaged in, how their economy might be characterized, what types of social relations they had and how their polities were organized. In this regard, it should be noted that Jamaican researchers were at the forefront in technical studies. They were among the first to seek the specific identification of animal bones found in sites in order to determine what people ate and where the foods were captured (Johnson 1976; Wing 1977). They used petrographic analysis to identify the sources of stone artefacts in the sites (Robool and Lee 1976, reprinted in this volume); and they used X-ray diffraction to characterize the clays from which pottery vessels were made at the Bellevue site (Medhurst 1976a, 1976b, 1977a, 1977b). In addition, the study of wooden artefacts and of the petroglyphs and pictographs that decorated cave walls provided information about the makers' belief systems and world view (Aarons 1994; Watson 1988; Saunders and Gray, this volume).

Jamaican archaeology has a long and rich heritage. In fact, its early practitioners equalled and in some cases surpassed their peers in the United States. Yet for many years Jamaica was isolated. Caribbean archaeologists tended to emphasize the earliest Ceramic Age culture, known as Saladoid, and the contact period "Classic Taíno" cultures of eastern Cuba, Hispaniola and Puerto Rico. Because these cultures did not occur in Jamaica, Jamaican archaeology was viewed as peripheral to the main archaeological interests in the region. This lack of interest was initially expressed by calling the peoples of central Cuba, the Bahamas, the northern Lesser Antilles and Jamaica "sub-Taínos" (Lovén 1935). Although the term *Western Taínos* has now been adopted for the contact period peoples of central Cuba and Jamaica, the legacy of past research orientations has maintained their peripheral position.

Despite a general lack of interest on the part of foreign archaeologists, Jamaica developed a model programme of national archaeology through the combined efforts of the Institute of Jamaica, ASJ, the University of the West Indies and the Jamaica National Heritage Trust. During the past decade, archaeologists working throughout the West Indies have begun to recognize that we need a more comprehensive view of the past. This new perspective does not focus on a single island, but instead takes an "archipelagic" view (Watters 1997). In this regard, there is renewed interest in the archaeology of the periphery, and Jamaican archaeology stands poised to make significant contributions to our understanding of the native peoples of the West Indies.

Appendix

Table 1.1 Midden Sites Reported by Robert Howard and Reference to Their Original Description

Site	Parish	Reference
Great Goat Island	St Catherine	Duerden 1897
Jackson's Bay	Clarendon	MacCormack 1898
Jackson's Bay	Clarendon	MacCormack 1898
Portland	Clarendon	MacCormack 1898
Portland Ridge Midden 1	Clarendon	MacCormack 1898
Portland Ridge Midden 2	Clarendon	MacCormack 1898
Harmony Hall	Clarendon	Duerden 1897
Salt River	Clarendon	MacCormack 1898
Round Hill	Clarendon	Howard 1950
Pedro	St Elizabeth	Reichard 1904
Hounslow	St Elizabeth	Duerden 1897
Black River	St Elizabeth	Reichard 1904
Bluefields	Westmoreland	C.B. Lewis, Howard 1950
Newfound River	Hanover	Duerden 1897
Rhodes Hall	Hanover	Duerden 1897
Haughton Hall	Hanover	Duerden 1897
Kew	Hanover	Duerden 1897
Fairfield, Montego Bay	St James	Reichard 1904
Montego Bay Point	St James	Reichard 1904
Williamsfield	St James	Duerden 1897
Mammee Hill	St James	Duerden 1897
Spotty Hill	St James	Duerden 1897
California	St James	Duerden 1897
Wales	Trelawny	Duerden 1897
Stewart Castle	Trelawny	Duerden 1897
Rio Bueno	Trelawny	Howard 1950
Dry Harbour	St Ann	Howard 1950
Retreat	St Ann	Duerden 1897, De Booy 1913
Mahogany Hill	St Ann	Longley 1914
Scarborough	St Ann	Longley 1914
Logie Green	Clarendon	Longley 1914
St Jean D'Acre	St Ann	Longley 1914
Culloden	St Ann	Longley 1914
Green Hill	St Ann	Longley 1914

Table 1.1 continues

Table 1.1 Midden Sites Reported by Robert Howard and Reference to Their Original Description *(cont'd)*

Site	Parish	Reference
Armordale	St Ann	C.S. Cotter, Howard 1950
Boston	St Ann	C.S. Cotter, Howard 1950
Orange Valley	St Ann	C.S. Cotter, Howard 1950
Southfield	St Ann	Howard 1950
Cranbrook	St Ann	Duerden 1897
Seville	St Ann	C.S. Cotter, Howard 1950
Liberty Hill	St Ann	Howard 1950
Windsor	St Ann	C.S. Cotter, Howard 1950
New Ground	St Ann	C.S. Cotter, Howard 1950
Greenwich Park	St Ann	C.S. Cotter, Howard 1950
Tydenham	St Ann	Howard 1950
Prosper Hall	St Ann	C.S. Cotter, Howard 1950
Trafalgar	St Ann	C.S. Cotter, Howard 1950
Friendship	St Ann	Duerden 1897
Belle Vue	St Ann	Duerden 1897
Shaw	St Ann	Howard 1950
Dunlookin	St Mary	Howard 1950
Prospect	St Mary	C.S. Cotter, Howard 1950
Llanrumney	St Mary	C.S. Cotter, Howard 1950
Clitos Point	St Mary	Howard 1950
Port Antonio	Portland	C.S. Cotter, Howard 1950
Duckenfield	St Thomas	C.S. Cotter, Howard 1950
Rozelle	St Thomas	C.S. Cotter, Howard 1950
Creighton Hall	St Thomas	Howard 1950
Cambridge Hill	St Thomas	Duerden 1897
Sugar Loaf Hill	St Thomas	Howard 1950
Seven Mile Hill	Kingston & St Andrew	Howard 1950
Fort Nugent	Kingston & St Andrew	C.B. Lewis, Howard 1950
Tower Hill	Kingston & St Andrew	C.B. Lewis, Howard 1950
Long Mountain	Kingston & St Andrew	Duerden 1897
Hope	Kingston & St Andrew	Duerden 1897
Iver	Kingston & St Andrew	Howard 1950
Norbrook	Kingston & St Andrew	Blake 1895; Duerden 1897
Chancery Hall	Kingston & St Andrew	C.B. Lewis, Howard 1950
Ferry Hill	St Catherine	Howard 1950
Waterloo	St Catherine	Howard 1950
White Marl	St Catherine	Duerden 1897; Howard 1950
Port Henderson	St Catherine	Howard 1950

Source: Howard 1950.

Table 1.2 Cave Sites Reported by Robert Howard and Reference to Their Original Description

Site	Parish	Reference
Great Goat Island	St Catherine	Duerden 1897
Portland Cave	Clarendon	C.B. Lewis, Howard 1950
Portland Ridge Cave No. 1	Clarendon	C.B. Lewis, Howard 1950
Portland Ridge Cave No. 3	Clarendon	Howard 1950
Portland Ridge Cave No. 4	Clarendon	Howard 1950
Portland Ridge Cave No. 5	Clarendon	C.B. Lewis, Howard 1950
Portland Ridge Rock Shelter	Clarendon	Howard 1950
Little Miller's Bay	Manchester	MacCormack 1898
Little Miller's Bay	Manchester	MacCormack 1898
Little Miller's Bay	Manchester	MacCormack 1898
Jackson's Bay	Clarendon	MacCormack 1898
Pedro	St Elizabeth	Duerden 1897
Hounslow	St Elizabeth	Duerden 1897
Ipswich	St Elizabeth	Howard 1950
Drummond	Westmoreland	Duerden 1897
Negril	Westmoreland	Duerden 1897
New Market	St James	Reichard 1904
California	St James	Duerden 1897
Windsor	Trelawny	Howard 1950
Alexandria	St Ann	Longley 1914
Botany Bay	St Thomas	Duerden 1897
Cambridge Hill	St Thomas	Duerden 1897
Cambridge Hill	St Thomas	Duerden 1897
Halberstadt	Kingston & St Andrew	Duerden 1897
Bloxburgh	St Thomas	Duerden 1897
Dallas Castle	St Andrew	Duerden 1897

Source: Howard 1950.

Table 1.3 Cave Art Sites Reported by Robert Howard and Reference to Their Original Description

Site	Parish	Reference
Canoe Valley	Manchester	C.B. Lewis, Howard 1950
Canoe Valley	Manchester	C.B. Lewis, Howard 1950
Canoe Valley	Manchester	C.B. Lewis, Howard 1950
Kempshot	St James	Duerden 1897
Pantrepant	Trelawny	Duerden 1897
Salisbury	St Ann	C.S. Cotter, Howard 1950
Walkerswood	St Ann	C.S. Cotter, Howard 1950
Dryland	St Mary	Duerden 1897
Mountain River Cave	St Catherine	Duerden 1897

Source: Howard 1950.

Notes

1. There are similar problems with access to archaeological research conducted on other islands, including Cuba and the Dominican Republic, where the results are published locally and are not widely disseminated, especially to the English-speaking world.
2. Vanderwal (1968a) called it the "Fairfield style" and reported that it was found only on the north coast in western Jamaica. Montego Bay–style pottery recently was discovered on the south coast at the Sweetwater site, Paradise Park, Westmoreland, just east of the town of Savanna-la-Mar.

2  The Taíno Settlement of the Kingston Area

Philip Allsworth-Jones
Gerald Lalor
George Lechler
Simon F. Mitchell
Esther Z. Rodriques
and
Mitko Vutchkov

Introduction

THE PRESENCE OF Taíno sites in the Kingston area has been recorded from the last years of the nineteenth century onwards, and important excavations have been conducted at some of them, particularly by amateurs in the 1970s. Dr James Lee included them in his general mapping project of the island, the results of which were mentioned in the newsletter, which he edited from 1965 to 1986. As a result of the development and spread of Kingston in recent times, some new sites have been discovered, but they and some of the old ones have also been wholly or partially destroyed. The number of people who are aware of the exact location of some of these sites is limited, and it seemed desirable to record this information before it was lost. A survey of all known sites was therefore carried out in order to ascertain their current status and assess possible opportunities for future work. The results can be seen in the accompanying map (see Figure 2.1) and annotated list (see Table 2.3). In addition, two pilot studies were undertaken to explore the possibilities of scientific analysis of some of these materials. First, following a small trial exca-

---

Originally published in 1999, in *Proceedings of the Eighteenth International Congress for Caribbean Archaeology, Grenada, 1999*: 115–27.

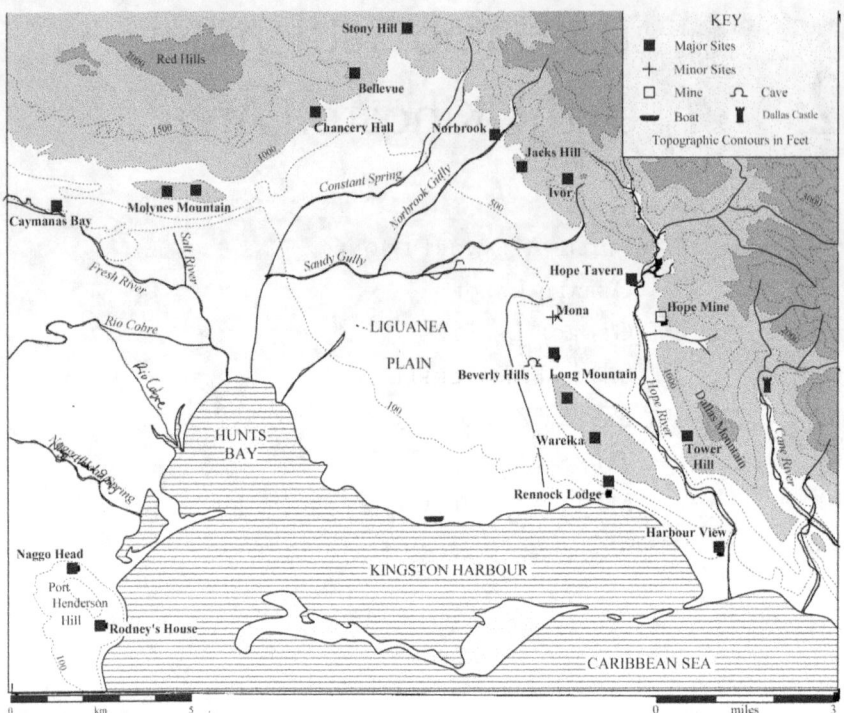

Figure 2.1 Taíno sites in the Kingston area

vation at Chancery Hall in 1998, the molluscs from that excavation were examined, and the results are compared with the material already published from Rodney's House and Bellevue. Second, an initial study of pottery from six of the sites has been carried out using neutron activation analysis (NAA), and preliminary results from that study are also presented here. It is hoped that the pattern of interdisciplinary investigation employed in this study, using geographical units larger than the individual site, can be extended to throw light on the pre-Columbian occupation of Jamaica in general.

The Kingston Area: Geographical Background

The area with which this study is concerned is illustrated in Figure 2.1. In the centre is the Liguanea Plain, crossed by a number of gullies, and now occupied by the sprawling mass of the city of Kingston itself. To the north and east it is bounded by an arc of hills, notably the Red Hills, Jacks Hill, Dallas Mountain and Long Mountain. The Hope River runs to the sea in a gorge between the last two. To the west, where once there was a morass, the Salt and Fresh rivers and the Rio Cobre enter the sea at Hunts Bay. The Rio Cobre, canalized in the mid-nineteenth century, once joined the Fresh River in its course to the sea (Edward Robinson, personal communication, 1999). Port Henderson Hill lies to the south, opposite the present Port Royal. Geologic-ally, Port Henderson Hill, the Red Hills, Dallas Mountain and Long Mountain are all formed of Tertiary limestone, whereas Jacks Hill and the mountains rising to the northeast are of Cretaceous-Tertiary granodiorites, andesites and volcaniclastic and clastic sediments (Matley 1951; Green 1977; Gupta and Ahmad 2000).

The Liguanea Plain represents an alluvial fan that was produced by sediments carried by the Hope River before it was diverted into its present channel (Wood 1976). It is possible that Sandy Gully marks its former course. It is not known exactly when the drainage took on its present form, but presumably it was essentially as it is now during the time of the Taíno occupation. According to Claypole (1973), the Liguanea Plain was largely unsettled and uncultivated immediately prior to the English occupation in 1655: "No springs or rivers flowed in or across the centre portion which was composed mainly of a dry savanna area". One result of the Hope River capture was the formation of the Palisadoes tombolo, made up of increased sediment entering the sea southeast of Long Mountain and transported west by longshore drift. According to Hendry (1978), Port Royal has at times been joined to the rest of the Palisadoes and at times been separated from them.

Taíno Sites in the Kingston Area

The sites are arranged in an arc around Kingston, and are listed in Table 2.3 in their approximate order from west to east (Figure 2.1). The code names (where applicable) are those assigned to them by Dr J.W. Lee. If Molynes Mountain and Long Mountain are both considered as two sites, then there are eighteen major open-air locations characterized as shell middens, two burial caves, one stray find of a petaloid celt, one known raw-material source and one site where a canoe considered to be of Taíno origin was found. Some of the open-air sites were already known by the end of the nineteenth century and were commented on by Duerden (1897). Now they either are difficult to access because they are in socially volatile areas (Wareika and Rennock Lodge) or have been partially or totally built over (Norbrook and Hope Tavern). Of the sites discovered later, Harbour View is also largely inaccessible, Naggo Head has been totally destroyed by quarrying, and the few finds from Stony Hill were found only after the house on the site "Fort George" had been demolished. Other sites (Caymanas Bay, Molynes Mountain, Jacks Hill, Ivor, Long Mountain) are apparently still largely intact but have not been systematically investigated and are known only thanks to the work of interested amateurs. The major excavated open-air sites are Rodney's House, Chancery Hall, Bellevue and Tower Hill, and these have produced both artefactual and environmental evidence. Chancery Hall has also produced the only radiocarbon date from the area, of 690 ± 50 BP (uncalibrated, which is equivalent to AD 1260 ± 50). Very little is known of the two burial caves (Beverly Hills and Dallas Castle), and the exact whereabouts of the second are not certain. Hope Mine certainly functioned as a source of galena until recently, and the locality was known to the Taínos, since pieces of this material, presumably prized for their decorative effect, have been found at both Bellevue and Chancery Hall. The wooden canoe is an unusual find quite unlike any of the others. It was discovered by National Water Commission (NWC) workmen in 1993–94 at the corner of Harbour and Pechon streets in downtown Kingston and is now in the custody of the Jamaica National Heritage Trust. It consists of a single piece of wood, is rounded at both ends and has a flat bottom with markings (presumably resulting from its construction) on both sides. It is considered to be of Taíno origin, but dating of the material, as well as full publication by the Jamaica National Heritage Trust, is still awaited.

A distinct pattern of settlement is apparent from the study of the map. One of the major open-air sites is at an altitude of more than 610 m, eight are more than 305 m, and nine are between 305 m and 61 m above sea level. The tendency to settle on hilltops is clear. The stray find of a petaloid celt from the former grounds of the Mona Great House, as well as that of the canoe near the present day shoreline, provides a hint, however, that the Liguanea Plain was not entirely neglected, and the people must have traversed it to collect the marine molluscs which they evidently so much enjoyed, as well as for other purposes.

Analysis of Shells from Chancery Hall

A small excavation took place at Chancery Hall on 12–13 April 1998 as a joint project between the University of the West Indies and the University of Leicester. Work was carried out in two lots. On lot 340, a 1-m² quadrant was excavated to a depth of 15 cm. Apart from shells, artefacts recovered included ninety-six potsherds and one limestone flake. In addition, a section was cut in lot 386, by the boundary wall between it and lot 340. Layer 3 contained abundant shells and artefacts comparable to those from the excavated quadrant. There were twenty-three potsherds, fifteen chert flakes and a limestone core. This study related to the totality of the molluscan material recovered at that time.

Methods

All material recovered from the site was washed and dried. Molluscs were counted, counts being based on apices for gastropods and umbones for bivalves. Single gastropod valves were counted as one (operculae were ignored), while bivalve valves were counted as 0.5 (thus reflecting the fact that each animal has two valves). Identification was based on standard texts (for example, Abbott 1954; Humfrey 1975; Warmke and Abbott 1961).

We divide the material into two separate groups: terrestrial molluscs and marine molluscs. While marine molluscs must have been transported to the site, terrestrial molluscs may have lived on the site and may have had little value to the Taíno people.

Results

The results of mollusc identifications are presented in Table 2.1. Representative samples have been deposited in the Geological Museum, University of the West Indies, with catalogue numbers ranging from UWIGM.1999.5 to UWIGM.1999.44. Eighty-five per cent of the terrestrial gastropods on the site are represented by *Pleurodonte lucerna* (Müller).

Eighteen species of marine bivalve and nine species of marine gastropod were identified from Chancery Hall. Only five of the marine species [*Neritina (Vitta) reclivata* (Say), *N. (V.) piratica* (Russell), *Anadara ovalis* (Bruguière), *Chione intapurpurea* (Conrad) and *Crassostrea rhizophorae* (Guilding)] are numerically important, accounting for 90 per cent of the total marine species recovered (Table 2.1).

Discussion

The concentration of shells on the Chancery Hall site is likely to reflect both the dietary preference of the Taíno people and the resources available to them. The five most abundant marine molluscs found on the site probably formed a significant part of their shellfish diet. The species of *Neritina* occur in brackish water on intertidal mudflats (Warmke and Abbott 1961, 50–51), while the bivalves *A. ovalis* and *C. intapurpurea* are semi-infaunal (partially buried) inhabitants of mudflats, and *C. rhizophorae* lives attached to mangrove roots. Kingston Harbour, with its protected mudflats and shallow water, is the main site on the central south coast of Jamaica where mudflat molluscs occur, and it seems likely that the Chancery Hall Taíno people collected their shellfish from these mudflats.

The modern mudflat fauna in Kingston Harbour is dominated by abundant examples of *N. virginea* Linné and *C. cancellata* Linné, while *N. (V.) piratica, N. (V.) reclivata, A. ovalis* and *C. intapurpurea* are rare. The abundance of the latter four species on the Chancery Hall site suggests that at the time

Table 2.1 Shells Collected from Chancery Hall

Species	Lot 340		Lot 386, Layer 3		Both Sites	
Marine Gastropods	Count[1]	Per cent[2]	Count[1]	Per cent[2]	Count[1]	Per cent[2]
Cittarium pica	1	0.1	0	0.0	1	0.04
Fasciolaria tulipa	1	0.1	0	0.0	1	0.04
Littorina sp.	0	0.0	1	0.2	1	0.04
Melongena melongena	21	1.2	10	1.6	31	1.30
Murex brevifrons	12	0.7	7	1.1	19	0.80
Nerita fulgurans	1	0.1	0	0.0	1	0.04
Neritina (Vitta) piratica	487	27.8	111	17.7	598	25.13
Neritina (Vitta) reclivata	771	43.9	198	31.7	969	40.71
Neritina (Vitta) virginea	7	0.4	6	1.0	13	0.55
Total marine gastropods	1,301	–	333	–	1,634	–
Terrestrial Gastropods	–	–	–	–	–	–
Pleurodonte lucerna	288	n/a	129	n/a	417	n/a
Dentellaria sloaneana	13	n/a	4	n/a	17	n/a
Other terrestrial	0	n/a	59	n/a	59	n/a
Total terrestrial gastropods	301		192		493	
Bivalves	–	–	–	–	–	–
Anadara notabilis	1	0.0	3	0.2	4	0.08
Anadara ovalis	324	9.2	287	22.9	611	12.84
Anomalocardia brasiliana	3	0.1	2	0.2	5	0.11
Arca umbonata	35	1.0	10	0.8	45	0.95
Arca zebra	72	2.1	26	2.1	98	2.06
Barbatia candida	2	0.1	0	0.0	2	0.04
Brachidontes citrinus	2	0.1	6	0.5	8	0.17
Chama macerophylla	50	1.4	18	1.4	68	1.43
Chione cancellata	5	0.1	8	0.6	13	0.27
Chione granulata	60	1.7	19	1.5	79	1.66
Chione intapurpurea	215	6.1	123	9.8	338	7.10
Chione sp.	0	0.0	1	0.1	1	0.02
Codakia (s.s.) *orbicularis*	7	0.2	1	0.1	8	0.17
Crassostrea rhizophorae	117	3.3	79	6.3	196	4.12
Isognomon alatus	6	0.2	2	0.2	8	0.17
Ostrea frons	4	0.1	0	0.0	4	0.08
Semele proficua	3	0.1	0	0.0	3	0.06
Trachycardium muricatum	1	0.0	0	0.0	1	0.02
Total bivalve valves	907	–	585	–	1,492	–

[1]Individual bivalve and gastropod counts.
[2]Percentage of marine shells based on complete animals (gastropods count 1, bivalves count 0.5).

of Taíno occupation these species were dominant elements of the Kingston Harbour shellfish assemblage. Over-collection of these species by the Taíno people may have been responsible for the demise of the natural populations. In this context, it is interesting to note that the species favoured by the Taíno were replaced by species of smaller size (judging from modern populations) and therefore less nutritional value (more need to be collected for the same food quantity).

One notable rarity on the Chancery Hall site is the *Strombus gigas* Linné (queen conch), only a single fragment having been found on a subsequent visit. This gastropod species is an important part of the modern shellfish diet in the Caribbean and was almost certainly collected for food by the Taíno people. *S. gigas* is a very large marine gastropod with an impressive shell. Its absence at Chancery Hall might be due to the fact that the shell is very heavy. (Why carry animal and shell up to the site when the muscle can be cut and only the meat transported?) Modern Jamaican beaches are littered with piles of *S. gigas* shells which have been culled for food; the antiquity of some piles may not even be guessed.

The terrestrial gastropod *P. lucerna* is abundant on the Chancery Hall site. However, there are many places in Jamaica where extensive accumulations of terrestrial gastropods (often *P. lucerna* – Mitchell, personal observation) are concentrated in soil profiles with no evidence of archaeological occupation. Furthermore, a Taíno rubbish tip may have been a highly desirable habitat for such omnivorous terrestrial gastropods. It is therefore premature, without further investigation, to assume that the Taíno people ate these terrestrial molluscs, and they may be present on Taíno sites simply because they lived there. We therefore suggest that the presence of land snails on Jamaican archaeological sites should not necessarily be taken as evidence that they formed part of the diet of the Taíno people.

Excavations at the Bellevue site (Wing and Medhurst 1977; Medhurst 1977a, 1977b) recorded abundant marine and terrestrial shells. The most abundant marine taxa recorded by these authors were species of *Neritina, Arca zebra* Swainson, *Chione granulata* Gmelin and *Anadara brasiliana* Lamarck. This is clearly a similar assemblage to that recorded from Chancery Hall, which is only about 1.5 km from Bellevue.

The assemblages of shells from Chancery Hall and Bellevue contrast markedly with those collected at Rodney's House. Wilman (1978) recorded abundant marine (3,394) and terrestrial (371) shells from Rodney's House with the marine assemblages dominated by *A. zebra, A. imbricata* Bruguière, *Chama macerophylla* Gmelin and *Donax denticulatus* Linné. The first three species are either cemented or attached by a byssus to hard substrates such as rocks, while the fourth is a shallow infaunal (living within the sediment) bivalve inhabiting intertidal sands. Thus the assemblage from Rodney's House typifies the coastal environments of Port Henderson Hill, with its rocky headlands and sandy beaches.

In summary, we conclude that while the molluscs preserved on Taíno sites undoubtedly give some valuable insight into the Taíno diet, this may be to some extent distorted by spurious additions (terrestrial molluscs living on the site) and absences (large molluscs which were butchered on the shore). Arguments concerning human population size that are based solely on shellfish found on archaeological sites may, therefore, be unsound.

Neutron Activation Analysis of Pottery

Twelve pottery samples from six sites in the area (Jacks Hill, Harbour View, Bellevue, Chancery Hall, Rodney's House and Norbrook) were chosen for the study at the International Centre for Environmental and Nuclear Sciences at the University of the West Indies, to be carried out with the technique of neutron activation analysis (NAA). The objective was to determine whether the potters employed the same clay source and, if variations were detected, whether these reflected different clay sources or some other factor – for instance, different vessel types. Hence, there was an attempt to include as varied a selection as possible from each site, including rims and body sherds with different inclusions, and two griddles.

Results

A total of twenty-seven major, minor and trace elements was found. The concentrations of these elements are summarized in Table 2.2.

Discussion

Two striking points emerge from a study of these figures. First, there is a general homogeneity in the quantity of each element present in each sample site. The degree of homogeneity is particularly clear if only the four major elements (Al, Fe, Ti and Ca) are considered. Second, the values for these elements are consistent with their known occurrence in the soils of the Kingston area. Aluminium has an appropriate occurrence of between 8 and 10 per cent; iron, less than 1 per cent; titanium, between 0.49 and 0.7 per cent; and calcium, between 1 and 2 per cent (Lalor 1995). Histograms of the major elements in the sampled sites compared with the levels in the soils of the Kingston area are shown in Figure 2.2.

Table 2.2 Neutron Activation Analysis of Pottery Samples from Sites 1–6 (concentrations in ppm, unless otherwise noted)

Element	Jacks Hill	Harbour View	Bellevue	Chancery Hall	Rodney's House	Norbrook
Aluminium (%)	10.3	8.98	6.23	9.06	8.85	9.77
Vanadium	110	196	117	130	106	70.1
Titanium	4,830	5,310	3,920	3,370	3,440	3,860
Calcium (%)	0.808	1.12	1.5	1.21	0.997	1.26
Manganese	447	417	439	678	268	261
Dysprosium	2.72	2.08	2.06	2.31	1.08	1.46
Europium	0.99	0.635	0.727	0.825	0.50	0.65
Barium	582	1,330	589	470	672	792
Cadmium	2.24	3.29	5.16	6.91	1.13	2.25
Lanthanum	17.7	12.1	14.6	13.5	8.55	12.9
Samarium	4.00	2.39	2.75	2.76	1.39	2.12
Arsenic	4.32	10.1	5.08	5.23	5.79	2.12
Sodium (%)	2.12	1.76	1.86	2.45	1.54	2.32
Bromine	3.77	3.28	1.92	3.98	2.57	2.54
Uranium	2.52	1.87	1.55	1.90	1.39	1.3
Potassium (%)	2.65	1.90	2.03	1.65	1.95	2.18
Antimony	0.60	1.88	0.76	0.88	1.20	0.86
Lutetium	0.33	0.245	0.223	0.20	0.50	0.24
Chromium	24.5	50.9	34.3	<5	20.7	33.8
Iron (%)	4.67	6.16	3.89	4.43	2.88	3.87
Cobalt	15.3	10.0	10.2	15.6	4.44	6.20
Selenium	14.5	13.7	12.4	15.1	7.96	10.7
Cerium	53.0	22.8	33.2	26.4	11.1	35.2
Caesium	3.33	2.69	<1	<1	2.29	<1
Zinc	73.7	56.9	51.9	67.2	52.6	70.9
Thorium	10.9	5.10	8.95	1.80	4.37	10.6
Hafnium	6.26	5.86	5.72	4.55	4.04	6.40

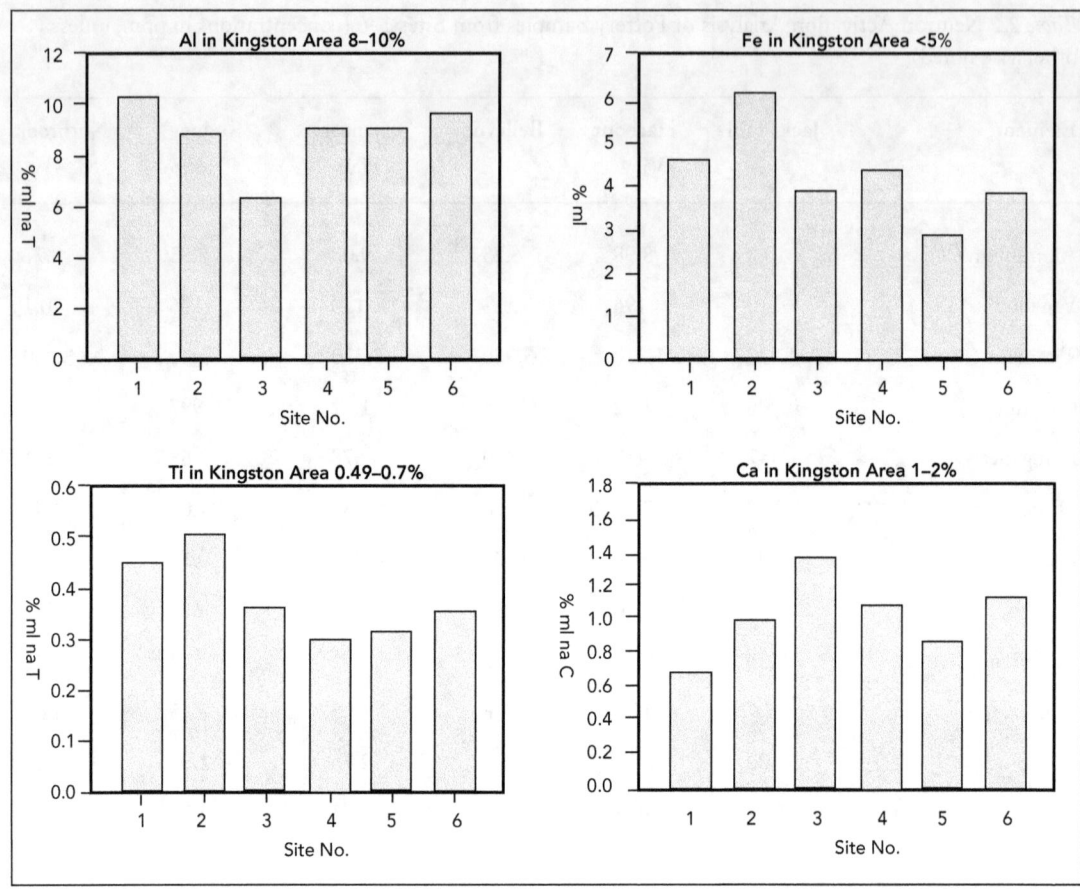

Figure 2.2 Histograms of the major elements in the pottery samples compared with the levels in the soils from the Kingston area

We believe that there probably was a single clay source for these samples. It may have been in Hunts Bay, as suggested by Medhurst and Clarke (1976a), but this remains to be tested, and other sources within the area are known (Hill 1978). A check will also be made to see whether the buff-yellow sherds found in the excavations at Bellevue (distinct from the majority red-brown wares, which alone formed part of this study) conform to the general pattern. They are thought to represent water containers, and are said to have been found at various other places on the island; hence, they may show evidence of long-distance contacts in what otherwise appears to be a homogeneous local industry.

Conclusion

The Taíno settlement of the area had a definite pattern. Most of the known sites are on hilltops, although there are some indications that the Liguanea

Plain may have played a role in the economic network of the time. The analysis of the shells from Chancery Hall revealed a definite concentration of certain species, which may be typical of inland sites as opposed to coastal sites such as Rodney's House. Further study (coupled with an examination of vertebrate remains) at other sites in the area may reveal interesting local variations in the Taíno patterns of faunal exploitation. There are indications that certain molluscs may have been over-collected, leading to a lasting diminution of the natural populations. Neutron activation analysis of selected potsherds showed that they possessed a significant degree of homogeneity, perhaps suggestive of a single clay source. We intend to follow up with further studies on possible clay sources, and also with an approach using X-ray fluorescence, before drawing definitive conclusions. The likelihood of raw-material exchange is demonstrated for the area by evidence of exploitation, or at least collection, of galena at the Hope Mine, and study of the petrography of the celts found at the sites would undoubtedly also reveal much about source materials (Roobol and Lee 1976, reprinted in this volume). This study is hence not an end but a beginning to what it is hoped will be a larger work.

Acknowledgements

Thanks go to Mrs Margaret Hodges and Mr Michael Gardner for showing us the sites on Plantation Heights and Long Mountain, and to the Jamaica Defence Force for their permission to visit Rodney's House. For help in the excavation at Chancery Hall in 1998, thanks go to Dr Rob Young and Dr Jane Webster of the University of Leicester, to Dr Silvia Kouwenberg and Ms Susan Chung of the University of the West Indies, who participated in the work, and to Mr Tony Gouldwell of the University of Leicester, who studied and presented a report on some of the finds. Mr John Wilman provided information about the excavations at Bellevue and Rodney's House, Mr Douglas Aitken kindly showed us his collection from Ivor, and Professor Maureen Warner-Lewis told us about the finds made at her property near Mona Great House. We are also grateful to Dr James Lee, who indicated on the map the precise locations of some of the sites that he investigated or relocated from the 1960s onwards.

Appendix

Table 2.3 Taíno Sites in the Kingston Area

Site	Code	Comments
Rodney's House	S-5	Excavated by Wilman in 1978 and by Medhurst in 1979. Six middens. Faunal remains. 3,394 marine and 371 terrestrial molluscs, most common marine *Arca zebra, Donax denticulatus, Arca imbricata, Chama macrophylla*. 6,728 bone fragments, MNI 747. Four species of mammals, three species of reptiles, four families of birds, twenty-five families of fish, six of crabs and lobsters. Typical West Indian dry coastal and shallow-water faunal communities. (Medhurst 1980; Scudder 1992; Wilman 1978, 1979)
Naggo Head	S-12	Investigated 1972–73, now destroyed by quarrying. Child burial. (Lee 1972a, 1972b; Aarons 1983a)
Caymanas Bay	S-14	Investigated 1972–75. Small site on low hill. (Lee 1976b)
Molynes Mountain	K-14	Two sites, including Plantation Heights, investigated by Lee and Hodges, 1967 and 1985. Pottery of White Marl style. (Lee 1967a, 1967b, 1983a, 1985b)
Chancery Hall	K-11	Investigated by Lechler from 1990 onwards, excavated by the Jamaica National Heritage Trust in 1996 and by a University of the West Indies–University of Leicester team in 1998. Seven human burials. Faunal remains. Charcoal sample dated in 1992 by Beta Analytic Inc. at 690 ± 50 BP (uncalibrated). (Lechler 2000)
Bellevue	K-13	Excavated by Medhurst and Clarke in 1974–75 and by Medhurst and Wilman in 1976–77. House foundation 4.5 m in diameter. Four human burials. Pottery principally red-brown, a little buff-yellow ware. Faunal remains. 1974–75: 474 marine and 717 terrestrial molluscs; 1976–77: 2,500 marine and 2,341 terrestrial molluscs. Most common marine *Neritina piratica reclivata* and *virginea, Arca zebra, Chione granulata, Anadara brasiliana*; 1,207 bone fragments from the first excavation, MNI 126, predominantly land species. (Medhurst 1976a, 1976b, 1977a, 1977b; Scudder 1992; Wing and Medhurst 1977)
Stony Hill		Investigated by Gardner in 1997 when "Fort George", Miss May Farquharson's house, was demolished.
Norbrook	K-5	Investigated in 1890 by Lady Blake and therefore of considerable historical importance. Artefacts are still in evidence, but the site (hitherto owned by the National Water Commission) is undergoing development. (Duerden 1897)
Jacks Hill	K-1	Investigated by Lee and Lechler. Artefacts still in evidence.
Ivor	K-10	Investigated by Lee in 1971. Some excavation during construction work. (Lee 1971)

Table 2.3 continues

Table 2.3. Taíno Sites in the Kingston Area *(cont'd)*

Site	Code	Comments
Hope Tavern	K-3	Investigated by Duerden and subsequently relocated by Lee in 1966. (Duerden 1897; Lee 1966)
Tower Hill	K-7	Excavated by R.P. and A.K. Bullen in 1961. Faunal remains. Marine and terrestrial molluscs, sea turtles, fish including sharks, birds, and abundant *hutia*. (Bullen and Bullen 1974)
Mona		A stray find of a petaloid celt within the former grounds of the Mona Great House.
Long Mountain	K-8	Duerden stated that shell middens were widely spread on the elongated top and on less elevated portions of the mountain. Two distinct sites were subsequently identified by Lee and by Gardner. (Duerden 1897)
Wareika	K-2	Recorded by Duerden as being behind the then newly built Wareika House. (Duerden 1897)
Rennock Lodge	K-9	Marine shells, pottery, and two amulets reported by Duerden. (Duerden 1897)
Harbour View	K-6	Site in the vicinity of the Martello Tower, investigated by Lechler. (Lee 1984; Wallace 1992)
Hope Mine		Galena (lead and zinc ore) mined here from the time of the Spanish occupation onwards. Source of material found at Bellevue and Chancery Hall. (Matley 1951; Hughes 1973)
Beverly Hills	KC-7	Reported as a burial cave by Lewis. (Lee 1970a)
Dallas Castle	KC-2	Reported as a burial cave by Duerden, could not be relocated by Lee. (Duerden 1897)
Downtown Kingston		Canoe found in 1993–94 by National Water Commission workmen at the corner of Harbour and Pechon streets. Considered to be of Taíno origin. Made of a single piece of wood.

3  The Pre-Columbian Site of Chancery Hall, St Andrew

Anthony Gouldwell
Philip Allsworth-Jones
George Lechler
Simon F. Mitchell
Selvenious Walters
Jane Webster
and
Robert Young

ONE OF THE TAÍNO sites discovered in recent years on the outskirts of Kingston is Chancery Hall, in Red Hills. In 1991, Mr George Lechler, past president of the Archaeological Society of Jamaica, reported the existence of the site and managed to salvage several important finds from it. In 1996, the Jamaica National Heritage Trust conducted test pit excavations on four of the Chancery Hall lots and retrieved further significant material. In 1998, another small excavation was carried out by a combined team from the University of the West Indies and University of Leicester, primarily for providing stratigraphic control and recovering environmental data. This three-part report covers the discoveries made at the site so far. Much of Chancery Hall remains well preserved and it is hoped that further work can be done there.

I. Discovery and First Investigation of Chancery Hall (1990–1994)

Chancery Hall is about 8 km inland and at an elevation of about 240 m on gentle slopes facing southeast. The site was discovered in 1990 when George Lechler's company, Explosive Sales and Services Ltd, was employed as subcontractors to drill and blast for roadways, storm drains, pipe trenches and so on, in connection with a new housing development in the area. The site was divided into lots, which have been sold and on many of which houses have been constructed. In subsequent years salvage archaeology was carried out on an amateur basis, particularly in the vicinity of Horatio Drive. Most but not all of the finds reported here come from lot 340 to the north of Horatio Drive.

Human Burials

Seven burials were discovered (Figure 3.1). One consisted of an adult with a child buried on top and three bowls on top of the child. A bulldozer had crushed two of the bowls, but the third was recovered intact and contained fragmented bones (Figure 3.2).

Figure 3.1 Taíno skulls *in situ*. (Archaeological Society of Jamaica.)

Figure 3.2 Earthenware pot containing infant remains. (Archaeological Society of Jamaica.)

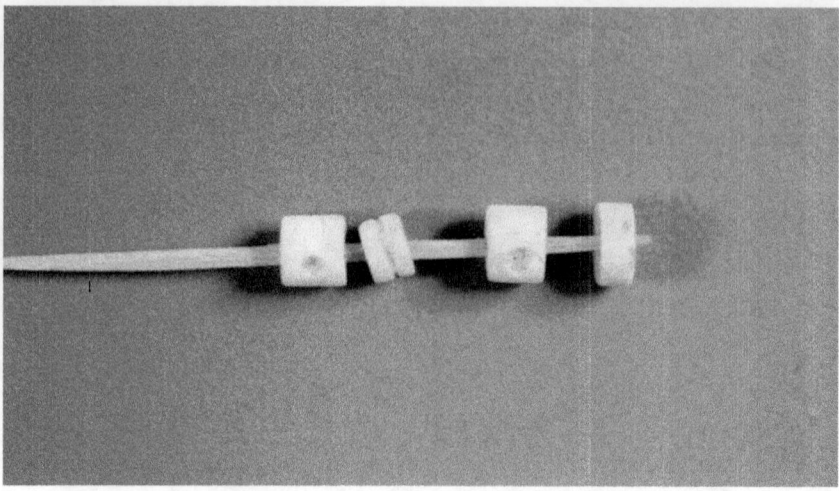

Figure 3.3 Beads associated with the skull. (Archaeological Society of Jamaica.)

The bones were sent to Dr Elizabeth Wing (University of Florida), who identified them as belonging to a human infant. They included the distal end of a femur and the proximal ends of an ulna and radius. There were several ribs. Also present were bones belonging to a *hutia* (*Geocapromys brownii*, right acetabulum) and molluscs, including two large land snails (E.S. Wing, letter to author, 10 December 1991).

Also unearthed was a single skeleton – the skull of which was rescued by Mr Errol Rhone, one of the workers on the site. His fellow workers, thinking that he was going to work obeah with the skull, crushed it into pieces, but the shattered remains were brought to George Lechler. On later examination, Lechler found four small beads associated with these remains (Figure 3.3), which convinced us that this was indeed a Taíno burial.

Faunal Remains

There were thousands of shells on the site, as is the case on many Taíno middens. But in addition, this site contained some unusual remains. In mid-1993, Lechler was given a fragmented animal skull, which was badly broken and clearly not complete. Lechler was puzzled by what appeared to be a double row of molars in the lower jaw. A portion of the skull was sent to Dr Wing, who identified it as a young manatee, measuring 1.5 to 1.8 m in length (Wing 1994). As far as Lechler is aware, this is the first time the remains of a manatee have been discovered on a Jamaican Taíno site.

A triton shell about 11 cm in diameter at its widest part and 19 cm long was also discovered (Reid and Lechler 1993). The apex, or narrow end, was chipped away. It is believed that this was a musical instrument, a horn that could have been used for signalling over long distances. A second shell, similar to the first but smaller, was also found. Conch-shell horns are, of course, still known in both Jamaica and Haiti, and Lechler has used them as a means of informing people that blasting is about to take place.

Artefacts

Many petaloid celts of various sizes, grinding stones, pottery sherds and griddles, amulets, pendants, beads and other objects have been found. A piece of bone carved to represent a dog's head was recovered, as was a round, grooved sandstone object of unknown significance.

In addition, three clay *zemís* and a sandstone *zemí* were found, as well as bits and pieces of several more *zemís* of the same type. The sandstone *zemí* is 9 cm high, 6.8 cm wide, and 5.3 cm thick from front to back. It has round inlet eyes, which Lee suggested might have been designed to hold gold leaf, and an elaborate crosshatched hair design. One of the clay *zemís* is particularly striking. It is 8.6 cm high, with a typical Taíno "skull face" encircled by a dotted headdress. The body has no arms or legs, and is rounded at the bottom.

A piece of galena (lead-zinc ore), probably originating from the Papine area, was recovered. This ore is also known to be found elsewhere in the St Andrew area – for instance, at Smokey Vale, Belvedere.

Dating

In 1992, a charcoal sample was collected from the deposits just north of Horatio Drive near the boundary between lots 340 and 339 and sent to Miami for carbon-14 dating. Dr Jerry J. Stipp of Beta Analytic Inc., where the tests were carried out, reported a date of 690 ± 50 BP or AD 1260 ± 50.

Dr Stipp's report revealed that

> some intrusive rootlet contamination was present in the initial sample. After washing away all associated and adhering mineral matter, the charcoal pieces were lightly crushed for increased surface exposure; all remaining rootlets were removed by combination of flotation and handpicking. The charcoal was then chemically treated by repeat-soakings in dilute hot acid and alkali solutions to remove any carbonate or humic acid contaminants. After final thorough rinsing to neutrality in hot distilled water, the clean charcoal was gently dried, synthesized to benzene, and counted for radiocarbon content. The sample was of good quality and quantity, and all analytical steps proceeded normally.

Conclusion

This site is one of many circling the Liguanea Plain – Smokey Vale, Belvedere, Norbrook Gully, Skyline Drive, Wareika Hill and Harbour View. It is anticipated that more will be done to extract information from the Chancery Hall site before it is too late.

II. Jamaica National Heritage Trust Excavations in 1996

In view of the potential that the site clearly possesses and the threat posed to it by development in the area, the Jamaica National Heritage Trust undertook excavations at Chancery Hall in the period from 17 June to 2 July 1996. Mr Selvenious Walters (field coordinator) conducted the excavations under the overall supervision of Mr Roderick Ebanks (technical director and project coordinator) and with the participation of Ms Evelyn Thompson (acting deputy technical director and conservator). Other Jamaica National Heritage Trust members who took part were Ms Dorothy Griffiths, Mr Clifton McKen, Mr Ricardo Tyndall, Mr Ryan Murphy, and Mr R. Talbot. Two volunteers, Mr K. Farmer and Ms K. Redwood, accompanied them.

The objective was to obtain a general idea of the site by putting down preliminary test pits in some of the lots scheduled for development immediately north and south of Horatio Drive. In itself, this area is no more than a fraction of the site as it originally existed, but it is the area from which Mr George Lechler and his associates rescued some of the most significant finds. Six 1-m^2 test pits were dug, five in lots 340, 339 and 338 (north of Horatio Drive) and one in lot 308 (south of Horatio Drive). The arrangement of the test pits is shown in Figure 3.4.

The maximum depth of deposit in test pit 1 was 90 cm and in test pit 3 was 110 cm, whereas the others varied between 40 and 60 cm. All the pits were dug in horizontal 10-cm levels. A few historic artefacts (mostly glass bottles) were encountered near the surface in test pits 2, 4 and 5, but the overwhelming bulk of the material was pre-Columbian. Individual details of the excavated test pits follow.

Test Pit 1

Depth 90 cm. The most significant feature here was the discovery of human bones at a depth of 59–71 cm in the southeast corner of the pit. They were

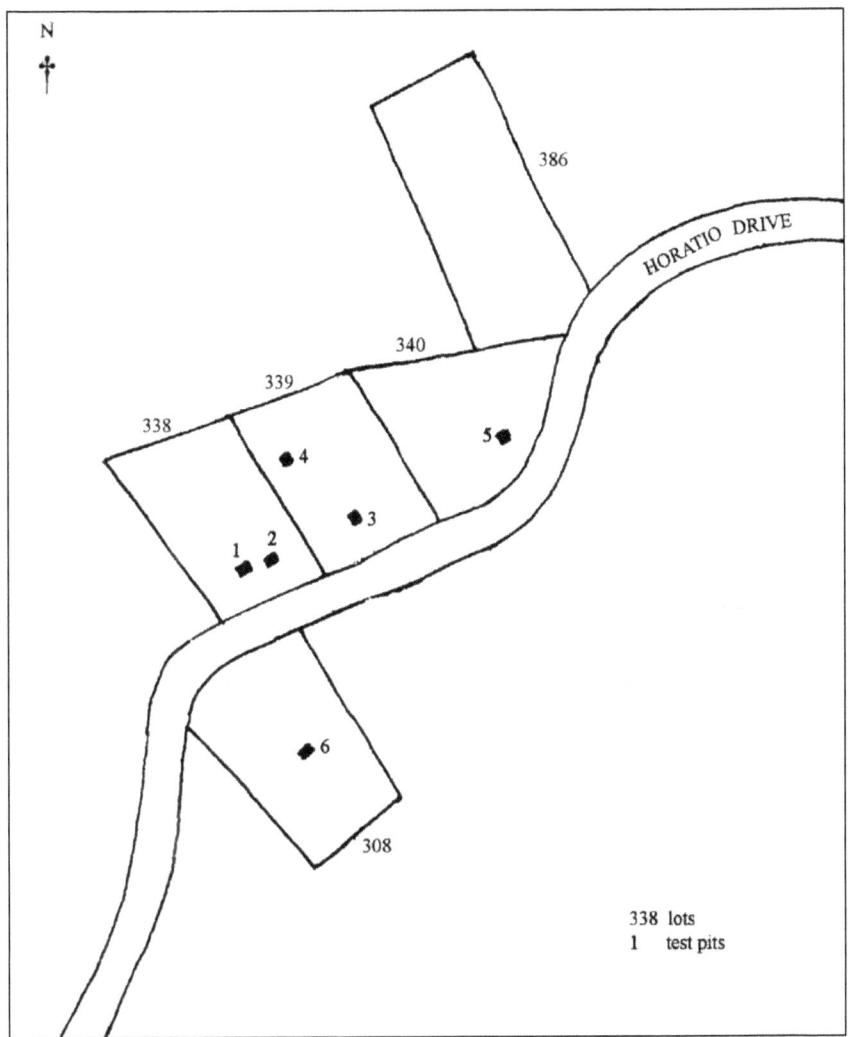

Figure 3.4 JNHT excavations at Chancery Hall. (Illustration by Selvenious Walters.)

preserved upon a pedestal as excavation elsewhere proceeded to what was believed to be an archaeologically sterile horizon at the base. The human remains include a skull with mandible and teeth, and limb bones. But what was found was evidently not the entire skeleton. The remainder extended eastwards and southwards into the side of the pit. Conservation measures were undertaken on the spot, but no attempt was made to lift the bones, in view of the fact that part of the skeleton still remained buried. A further excavation would be needed to complete this operation, if it were felt to be desirable. On the basis of what was observed, it can be concluded that this was a deliberate burial. If the body had merely been left on the ground to decompose, the bones would have been more scattered than they were. In fact, they were confined to a small area and placed in such a way as to suggest that the body was buried in a flexed position.

Test Pit 2

Depth 60 cm. Some historic artefacts (green glass bottle fragments and a creamware sherd) were found in levels 1 and 2, but there were (comparatively sparse) pre-Columbian artefacts beneath, in a context generally characterized as terra rossa in type. Excavation stopped when an archaeologically sterile horizon appeared to have been reached.

Test Pit 3

Depth 110 cm. Significant concentrations of ash were detected, particularly in levels 4 to 7 but continuing deeper than that in places. They were associated with increased concentrations of shells, both marine and terrestrial. In levels 5 and 6 a large portion of a griddle was found, including the rim. Again, it was excavated separately on a pedestal. It was treated *in situ* with a solution of consolidant before being carefully removed and transported to the conservation laboratory at the Jamaica National Heritage Trust. In the light of the general stratigraphic situation, it is considered that the griddle probably pre-dates the skeletal remains found in test pit 1. When a depth of 110 cm was reached in this pit, the soil was sterile.

Test Pit 4

Depth 40 cm. A few historic artefacts (green glass bottle fragments) were encountered in level 1. The pre-Columbian artefacts beneath were not numerous, but included a stone object the size and shape of a sewing-machine bobbin. Sterile soil was encountered at a shallow depth, indicating that as one goes up the hill the occupation deposits thin out. Limestone rocks are frequent, indicating that bedrock is near.

Test Pit 5

Depth 50 cm. Some historic artefacts (green glass bottle fragments) were found in levels 1 and 2. The matrix beneath, characterized as red bauxite in type, contained relatively few pre-Columbian artefacts. At the base it had become completely sterile.

Test Pit 6

Depth 40 cm. This is a steeply sloping area. Very few artefacts were found, and we believe that even these were displaced by erosion from their original place of deposition farther up the hill. Sterile soil was very quickly reached.

In general, it appears that the major deposits with signs of Taíno occupation occur immediately north of Horatio Drive (test pits 1, 2, 3 and 5). Test pits 1 and 2 yielded relatively few artefacts compared with test pit 3, perhaps corresponding to a gardening area. The flat aspect that this part of the site currently possesses probably is a result of later agricultural levelling, attested to by the presence of some historic artefacts. The fact that no signs of a burial were discovered in test pit 2 indicates that this area as a whole did not function as a cemetery in Taíno times. Although the excavation in test pit 5 did not produce many finds, there are in fact large numbers of shells and artefacts now strewn on the surface of lot 340. There is no doubt that this area supported the bulk of the Taíno houses which once existed here. The part of the site around test pit 4 could also have been a gardening area, or it might have served as a stone tool–manufacturing centre.

The preliminary investigation conducted by the Jamaica National Heritage Trust in 1996 revealed Chancery Hall's importance as a major Taíno site worthy of thorough examination. Unquestionably there is more to be done here before the completion of the current development renders it no longer available.

III. Excavations at Chancery Hall, 1998

A small excavation took place at Chancery Hall on 12–13 April 1998 as a joint project between the University of the West Indies and the University of Leicester. Work was carried out in two lots. On lot 340, a 1-m² quadrant was excavated to a depth of 15 cm. Apart from shells, artefacts recovered included ninety-six potsherds and one limestone flake. In addition, a section was cut in lot 386, by the boundary wall between it and lot 340 (see Figure 3.4). Layer 3 contained abundant shells and artefacts comparable to those from the excavated quadrant. There were twenty-three potsherds, fifteen chert flakes and a limestone core. A visit to the site in 1999 revealed that there were still many artefacts and other traces of human activity eroding from the sediments in lot 340, including five human teeth.

The molluscan material from the two lots excavated in 1998 has been described in detail in Allsworth-Jones et al. (2001, reprinted in this volume, Table 2.1). In addition, a 7.5-kg sample of material from layer 3 in the section on the edge of lot 386 was subjected to microscopic analysis in the laboratory at the School of Archaeological Studies in Leicester. A.J. Gouldwell reports on the results of this analysis (see appendix). These two studies are of interest primarily for the light that they cast on the Taínos' environment and their exploitation of it. The principal points may be summarized as follows.

It is clear from the analysis that the marine gastropods and bivalves at the site are dominated by only five species: *Neritina reclivata* and *N. piratica*, *Anadara ovalis*, *Chione intapurpurea* and *Crassostrea rhizophorae*. Both species of *Neritina* occur in brackish water on intertidal mudflats, which also serve as the habitat for the first two bivalves. *Crassostrea rhizophorae* lives attached to mangrove roots. Hence, it is evident that the inhabitants collected their shellfish mainly from what is now the Kingston Harbour. The terrestrial gastropods at the site are dominated by *Pleurodonte lucerna*, but there is some doubt as to whether this really constituted an item in the human diet, since, as remarked earlier (Allsworth-Jones et al. 2001, reprinted in this volume), "there are many places in Jamaica where extensive accumulations of terrestrial gastropods are concentrated in soil profiles with no evidence of archaeological occupation", and "a Taíno rubbish pit may have been a highly desirable habitat" for them.

Several salient points emerge from the study carried out by Gouldwell. The study clearly shows the potential for microscopic work of this kind in recovering evidence which might not otherwise be available. Caution, however, is needed in the interpretation of the results. Even in well-stratified conditions such as this, there is a possibility of contamination and intrusion by fibrous roots. Thus, the interesting and well-preserved insect and scorpion remains are probably of recent origin, and the same goes for the two seeds. There is no need to doubt the antiquity of the wood charcoal, which is assumed to be an indication that the inhabitants used wood as fuel for cooking. There is an approximately equal representation of mammalian and fish bone fragments, though the minimum numbers of individuals represented are obviously much less than the fragments in the count. The mammalian remains probably all belong to *hutia*, but a limitation of this study is that no specific identification of the fish remains could be made. Some of the fish bones show signs of contact with fire, consistent with the hypothesis advanced to account for the presence of charcoal. Interestingly enough, the fish bones showed no sign of cracking caused by chewing, or of etching by gastric juices. The conclusion is that the fish were filleted before being eaten, but it is desirable that this suggestion be tested elsewhere. As Gouldwell says, the conclusion in general is that this was "a midden of food waste".

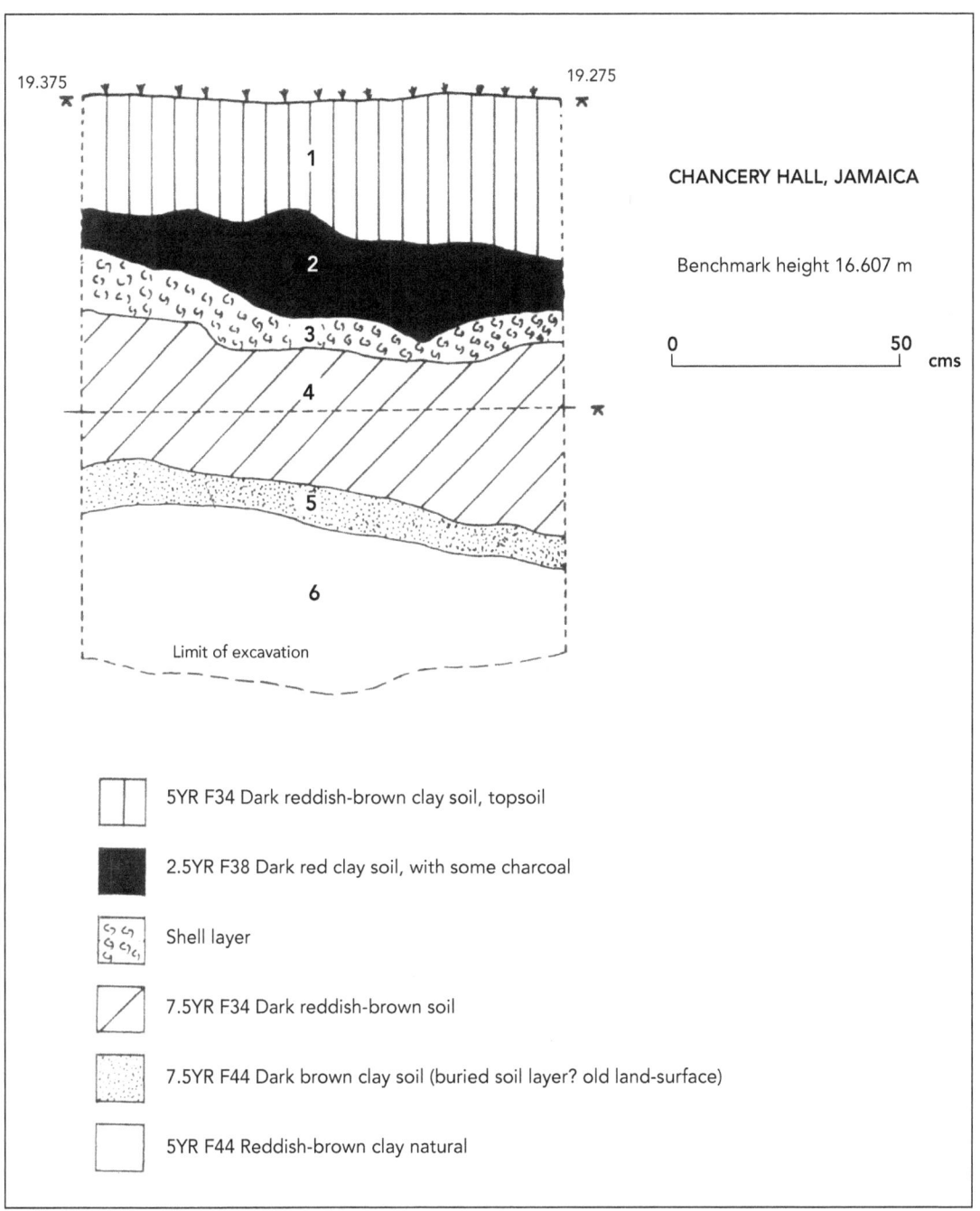

Figure 3.5 Stratigraphy of Chancery Hall

Summary and Conclusion

Following development of the Chancery Hall area, Mr George Lechler and his associates rescued some finds from the site. These included the remains of seven human burials, as well as a number of artefacts. In 1992, a charcoal sample from the deposits just north of Horatio Drive, near the boundary between lots 340 and 339, was dated by Beta Analytic to 690 ± 50 BP, equivalent to AD 1260 ± 50.

Six test pits in four of the lots were excavated by the Jamaica National Heritage Trust in 1996 (Figure 3.4). The remains of another human burial were discovered in lot 338, as were additional artefacts including a large portion of a griddle. The great majority of the finds were pre-Columbian, but there were also a few historic pieces at the top of the sequence. The depth of deposits in the test pits varied between 40 and 110 cm.

In 1998, a team from the University of the West Indies and the University of Leicester undertook a small excavation. A 1 m² quadrant was excavated to a shallow depth in lot 340, and a section was drawn at the boundary between lots 386 and 340. The material recovered is mainly of environmental interest, showing how the Taínos exploited the resources in their immediate surroundings. A 7.5-kg sample from layer 3 in the section was analysed in the laboratory at Leicester, confirming that this was a midden largely composed of food waste.

While a certain amount of information has been recovered from the site, undoubtedly much more has been destroyed or is no longer available for study as a result of the development that has taken place. It is hoped that in future, when a proposed development will have an impact on an archaeological site, a concerted effort will be made to recover data in advance of construction.

Acknowledgements

Thanks go to Dr Silvia Kouwenberg and Ms Susan Chung for their assistance with the excavation at Chancery Hall in 1998.

Appendix

A Laboratory Study of the Remains from Layer 3, Lot 386, Chancery Hall

A.J. Gouldwell

Introduction

A pre-Columbian shell midden at Chancery Hall was sectioned and excavated to a very limited extent in 1998 by a team from the University of the West Indies and the School of Archaeological Studies at the University of Leicester. A sample of the layer, context CH 98 lot 386: 3, was brought to Leicester for analysis and evaluation of macrofossil content. It was already apparent that the material contained substantial quantities of bone of small mammals and fish, and terrestrial and marine shell. The site is not situated on the coast, hence the marine shell, and very probably the fish, was transported to the site by the inhabitants of the time. Some large land snails were present, and small pieces of charcoal were also observed. Examination of the contents should suggest what resources were being exploited, and this in turn can be expected to raise questions about the relationship between the human inhabitants, their economy and the environment.

The macrofossils were divided into classes suitable for analysis. Particular categories of material looked for included wood and other charcoal; crop residues; seeds representing the background vegetation; insects and other arthropods; molluscan shells; and bones of fish, amphibians, reptiles, birds and mammals.

Materials and Methods

The sample was reddish-brown, loamy, with gritty inclusions of charcoal, shell, bones, stone and pot. The total mass was 7.50 kg. The consistency and colour of the sediment, together with the obvious presence of roots, suggested well-oxygenated conditions. This means that the primary mode of archaeological preservation of seeds would be charring rather than waterlogging or desiccation.

The basic principle of separation of macrofossils employed was that of dispersion, wash-over and flotation (Kenward, Hall and Jones 1980).

In the present case, successive subsamples were weighed out in 0.50-kg lots and dispersed in a 5-litre bucket of water. The material was stirred in with the water to ensure thorough mixing, and large inclusions such as stones, pot and large shells were removed manually.

Floating and suspended material was decanted into nested sieves, the heavier residue remaining in the bottom of the bucket. Flot was collected in a 500-μm mesh, which was adequate for retaining most seeds. A 4.75-mm mesh was placed on top to screen out roots and other coarse matter.

Flot was resuspended in water when necessary, to clean it before decanting it into sieves to rinse out the silt. The flot was then allowed to dry on newspaper before sorting.

Residue remaining in the bottom of the original bucket used for flotation was washed through nested sieves to facilitate sorting. Clogging of the sieves was a problem, so it was necessary to experiment with additional, coarser sieves to retain slowly disaggregating, coarse particles as well as a few remaining fibrous roots. Choice of meshes was pragmatic: the finest used was 500-μm. Coarser ones used ranged through 2 mm up to 4.75 mm. Different sieve fractions were allowed to dry on separate sheets of newspaper to aid subsequent sorting of contents.

All the material thus obtained was sorted into categories using a low-power lens for coarser material (larger pieces of charcoal, bone and shell), and a stereoscopic microscope with a zoom magnification set at × 0.7 or slightly higher for fine material (seeds, insects, smaller shells and charcoal fragments).

Identifications are provisional, but every attempt was made to check with local specialists where appropriate.

Results

Fibrous roots formed a conspicuous component of the sample, warning of the likelihood of recent organic intrusion. Of the botanical remains, the most interesting finds are the fragments of wood charcoal. Two seeds that were found were probably of recent origin. Of the zoological remains, the bones and shells are probably reliable indicators of ancient human activity. The insects and other arthropods can probably be safely dismissed as more recent intrusions. Quantities are listed in Table 3.1.

Table 3.1 All Recovered Organic Materials

Class of Material	Specimens	MNI[1]
Plant Material		
Roots	+++	n/a
Wood charcoal	*ca.* 125	n/a
Seeds	2	
Animal Material		
Arthropods	19	5
Molluscs	350	223
Marine worms (serpulids)	3	2
Bone	748	5
Total	1,247	235

[1]MNI = minimum number of individuals

Wood Charcoal

Quantities are listed in Table 3.2. The vascular tissue of wood represented as charcoal was of diffuse, porous type, with vessels (seen in transverse section) distributed singly or in radially aligned groups of two. These are visible at a magnification of × 10. Seasonal, presumably annual, rings are discernible. The largest fragment (30 mm long) showed vessels grouped in a cluster of six, mostly in a radial line, with a couple of cells offset from that line. The fragments were not broken to produce clean surfaces to be examined; destructive analysis has been left to whoever does the final identification.

The charcoal fragments were all of irregular shape and of insufficient size to reveal any indication of workmanship or stem growth form. The size range is indicated in Table 3.2.

Table 3.2 Size Distribution of Charcoal Fragments

Size	25–30 mm	15–25 mm	10–15 mm	5–10 mm	2–5 mm
Fragments	2	2	6	25	*ca.* 90

Seeds

Two seeds were recovered. They were superficially similar to those of *Ranunculus* in outline, but are not flattened, and possess a warty surface and squarish base. Length 1.6 mm. Colour: light yellowish-brown. The appearance of the seeds is fresh, and it is strongly suspected that they are of comparatively recent origin.

Insects and Other Arthropods

Finds of arthropods are listed in Table 3.3. Most are disarticulated parts of insects: beetles (order Coleoptera); earwig (order Dermaptera) and what appears to be the head of an ant (order Hymenoptera). Additionally, there are components of claws of chelicerate arthropods, presumably scorpions. The remains appear to be in good condition: some of the body parts remain articulated, and the individual sclerites and other exoskeletal parts do not show obvious signs of degradation such as discolouration, cracking, perforation or abrasion (Kenward and Large 1998). In short, they look fresh (though a comparison with modern reference material of the taxa has not been made), with the earwig being the most complete.

The earwig possesses intact cerci (posteriorly situated pincers or "forceps")

Table 3.3 Arthropod Remains

Anatomical Part	Number
Insects	
Order Hymenoptera	
Head, antlike	1
Order Coleoptera	
Thorax, including fused elytra	1
Beetle femur/fibia, jointed	1
Pronotum	1
Ventral tergite	1
Order Dermaptera	
Earwig abdomen with part thorax	1
Miscellaneous (mostly Coleoptera?)	
More or less undiagnostic, chitinous plates	4
Cf. head	1
Scorpions	
Segments of ?same, disarticulated chelicera	4
~~Limb segments with 3 ?related chelicerae~~	~~4~~

of slim, more or less parallel shape, suggesting a female. There are nearly two thousand recorded species of Dermaptera worldwide (Sakai 1996).

Beetles usually form the most conspicuous component of subfossil insect assemblages because of the toughness of their exoskeletons. In the present case, other groups seem to be present. The representation may not be abnormal, but experience of local subfossil insect assemblages would help in judging whether this collection is typical. Of the scorpions, the three "related" chelicerae (claws) in Table 3.2 are all pale yellowish-brown, while the four segments of the "same" chelicera are darker and more reddish-brown. All the chelicerae are fairly small, with the paler ones being clearly smaller than the darker. For secure identification, these should all be compared with reference material of different species and different age stages of scorpion.

Molluscan Shell (and Serpulid Worm Cases)

The presence of large molluscan shells was obvious, and some specimens were large enough to be extracted by hand. Among these larger shells were a mixture of thin-walled terrestrial specimens and a range of thick-walled marine or at least littoral species. The smaller molluscs were viewed under magnification.

Total fragments amounted to 350, divided (for gastropods) into apices, apertures and whorl fragments and (for bivalves) into left and right umbones and valve fragments. In terms of minimum numbers of individuals, 225 specimens were recognized. Of these, 79 were marine gastropods, 74 were terrestrial gastropods and 70 were marine bivalves. The species represented were identified by means of voucher specimens returned to Jamaica for that purpose. The species so recognized were added to the rest of the sample from lot 386 layer 3, and the grand totals appear in Table 2.1. The samples identified in Leicester were a recognizably similar subset of the totals for the site as a whole.

There were at least two serpulid worms (class Annelida: family Serpulidae) represented by three fragments. These form a chalky, loosely whorled, tubular casing. Height *ca.* 3.5 mm. Serpulids are segmented worms, not molluscs.

Bone: General

Bone (Table 3.4) was mostly fragmented and ranged from 1.25 to 21 mm in size. The systematic groups represented included fish, possibly amphibian, and small mammal. Because of the comminuted nature of the material there was much that could not be identified. Reptilian bone was not recognized.

Table 3.4 All Bone

Bone material	Specimens
Piscean	390
Cf. amphibian	3
Mammalian	355
Total	748

Fish Bone

Fish bone (Table 3.5) ranged from 16 mm to 1.25 mm in size. Of the total vertebral fish bones observed, nine (possibly more) showed signs of calcining, and seven showed partial or extensive blackening. Thus just over 8 per cent of the vertebrae showed signs of contact with fire.

Measurements of characterizable fish bone are as follows: prevomer: 3 mm wide, 6.5(+?) mm long; premaxilla 10.5 mm long; tooth curved; straight line connecting furthest points, 3 mm; ribs, fin spines, pterygiophores, etc. 2.5–16 mm long.

An attempt was made to classify fish vertebrae in terms of anatomical position: anterior abdominal, abdominal, caudal (Wheeler and Jones 1989). Much of the bone was damaged, in that vertebral processes were often incomplete and thin laminae of opercular bones were broken, but there was no cracking of vertebrae suggestive of chewing or of etching by gastric juices (hydrochloric acid). It seems reasonable to assume that damage to the bone is post-burial in origin. There was, however, some evidence of light burning. Caudal and abdominal bones are probably under-represented; a few abdominals may be damaged caudals, and the anterior abdominal figure might have been inflated if spiny processes have been broken from abdominals and caudals.

The number of recorded bone elements, 390, may seem substantial, but when looking at the more characterizable bone, very few specimens are indicated. Three premaxillae can be reduced to two individuals. It will take specific identifications to improve the estimate of number of individuals.

There were three anatomically unidentified bones, which may possibly have belonged to amphibians.

Table 3.5 Fish Bone

Anatomical Part	Number
Vertebrae: large	
Caudal?, centrum: L 8.5 mm, H 8.5 mm	1
L 3–6 mm	
Anterior abdominal vertebrae	6
Abdominal vertebrae	5
Caudal vertebrae	8
Other large	
Urostyle, anterior facet: H 4.75 mm	1
Smaller vertebrae, L 1.25–3.0 mm	
Anterior abdominal vertebrae, L 1.25–3.0 mm	77
Abdominal vertebrae: L 2–3 mm	38
Caudal vertebrae incl. one urostyle	27
Unplaced	29
Total vertebrae	**192**
Other bones	
Articular	2
Dentary	1
Premaxilla	3
Hyomandibular	1
Prevomer	1
Tooth	1
Pterygiophores	23
Fin spines	38
Ribs	6
Miscellaneous*	122
Total non-vertebrate	**198**
Overall total	**390**

Note: L = length of centrum, H = height of centrum.

*Miscellaneous includes unsorted ribs, fin spines and rays, detached neural and haemal spines, etc.

Mammalian Bone

All the mammalian bone (Table 3.6) seems to have come from small mammals, which should mean they are all of *hutia*, *Geocapromys brownii* (order Rodentia: family Capromyidae). The bones and fragments ranged in size from 2.5 to 21 mm. Of the two mammalian lower-jaw fragments, one contained three molariform teeth with one empty socket; all the teeth were missing from the other.

Table 3.6 Mammalian Bone

Anatomical Part	Number
Skull	1
Loose, molariform teeth	10
Dentary (both right side)	2
Vertebrae	6
Ribs	8
Scapula (blade/spine fragment)	1
Humerus (distal)	1
Ulna (proximal articulation)	1
Femur (proximal)	1
Tibia (distal part of shaft)	1
Calcaneum (tibiale)	1
Cf. metatarsal	1
Proximal phalanx	1
Total identified	35
Total unidentified	*ca.* 320

Discussion

The sediment is loose and friable and therefore apparently well suited for wash-over and flotation and subsequent wet sifting of the non-floating residue. Without flotation and sifting, most of the fragments of charcoal, bone and smaller shells, particularly of land snails, would probably have been lost in the course of manual extraction of finds. It was found, however, that particles tended to break down slowly and cause clogging of the meshes. Shell material needed cleaning after separation from the sediment.

Survival of arthropod exoskeletons normally depends on either desiccation or anaerobic waterlogging, neither of which condition seems to apply here. The remains of insects and other arthropods seldom survive as articulated, complete specimens. In the present case, such finds were predominantly of disarticulated units of chitinous exoskeleton, with the notable exception of the substantial part of an earwig and an articulated leg of a probable beetle. This suggests – particularly in such a small sample, and in the light of root penetration and the oxidation status of the sediment – that much of the insect fauna represents recent intrusion. In a larger sample, it might be possible to recognize a continuum through states of preservation, with recent additions being in near-perfect condition and the oldest specimens showing advanced decay.

Shells of small terrestrial molluscs are assumed to have arrived there more or less naturally, being too small to have been gathered intentionally. The concentration of larger shells, both terrestrial and marine, on the other hand, can most easily be explained as the result of intentional gathering for food. This also applies to the presence of bones of fish and *hutia*. Most of the marine shells span a size range that one might expect for molluscs harvested for human consumption, but there are also some very small specimens.

Charcoal in the present context is probably indicative of fuel for cooking, and a few fragments of bone show signs of burning. It might be interesting to obtain identifications of the woody species present in order to compare with present vegetation. Use of particular species for fuel can be a matter of definite choice rather than random collection (Prior and Tuohy 1987).

Only a small quantity of bone showed signs of burning, so combustion must have been part of the cooking process or a source of nighttime light and warmth, rather than a means of waste disposal.

Fish must have been brought to the site intentionally, presumably to be eaten, and filleted before consumption, as there is no evidence of chewing or of etching by digestive juices (hydrochloric acid).

Apart from bats, there is one surviving species of native mammal in Jamaica, a local species of *hutia*, *Geocapromys brownii*. The most economical interpretation is that the mammalian bone is all of *hutia*.

The remains were mostly broken up, and there may have been scavenging by dogs, though the bones are too small to show convincing tooth marks. It may be just possible that reptilian bones, such as those of iguana, were present and not recognized, given the fragmented nature of much of the assemblage, but teeth, characteristically durable parts, were all identifiable as mammalian, apart from the few fragments of mouth-parts of fish.

Statistics have been calculated to measure the usefulness of a range of sample sizes (Van der Veen and Fieller 1982). The present sample serves to provide a list of taxa present, but the statistical value of the figures varies for each class of material.

The sample of 1,247 objects gives an estimate, with a 98 per cent level of confidence, of the proportions of constituents of the midden overall. Fish and mammal bone occur in numbers of 390 and 355, respectively, but actually reduce to very few individual creatures, below any level at which statistical analysis has any meaning. Shell can be counted as something in the order of 225 individuals (rather less than the total number of fragments). Fortunately, in this case the results could be combined with the rest of the material from the site to give a satisfactory overall classification (Allsworth-Jones et al. 2001, reprinted in this volume).

Taking more samples would bulk up the sample sizes for all classes of material and would permit a determination of degree of homogeneity, on which normal statistical descriptors depend. It is plain, however, that a considerably greater quantity of material is needed for a satisfactorily detailed analysis of the bone content.

Conclusions

The sedimentary material is quite amenable to disaggregation and microscopic analysis. The oxidation state and presence of abundant roots suggests that the oxidizable remains recovered – arthropods and seeds – were probably of recent origin. The most useful classes of material are wood charcoal, molluscan shell and bones.

It seems clear that the deposit represents a midden of food waste, primarily of fish, mammal (*hutia*), and land and maritime shellfish, with charcoal fragments from a cooking fire. Insects and seeds seem to be contaminants from more recent levels. Statistically, the sample gives a promising prediction of the rest of the midden in terms of broad classes of data, but for a detailed description of the individual groups – bone, charcoal, shell – more material ought to be sampled. The maximum volume of material to be processed would probably be governed by considerations of cost rather than of statistical theory. In any case, a programme of taking pilot samples, similar in size to the present examples, for mutual comparison would help clarify longer-term needs.

It is apparent that the small terrestrial snails would be worth a more detailed examination for any clues to environmental, as opposed to economic, history. Seeds do not seem to be important as a source of evidence. It would be interesting to see whether future investigations will yield carbonized evidence of this class of material.

In general, it is clear that for satisfactory analysis a good collection of reference material is needed.

Acknowledgements

Thanks are due to Dr Robert Young for much practical assistance in the laboratory, and to Dr Frank Clark of the School of Biological Studies, University of Leicester, for confirming the identification of the scorpion remains.

4  Excavations at Green Castle, St Mary

Philip Allsworth-Jones
and
Kit Wesler

A JAMAICAN TAÍNO archaeological project was initiated in 1998 as a joint programme of the Department of History (University of the West Indies, Mona) and the Wickliffe Mounds Research Centre (Murray State University, Kentucky). The project is co-directed by Dr P. Allsworth-Jones and Professor K.W. Wesler, and excavations have so far concentrated on the site of Green Castle, near Annotto Bay (St Mary), on the north coast of the island. The purpose of this chapter is to provide a brief account of the results achieved so far.

Excavations at Green Castle

Following a survey of available sites, it was decided that the joint University of the West Indies–Murray State University Jamaican Taíno archaeological project would concentrate first on excavations at Green Castle, and these excavations ran for three seasons from 1999 to 2001. An advantage of the site was that it appeared to be largely undisturbed, and it was thought that it would permit questions to be addressed concerning both the settlement structure and the exploitation of the environment by the pre-Columbian inhabitants. The site was first reported by Ms Jean Crum-Ewing and was mapped by JamesLee in 1978 (Lee 1978b). The excavations were made possible thanks to the generous support of the landowner, Mr Duncan MacMillan, and the cooperation of the general manager, Mr Robin Crum-Ewing. Financial support was provided both by the University of the West Indies and by Murray

---

Originally published in 2003, in *Proceedings of the Nineteenth International Congress for Caribbean Archaeology, Aruba, 2001*: 186–93.

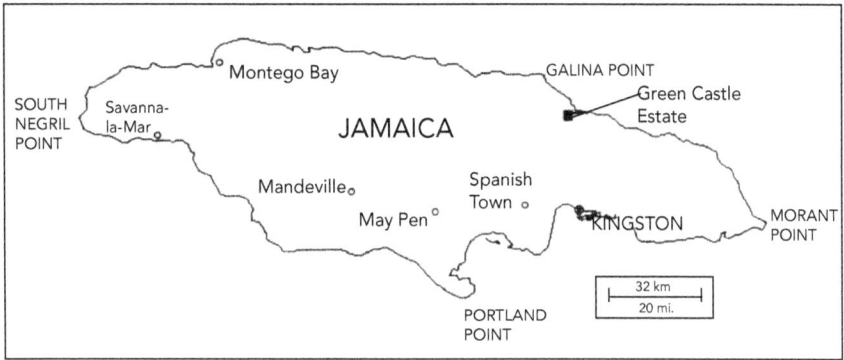

Figure 4.1 Location of Green Castle

State University, and during the last season by the National Geographic Society and the Reed Foundation. The details given below are taken from the preliminary annual reports on the excavations which have so far been submitted (Allsworth-Jones and Wesler 1999–2001).

The general position of the site is indicated on the map in Figure 4.1. It is a hilltop overlooking the sea, and the contours of the hilltop are shown in Figure 4.2. Over the three years, six trenches were excavated, designated according to their position in relation to site datum. The three westernmost trenches, excavated in 2000, were shallow and yielded very little information. The northernmost trench (0–2S 9–10E) was also quite shallow and was evidently affected by erosion and deflation. Conditions were quite different for the middle trench on the eastern side (30–31S 7–10E, later extended to east and north) and the southernmost trench on the eastern side (58–60S 5–6E). The southernmost trench produced the most complete stratigraphy, to a maximum depth of 1.5 m. On its eastern side, the middle trench reached a maximum depth of 80 cm. Three consecutive occupations were detected in the southernmost trench, separated by reddish, gravelly, more or less sterile layers. The difference between the two lowest occupations was particularly clearly marked, the basal level being completely sealed by a horizon of large loose rubble up to 25 cm thick. The situation was much more complex in the eastern part of the middle trench, where it became apparent from 2000 onwards that we were dealing with an artificially cut burial pit and probably other cut-and-fill features as well. In 2001 a complete adult burial was uncovered here, lying on bedrock.

A number of radiocarbon dates for the site have been obtained from the Beta Analytic laboratory. For the southern trench they are as follows.

Occupation 3 Level 2: 330 ± 60 BP (cal AD 1470–1645)
                 Level 3: 430 ± 80 BP (cal AD 1420–1616)
Occupation 2 Level 7: 760 ± 60 BP (cal AD 1221–1291)

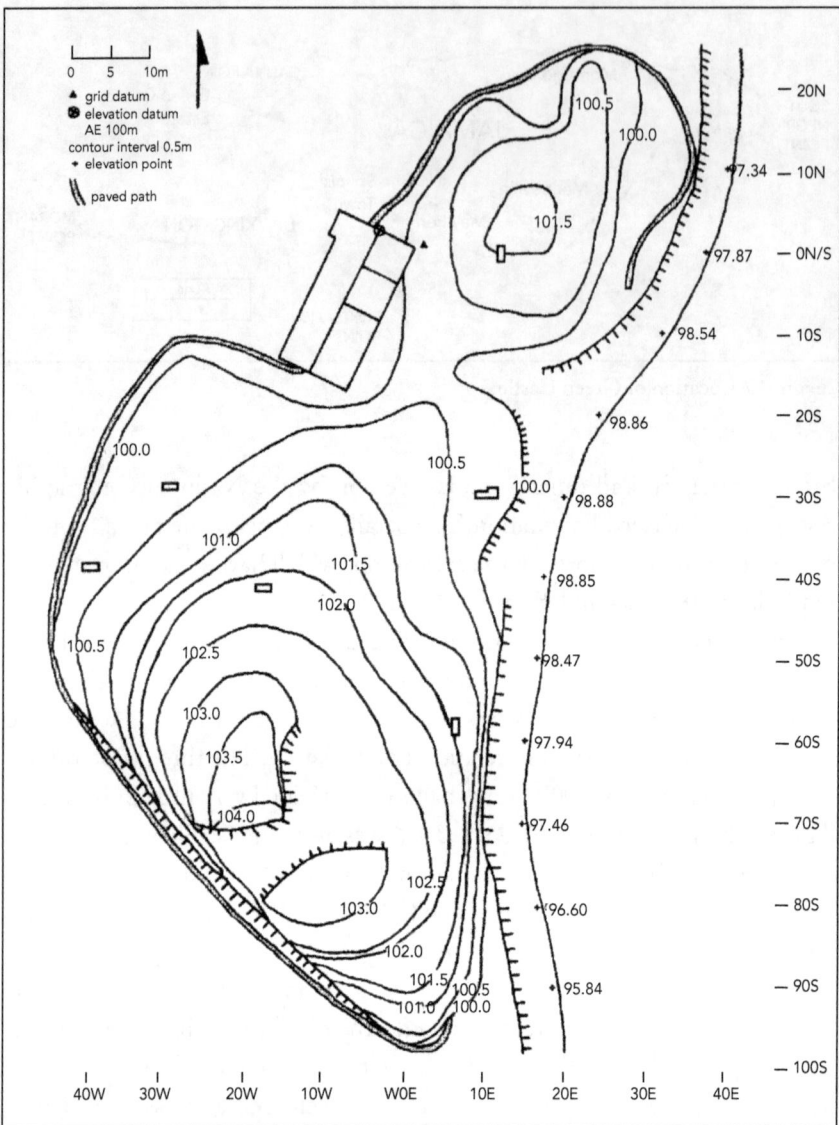

Figure 4.2 Green Castle contour map

Occupation 1   Level 13:   820 ± 60 BP (cal AD 1163–1277)
                      Level 13:   920 ± 60 BP (cal AD 1024–1209)

Rounding, as suggested by Kit Wesler, it can be stated that occupation 1 extended from about AD 1075 to 1250. There is an overlap here with occupation 2, but this is consonant with the hypothesis advanced by Dr Simon Mitchell (Department of Geography and Geology, University of the West Indies) that the rubble horizon separating the two may have represented a sudden event. Occupation 3 can be considered to have lasted from about AD 1440 to 1550, assuming that the latter is the practical upper limit for Taíno settlement of the site. There are no indications of Spanish contact, even in the uppermost deposits.

The dates in the middle trench are as follows.

Level 2:	70 ± 50 BP	modern
Level 3:	750 ± 60 BP	(cal AD 1223–1294)
Level 7:	480 ± 80 BP	(cal AD 1403–1469)
Burial 1:	670 ± 40 BP	(cal AD 1286–1385)

The date for burial 1 is a date determined by accelerator mass spectrometry (AMS). As can be seen, the dates for the burial and level 3 are similar, and are broadly comparable to those for occupation 2 in the south trench. The date for level 7 corresponds with that for occupation 3 in the south trench, and, on the face of it, there is a stratigraphic inconsistency here. As mentioned above, however, there is a cut-and-fill situation in this part of the trench, and we also observed possible signs of disturbance by roots and rodents. These factors may explain the apparent discrepancy.

In addition to these dates, a number of oxidizable carbon ratio (OCR) age determinations were obtained for the site, according to the method described by D.S. Frink (1994). In his work at the Wickliffe site in Kentucky, Kit Wesler found these determinations reliable and consonant with the radiocarbon dates (Wesler 2001). At Green Castle there are evident discrepancies between the two methods, which may be due to the fact that the model used for OCR dating tends to assume a steady build-up of deposits, and the mode of formation at Green Castle may have been quite different.

Apart from burial 1 in the middle trench, a burial of a child was discovered in the south trench, and a small extension on its western side was excavated so that the inhumation could be uncovered and, eventually, removed. Burial 2 occurs at a depth of about 35 cm. The date of 430 ± 80 BP (cal AD 1420–1616) was obtained on material in immediate proximity to it; hence evidently it belonged to occupation 3.

The two burials were analysed and partly excavated by Dr Ana Luisa Santos, of the Department of Anthropology, Coimbra University (Santos 2001). They are shown in Figures 4.3 and 4.4. Burial 1 is that of an adult, probably a male, who was interred in a flexed position, with an associated ceramic vessel at his feet. The individual was lying on his left side, with the right hand gripping the left forearm. The individual recovered in burial 2 is a child, with an estimated age at death of about seven years. The inhumation was in a flexed position, with all the bones from the lower limbs so contracted as to suggest that he or she may have been bound before burial. The child was

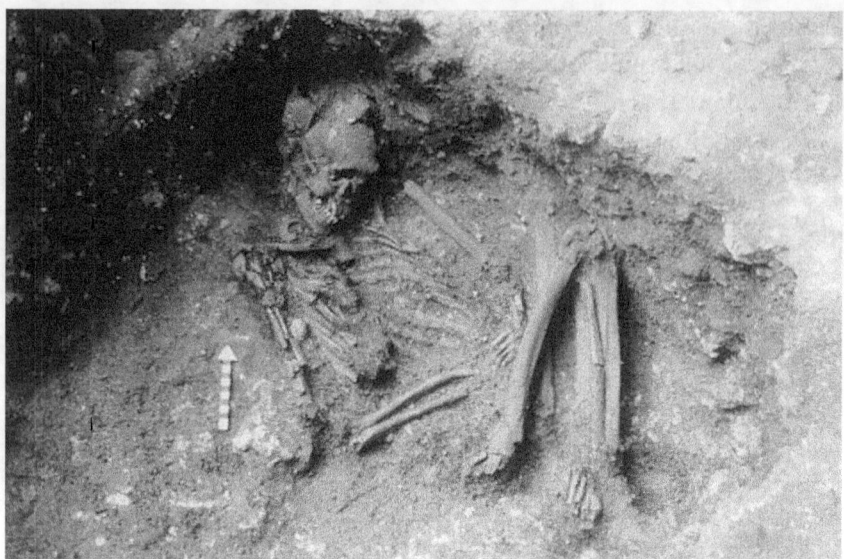

Figure 4.3 Burial 1

Figure 4.4 Burial 2

lying on its right side, with the left hand gripping the right elbow. In their general posture, therefore, there is a definite parallel between the two burials.

The bulk of the archaeological material consists of ceramic fragments as well as chert and other stone pieces. In general, the decoration would appear to indicate that this is a White Marl site, with no traces of Redware. Obviously this definition requires more sharpening up, which we hope to achieve by comparing the material to other collections in the island. Some of the more unusual pieces found include potsherd and shell discs, a bone needle, a ground stone artefact that may be a fragment of a monolithic axe, a fragment of a petaloid celt and several beads. There are large numbers of shells, which are being analysed by Dr Simon Mitchell. Apart from pleurodonts, which may well occur naturally at the site, the majority identified so far are marine gastropods which live mostly in the intertidal zone on the rocky shore, about 3 km from the site. In the first year, more than seven thousand fragments of bone were recovered. Jessica Allgood completed a study of these bone fragments, using the resources of the University of Southern Mississippi and the Florida Museum of Natural History (Allgood 2000). In her study she identified at least twenty-seven species of fish, as well as land mammals including, for the first time in Jamaica, the remains of guinea pig. Dr Betsy Carlson (Southeastern Archaeological Research Inc., Gainesville) is presently conducting the faunal analysis recovered from the later excavations.

Conclusion

In future, we intend to investigate another hilltop occurrence on the Green Castle estate, that of Newry. Mr Robin Crum-Ewing discovered this site in 1985 and it was mapped by Lee in that year (Lee 1985a). To all appearances, it could well turn out to be as extensive and productive as the first site. We also hope to examine other localities in the area, such as Coleraine and Iter Boreale (Lee 1970b, 1970c). A suggestion originally made by Lee about Coleraine raises the possibility that all these sites formed part of the *Guayguata* settlement noted by Gonzalo Fernández de Oviedo in the Annotto Bay area, a settlement whose name was later corrupted to Wagwater (Padron 1952; Fernández de Oviedo 1959). We hope that a broader study of this type will allow us to address general questions about Taíno regional political organization on the eve of the Spanish conquest.

5 The Impact of Land-Based Development on Taíno Archaeology in Jamaica

Andrea Richards

The destruction of archaeological sites is a worldwide problem. The issue of striking a balance between site preservation and development is common to many countries, in particular developing countries such as Jamaica. It has become apparent that with each passing year sites are being destroyed, and site destruction as a result of development will continue.

The threats to sites in Jamaica are numerous. Archaeological sites have to contend with looting, not just by the average citizen, but also by professionals who seek to build their private collections of artefacts. Other major threats are vandalism (as a result of insensitivity and ignorance), real estate development, raw-material extraction (mining), farming, natural disasters, tourism and infrastructural development. Examples of these threats are illustrated in Table 5.1.

This chapter seeks to examine two major threats to Taíno sites in Jamaica

Table 5.1 Examples of Threats to Taíno Sites

Threats	Sites Affected
Housing development	Harmony Hall, Clarendon
	Treasure Beach, St Elizabeth
Quarrying	Old Harbour Hill, Clarendon
Farming	Old Harbour, St Catherine
	Bull Savannah, St Elizabeth
Wave erosion	Little Miller's Bay, Manchester
	Long Acre, St Elizabeth
Tourism development	Auchindown, Westmoreland
Infrastructural development	Canoe Valley, Manchester

– infrastructural development through major road construction (such as the Old Harbour Bypass, the North Coast Highway Project and Highway 2000) and real estate development, particularly housing solutions. These threats are collectively referred to as land-based development. Solutions for all parties involved in the preservation of Jamaican archaeological resources will also be examined.

Table 5.2 illustrates that the total number of recorded Taíno sites in Jamaica is 357; of this total, 53 or 14.9 per cent of these sites have been reported destroyed. Half of these were destroyed as a result of land-based development (infrastructural and real estate). Farming, natural disasters and raw-material extraction contributed towards the destruction of 26.3 per cent of the sites, and the cause of the destruction of 24.5 per cent is undetermined. These data suggest that land-based development is responsible for half of the various impacts on archaeological sites. This information is by no means complete and is based only on sites recorded to date in the Jamaica National Heritage Trust's Sites and Monuments Record (SMR). Taíno sites are still being located, and there may be many more sites that have been destroyed, but no record is evident.

Table 5.2 Recorded Number of Destroyed Taíno Sites in Jamaica by Parish

Parish	Parish Site Totals	Infrastruc-tural	Real Estate Development	Farming	Raw-material Extraction	Elements	Other/Uncertain
St Ann	71	2	2	1	3	–	1
St Mary	31	–	2	–	–	–	–
St Elizabeth	37	2	–	–	–	–	1
Portland	0	–	–	–	–	–	–
St Thomas	20	1	–	1	–	1	–
Clarendon	40	2	1	1	1	2	1
St Catherine	29	1	1	1	–	–	–
Hanover	23	3	–	–	–	–	–
Kingston and St Andrew	20	1	3	–	–	1	–
Trelawny	22	–	1	–	–	–	2
Westmoreland	19	1	1	1	–	1	2
Manchester	20	–	–	–	–	1	2
St James	25	–	–	–	–	–	3
Total sites	**357**	**13**	**13**	**5**	**4**	**51**	**3**

Source: Compiled by author from the Jamaica National Heritage Trust's National Inventory of Sites.

The Agents of Development and the Role of the Jamaica National Heritage Trust

The Government of Jamaica, through various agencies, promotes development work in Jamaica. The three primary agencies concerned with development are as follows:

1. The Urban Development Corporation is a statutory body created by the Government of Jamaica primarily to ensure that development takes place in an orderly manner throughout Jamaica.
2. The National Works Agency, formerly the Public Works Department, concentrates on managing government infrastructure through maintenance and construction.
3. The National Housing Trust was established in 1975, mainly to accelerate housing development throughout the island.

These agencies are the major players – through the Ministries of Transport and Works, Water and Housing, and Land and the Environment. There are other instrumental organizations, such as the Jamaica Bauxite Institute and the National Environment and Planning Agency, which also have input into development issues. Another organization that carries out real estate development is the National Housing Development Corporation, a merger of the Caribbean Housing Finance Corporation, the National Housing Corporation and Operation PRIDE. In addition, there are many private developers who handle the construction of housing schemes, hotels and resorts, and arterial and secondary roads.

Agencies carrying out large-scale development are required to conduct an environmental impact assessment. This assessment will sometimes include a cultural history component or an archaeological impact assessment. The archaeological impact assessment will give an estimation of the impact this particular development will have on the archaeological heritage of the area in question. The Jamaica National Heritage Trust is the government agency with the mandate of protecting the nation's historic and archaeological heritage.

The Jamaica National Heritage Trust Act of 1985 grants to this body the power to protect sites from inappropriate development. When the Jamaica National Heritage Trust is contacted, an archaeological impact assessment or a heritage survey is conducted and recommendations are made. Impact assessments were virtually nonexistent before the North Coast Highway project began in the late 1990s (Ainsley Henriques, personal communication, 2002). The Jamaica National Heritage Trust may recommend mitigation measures from a shift in the road alignment (so that the site can be spared if it is a significant find) to the initiation of rescue archaeology ahead of major soil removal. Sometimes what is required is simple monitoring of the site when it is being cleared – if the nature of the site was not ascertained previously or its boundaries established (this is called a watching brief).

In general, developers have been hesitant to report findings of artefacts to the relevant authorities, as the result could mean losing work time and having their projects delayed while the site is surveyed or excavated. An impact assessment is seen by some as being time-consuming, a waste of money and an unnecessary hindrance to the work of developers. The Jamaica National Heritage Trust has been contacted on some occasions; however, in many instances work goes on without its knowledge, approval or recommendations (Dorrick Gray, personal communication, 2002).

Another problem is that penalties for noncompliance are insufficient. A person who wilfully defaces, damages or destroys any national monument is guilty of an offence, and on conviction is liable to a fine not exceeding J$40,000 or imprisonment not exceeding two years – or both (Jamaica National Heritage Trust Act 1985). The fine seems low in relation to the priceless nature of historic and archaeological sites.

Many Taíno sites have already been destroyed, and many more sites unknown to researchers will continue to be destroyed as the bulldozers of development move in without the necessary and proper assessment of the land in question. The White Marl Taíno site in St Catherine is the only declared Taíno site in Jamaica (Roderick Ebanks and Lloyd Wright, personal communication, 2002). The Jamaica National Heritage Trust Act of 1985 gives the trust power to halt development through the issuance of preservation or declaration notices. This often occurs where there are visible structures remaining above the ground. However, the Taíno left no structures above the ground; the remnants of Taíno existence remain below the earth, and it is easier to destroy what is not seen. When structures are not present on a site, it is easier for developers to clear it. Soil removal on the 14.5-km Old Harbour Bypass led to the discovery of three Taíno sites. Many more Taíno sites were located along the North Coast highway route. These sites have been partially or completely destroyed. Sites, once destroyed, are irreplaceable and their material remains irretrievable.

The Impact of Road Construction

North Coast Highway, Highway 2000, the Old Harbour Bypass and South Coast Sustainable Development Study illustrate the effect of road construction on Taíno sites across the island.

The North Coast Highway Improvement Project

The North Coast Highway Project is a 255-km roadway extending from Negril, Westmoreland, to Port Antonio, Portland. The highway has three segments:

- Segment 1 – Negril to Montego Bay (71 km) – completed
- Segment 2 – Montego Bay to Ocho Rios (92 km) – not completed
- Segment 3 – Ocho Rios to Port Antonio (92 km) – not started

This highway project has affected several Taíno sites. Segment 1 saw the partial and complete destruction of Taíno sites at Mosquito Cove, Barbican and Kew in Hanover. The Jamaica National Heritage Trust conducted watching briefs and pre-development excavations on the sites at Rhodes Hall, Haughton Hall, Green Island, Cousins Cove, Flint River and Paradise (all in Hanover). Seven watching briefs were conducted during segment 1, as were three pre-development rescue excavations and eleven re-routings; two archaeological and historic sites were recorded and reconstructed.

A few sites that will be affected by segment 2 of the highway were reviewed. Jamaica National Heritage Trust archaeologists conducted a watching brief on the Taíno site at Little River, St Ann (one of the earliest dated sites in the island). The predicted impact of this highway development was not clear, as the boundaries of several sites were never established and some documented sites were not located. The proposed realignment also posed a threat to the site at Rio Bueno, Trelawny.

Barbican, Hanover

Archaeologists from the Jamaica National Heritage Trust located the Taíno site at Barbican in Hanover while carrying out surveys ahead of a major clearing of lands designated for the North Coast Highway Segment 1 project – Montego Bay to Negril. A field-walking exercise revealed a surface littered with Taíno pottery, some already fragmented by the tractor clearing the land. Rescue archaeology was conducted by the Jamaica National Heritage Trust, and several unique pottery pieces were found, along with a Taíno burial. The site is now a part of the highway (Figure 5.1).

Highway 2000

Highway 2000 is a 230-km toll highway being constructed to open the country to roads and highways and increase access to new territories. The largest

Figure 5.1 Road cutting through the Taíno site at Barbican, Hanover

infrastructural development to date in the country, it is designed to be Jamaica's pathway to the future (Highway 2000 Supplement, 2002). The highway is also designed to open the country's tourism "hotspots" by connecting the tourism centres in Montego Bay, St James and Ocho Rios, St Ann. Highway 2000 is intended to facilitate direct and efficient links between economic centres and to stimulate additional economic development in Jamaica.

- Phase 1 – Kingston to Mandeville (74 km)
- Phase 2 – Bushy Park to Ocho Rios (67 km)
- Phase 3 – Mandeville to Montego Bay (85 km)

The exact highway path has not been finalized, so the anticipated impact has not been ascertained.

The Old Harbour Bypass

The Old Harbour Bypass is a 14-km roadway linking Sandy Bay, Clarendon, and Nightingale Grove, St Catherine. It is a major part of the South Coast Highway development programme. Three Taíno settlements were noted – at Freetown, Inverness and Toby Abbott (all in Clarendon) – by Jamaica National Heritage Trust archaeologists conducting an archaeological impact assessment during the construction of the Old Harbour Bypass (Figure 5.2). Rescue excavations were conducted on all three sites. On the Inverness site, the developers and archaeologists reached a compromise. The intended road could not be moved from its planned location, so it was agreed that the road would be elevated into a gravel foundation, 2 m high, thus saving the site from destruction.

Figure 5.2 Road cutting through a portion of the Toby Abbott Taíno site

South Coast Sustainable Development Study

This study was undertaken by a team led by Sir William Halcrow and Partners to ascertain the feasibility of development along the south coast of Jamaica. The south coast is home to some of the least developed sections of the country and is considered "ripe for infrastructural development". It is also home to numerous historic and archaeological sites in the island, including many Taíno sites. Technical reports were prepared for the following areas: terrestrial resources, environmental audit and issues, marine resources, hydrology, geology and natural hazards, land use and planning, physical infrastructure, tourism, agriculture and aquaculture, socio-economic review, legal and institutional, and framework and cultural heritage.

A total of sixty-four Taíno sites, including villages, middens, burial/ritual caves and cave art sites, were identified in the study area, which ranges from Great Salt Pond, St Catherine, to the Negril Green Island, Westmoreland. The study area encompasses sections of the parishes of Westmoreland (five sites), St Elizabeth (nineteen sites), Manchester (fourteen sites), Clarendon (eighteen sites) and St Catherine (eight sites).

The Impact of Housing Developments

A great deal of land in Jamaica is allocated to housing developments, affecting archaeological sites throughout the island. Numerous houses have been built in the archaeologically sensitive Bluefields area of Westmoreland. The Taínos settled in locations that could be described as "prime settlement areas". Later on the Spanish settled in these areas, followed by the English (for instance, Seville and Bellevue sites in St Ann). The majority of these areas have been selected for housing development. The cases of Chancery Hall and Long Mountain, both in St Andrew, illustrate the impact of housing development on Taíno sites.

Chancery Hall Phase Two, St Andrew

The subcontractors for the Chancery Hall Phase Two housing development discovered the Chancery Hall Taíno site (Figure 5.3) in St Andrew in 1990, during drilling and blasting for the construction of roadways and pipe trenches. People who dealt with antiques reported that whole pots were recovered from the site, along with a well-preserved stone axe and a stone arrow point. A pot containing bones was also located. Seven burials were found at the Chancery Hall site.

In 1993, archaeologist Carey McDonald of the Jamaica National Heritage Trust visited the site and noted that it appeared to be a "major Amerindian site" (McDonald 1993). All but one of the middens had been dug unprofessionally. The archaeologist noted three areas:

- Area 1 – Three middens were located (one extensive and two moderate).
- Area 2 – This area was extensively cleared (topsoil clearing and extensive trenching) Three extensive middens were located. McDonald also noted that the contextual pattern of the soil might have been destroyed because of the tractor clearance of the land.
- Area 3 – This area was located along Lord Nelson's Drive, where tractors had exposed a large midden. Coney jawbones, flint, griddle fragments and potsherds were evident from this clearing.

In 1994, archaeologists from the Jamaica National Heritage Trust visited the site again, seeking information about the site boundaries and who was responsible for the current structural development, as the Jamaica National Heritage Trust had not received formal notification about the development project. The site was examined further and excavated. This examination revealed that a house was to be built in an area that had previously been identified as an archaeologically sensitive area. Another part of the site had been almost completely destroyed by treasure hunters and looters. Layers of topsoil had been removed by earth-moving equipment. Roads had been cut, and preparations were being made for housing construction. There was also extensive trenching in the area where the Taíno skeletons had been located. Chancery Hall is a major Taíno site which has yielded large quantities of artefacts. Radiocarbon dating of the site in 1992 had placed it at AD 1260 ± 50.

Figure 5.3 Chancery Hall Taíno site, St Andrew

The archaeological value of the site was diminished as a result of the developers' actions. It is unfortunate that the areas where Taíno sites are located are those that have been selected for real estate development. Archaeologists believe that many other Taíno sites have been destroyed in other hilly areas of Kingston and St Andrew, such as Norbrook.

Long Mountain, St Andrew

Concerns about the development of Long Mountain were not just archaeological in nature. In addition to housing several archaeological sites, in particular Taíno sites, Long Mountain is the only remaining locale of dry limestone forest in Kingston and St Andrew (see Figure 5.4). Archaeologists, land developers and environmentalists agreed that development would take place only on a section of the mountain behind Beverly Hills and facing Kingston Harbour. The area designated for the housing development was excavated ahead of development. Recommendations were made for changes in road alignment, and the developers followed these suggestions. The section facing the University of the West Indies, Mona, would be preserved, as this side was also the home of a number of larger Taíno sites that are in need of further professional research (JNHT Survey 2002).

Jamaican archaeologists have not been able to conduct long-term research on most Taíno sites. Long-term work was conducted at the White Marl Taíno

Figure 5.4 Long Mountain prior to development

Figure 5.5 Construction activity at the Long Mountain site. (Courtesy of Selvenious Walters.)

site in St Catherine, which to date is believed to be the largest Taíno site in Jamaica. Information from this site opened the gates to Taíno research in Jamaica, but island-wide, sites researched by professional archaeologists constitute a minority. It is possible that information about the Taínos, gleaned from properly researched sites, may be used to attract public interest and support for further research.

It is difficult in the context of development to properly investigate sites. When the sites become known, all that can be done is to record them, if they have not previously been recorded, and carry out rescue archaeology to retain what is possible. Preservation is done on sites that can be preserved in the hope that they will one day be effectively and systematically researched before becoming threatened by development once more.

Preservation and research of Jamaica's Taíno sites will undoubtedly provide insights into their culture and evolution as a people and society, and their interaction with the African and European cultures with which they came in contact. Only by researching the sites and making comparisons with other sites will archaeologists be able to draw academic conclusions on the life of the Taíno. Properly investigated, sites enable interpretations of the past that cannot be made otherwise (McManamon 2000, 5).

Recommendations

The Government of Jamaica, like the governments of many developing countries, is more concerned about managing unemployment, crime and other challenges of a growing population than about understanding the Taínos and their role in our history. Culture, at times, is perceived as expendable in the context of development.

The government and the Jamaica National Heritage Trust should require that impact assessments be carried out for any land-based development work in Jamaica. The Jamaica National Heritage Trust will have to become more proactive with developers regarding the destruction of sites, which should carry stiffer penalties. Public-sector agencies dealing with development projects should be informed of any archaeological heritage in the area and invited into partnerships with the Jamaica National Heritage Trust. The trust should also consider reviewing its policies to ensure that it becomes more proactive in carrying out its mandate. Decision makers should also seek the assistance of countries that have successfully solved at least some of the conflicts between development and preservation. Collaborative efforts will be required, and concessions will have to be made by both sides. For instance, the Inverness site in Clarendon, along the Old Harbour Bypass, was at risk of being destroyed. The developers met with archaeologists from the Jamaica National Heritage Trust, the two parties agreed that since the road could not be moved, it would be elevated onto a gravel foundation; no digging would take place, and the site would be preserved. Developers and cultural resource managers will have to sit at the same table, hammer out differences and make serious decisions. This was the case for the Long Mountain Steering Committee, which consisted of representatives from the University of the West Indies, the National Arboretum Foundation, the Jamaica National Heritage Trust and the National Environmental and Planning Agency as well as the developers;

among other collaborative efforts, the developers provided the Jamaica National Heritage Trust Archaeology Division with a weekly work plan.

Some sites will be preserved, and others will not. Where is the line to be drawn? Should attempts be made to preserve all sites or a select few? If only a few sites are to be preserved, how will their relative importance be evaluated? Sometimes a lack of communication is the only thing obstructing research on a site ahead of development. Incentives should be offered to developers to ensure that development does not severely damage sites, as sometimes developers are unaware of the options they have. One approach might be to collaborate with developers to create green spaces in sensitive areas and thereby preserve Taíno sites that would otherwise be destroyed or damaged.

The public cannot be excluded, as they constitute possibly the largest body of potential preservationists. Until individuals are properly educated about the Taínos, their culture (and its contribution to the Jamaican culture) and the importance of the Taíno legacy, the significance of the loss of Taíno sites will not be understood. Heritage parks should be set up depicting the life of the Taíno. Sites have already been lost along the Old Harbour Bypass and the north coast; however, educational exhibits could be set up to inform people that a Taíno site once existed there. The Jamaica National Heritage Trust should have a larger presence in schools, present more seminars, use the news media more effectively and take legal action against those who destroy archaeological and historic sites.

Protection of our Taíno sites cannot depend only on preservationists; it must be a nationwide initiative backed by effective government policies. "The greatest benefit of archaeological resources is what we can learn about the past from them and the links they have as material remains to important past events, individuals or historical processes" (McManamon 2000, 5).

Section 2

Taíno Exploitation of Natural Resources

THE TAÍNOS WERE heavily dependent on natural resources, and this was reflected in every aspect of their lives. Adaptation to a new environment is essential for survival. The floral and faunal remains from a site are useful indicators for the reconstruction of the natural environment as well as providing information on subsistence patterns, exploitation of plants for the creation of products, and human impact on the natural environment. This section illustrates the importance of natural resources for the Jamaican Taínos.

Wendy Lee's "Notes on the Natural History of Jamaica" introduces the reader to the natural history of Jamaica. Lee concisely discusses the geology and geography of the island, highlighting the flora and fauna.

The second chapter in this section is "The Exploitation and Transformation of Jamaica's Natural Vegetation", by Lesley-Gail Atkinson. In 1991, John Rashford published "Arawak, Spanish and African Contributions to Jamaica's Settlement Vegetation", identifying the human selective pressures on Jamaica's vegetation. Atkinson applies Rashford's principles to demonstrate the Taínos' impact on the natural vegetation and their role in the introduction of new flora.

Sylvia Scudder's chapter, "Early Arawak Subsistence: The Rodney Site of Jamaica", reports on the analysis of the faunal remains recovered in 1978 from Rodney's House, St Catherine, by John Wilman and Colin Medhurst. Scudder not only identified and analysed the faunal remains but also compared the results with those from the sites at Bellevue, St Andrew, and White Marl, St Catherine, to determine the subsistence patterns of the Jamaican Taíno.

6  Notes on the Natural History of Jamaica

Wendy A. Lee

The term *natural history* loosely refers to the study and appreciation of nature and natural resources, including both living species and their habitats. These notes include brief descriptions of Jamaica's geology, climate, landforms, major ecosystems, flora and fauna.

Size and Location of Jamaica

Jamaica is one of a group of four islands called the Greater Antilles, located in the Caribbean Sea. It is 235 km long by 82 km wide; its area is 11,400 km².

Geology

Jamaica is a land mass on the Caribbean Plate. The oldest rocks in the island are volcanic in origin and over 100 million years old, but most of the bedrock is limestone deposited on the seafloor between 45 and 12 million years ago, while the land mass was submerged beneath the sea. There have been two major periods of tectonic activity (uplifting, folding and faulting), the first starting about 65 million years ago and the second about 12 million years ago. Most major landforms of the island as we know it were formed within the past 5 to 10 million years, after the island finally emerged from the sea. Jamaica has never been connected to the mainland of North America, but when sea levels were much lower than present, about 18,000 years ago, there was a chain of islands between here and Central America. Table 6.1 describes major events in the island's formation.

Soils

Table 6.1 Geologic Time and Corresponding Events in the Formation of the Island of Jamaica

Geologic Time	Event
110 to 65 million years ago (± 45 million years)	Volcanic islands spew lava and ash into coastal waters, which over time form a thick layer of sedimentary rock.
65 to 50 million years ago (± 15 million years)	First major uplifting (tectonic activity) begins. Rocks are uplifted and folded, mountains rise up from the seafloor and some land areas sink under the sea. New rivers form and begin to erode the rocks and deposit new sediments on old rocks. Active volcanoes remain only in the Wagwater Trough, on a diagonal line between Port Maria on the north coast and Bull Bay on the south.
50 to 12 million years ago (± 5 million years to subside, 33 million years of deposition)	The land begins to subside beneath the sea and within about 5 million years is totally submerged. For the next 33 million years calcium carbonate is deposited from the skeletons of tiny marine organisms, forming a layer of pure white limestone up to 2,400 m thick that makes up two-thirds of the island's bedrock.
12 to 2 million years ago (± 10 million years)	Second major uplifting, folding and faulting of the land, followed by erosion as the limestone dissolves over the next 10 million years. This causes the island to emerge from the sea and results in the formation of the karst landscape in the Cockpit Country and the deposition of bauxite and "terra rosa" soils in limestone cavities. Large amounts of sand and gravel are also deposited along the north and south coasts, up to 150 m thick in places.
2 million years ago to the present time	The present-day river systems emerge from the older, underlying rocks. They erode and deposit tons of material downstream, forming broad alluvial plains, especially on the south coast.

Source: Porter 1990. Information summarized and tabulated by Wendy Lee.

Several different soil types are found in Jamaica, depending on the source material and the processes that have formed them. The main soil types and their locations are listed in Table 6.2.

Major Landforms and Vegetation Types

Table 6.2 Main Soil Types of Jamaica and Associated Landforms

Soil Type	Associated Landforms
Rich volcanic soils formed from igneous and metamorphic rock	Mountain ranges in the northeast and centre of the island
Limestone and "terra rosa" (red dirt), rich in bauxite	Interior hills and plateaus
Alluvial soils, sand, silt, gravel, clay	Lowlands (interior valleys and coastal plains)

Source: Porter 1990.

The major landforms of Jamaica are
- Mountain ranges
- Hills and plateaus
- Interior valleys
- Coastal plains
- Rivers
- Shoreline
- Cays and banks

Mountain Ranges

The Blue Mountains are the highest of Jamaica's mountain ranges, at 2,256 m. The John Crow Mountains are lower and further east. Both have patches of montane cloud forest and rain forest and are high in endemic species. The Port Royal Mountains form the foothills of the Blue Mountains. The Dry Harbour Mountains are found in the north-central part of the island. The Hellshire Hills in the southeast are important for endemic vertebrate species, including the endangered Jamaican *hutia* or "coney" (*Geocapromys brownii*) and the Jamaican iguana (*Cyclura collei*).

Hills and Plateaus

The Cockpit Country in the northwest is a fine example of karst topography (egg-box–shaped hills and valleys with many caves, formed as limestone was dissolved by acidic rain and groundwater). It has a mixture of wet evergreen forest and seasonally dry deciduous forest and is high in endemic species of plants (more than one hundred) and animals. There are many caves, and rivers that disappear into the ground and reappear further downstream.

A plateau is an area of relatively flat land on top of a range of hills or mountains. The Manchester Plateau is in the main central range. It consists of rolling hills, with hillsides and valleys mostly planted or in pasture. Parts of the area have been extensively mined for bauxite.

Interior Valleys

Major interior valleys include Lluidas Vale, St Thomas in the Vale, the Nassau Valley, Queen of Spain's Valley and Cave Valley.

Coastal Plains

An almost continuous strip of coastal lowland surrounds Jamaica. On the north coast there is a narrow coastal plain – usually less than 2 km wide – with lush vegetation nurtured by plentiful rainfall from the prevailing northeasterly trade winds. The south coast has a broad coastal plain, several kilometres wide in places, with a variety of ecotypes: semi-arid lands (for example, parts of the St Thomas, St Catherine and St Elizabeth coastlines), dry limestone scrub forests (St Catherine, Clarendon and Manchester coasts), mangrove forests (St Thomas, Kingston Harbour, St Catherine, Clarendon, St Elizabeth and Westmoreland), herbaceous swamps (Black River Upper and Lower morasses, St Elizabeth, Negril Morass, Hanover and Westmoreland), and marsh forests (Black River Lower Morass and Westmoreland).

Rivers

Major north-flowing rivers include the Rio Grande, Wagwater, Martha Brae, White River and Great River. Major south-flowing rivers include the Black River (the largest river in the island, navigable for 40 km upstream), Plantain Garden, Rio Cobre, Rio Minho, Cabaritta, and Milk River (all of which are longer than 32 km).

Shoreline

On the north coast, there are mainly white sand beaches derived from coral reefs close to the shore. Towards the east there are some rugged, pebbly beaches, derived partly from stones and sand washed down by rivers. Much of the south coast has black sand beaches, with particles of metallic oxides carried from the interior and deposited by south-flowing rivers. Many south coast coral reefs are far from shore (several kilometres in some areas) and contribute proportionally less to beach sands than on the north coast.

Climate

Jamaica has a maritime tropical climate. Trade winds blow from the northeast, especially in the summer. Hurricane season is July through November. Jamaica has frequent storms but few direct hits. There are two rainy seasons, in May and October/November. Kingston, Hellshire and southern St Elizabeth, in the rain shadow of the Blue Mountains and central ranges, receive the least rain. Portland, in the northeast, receives the highest rainfall in the island.

Average temperatures: 28° C (78° F) at sea level
15° C (56° F) at 2,000 m above sea level

Mean annual rainfall: Approximately 200 cm

Range of rainfall: 75–500 cm

Ecosystems

An ecosystem is a community of living creatures (plants and animals) and their non-living environment (soil, water, air, and so on) in a particular area, which together form a self-sustaining natural system. Ecosystems found in Jamaica are

- Forests
- Caves
- Rivers, streams and ponds
- Wetlands
- Coral reefs
- Banks and cays
- Seagrass beds

Biodiversity

Biodiversity refers to the variety and abundance of life forms in a particular place or ecosystem. Biodiversity comprises flora (plants) and fauna (animals). Indigenous species are plants and animals that naturally occur in a particular country but may also be found elsewhere in the world. An endemic species is any kind of plant or animal that is found only in a particular area (usually refers to a country). For a small island, Jamaica has a relatively large number of endemic species of flora and fauna – species that are found nowhere else in the world.

Examples of biodiversity include flowering plants such as grasses and palms, orchids, cacti and ferns, and fauna including mammals, birds, reptiles, amphibians, fish and invertebrates.

Flora

Jamaica is well known for its many species of flowering plants and ferns, more than four hundred of which are considered threatened or endangered due to clearing of land and other changes in habitat or over-harvesting. Flowering plants include numerous species of orchids, bromeliads, cacti, palms, trees, vines, shrubs and grasses. Approximately 30 per cent of the island's flowering plants are endemics. Indigenous plants include the national flower, the lignum vitae (*Guaiacum officinale*), pimento (*Pimenta dioica*), pawpaw or papaya (*Carica papaya*), sweet potato (*Ipomea batatas*), pineapple (*Ananas comosus*), cassava (*Manihot esculenta*) and guava (*Psidium guajava*). Many of the island's most familiar and useful plants have been introduced since European colonization in the sixteenth century. Introduced plants include ackee (*Blighia sapida*), breadfruit (*Atrocarpus altilis*), coconuts (*Cocos nucifera*), mangoes (*Mangifera indica*), bananas and plantain (*Musa* spp.) and a great many ornamental plants used in horticulture. The latter include hibiscus, bougainvillaea, oleander, anthuriums, and poinsettia. Many introduced plants have become so

Table 6.3 Total Number of Species

	Total Species	Endemic Species	Per cent Endemic
Flowering plants (all)	3,003	830	28
Orchids and bromeliads	267	82	31
Ferns	579	82	14

well established, especially in disturbed or urban areas, that they are replacing native species and threatening their survival in some parts of Jamaica.

Table 6.3 provides estimates of the total number of species and the number and per cent of endemic species of some distinctive Jamaican plant groups.

Fauna

Mammals

The Jamaican *hutia* or coney (Figure 6.1) is a rabbit-sized endemic rodent which is now very rare and hard to find. Three or four species of the more than twenty species of bats are endemic. The West Indian manatee (*Trichechus manatus*) occurs here as well as elsewhere in the region. The mongoose is an introduced mammal which has become a pest to farmers and indigenous wildlife, as have rats and mice and feral dogs and cats.

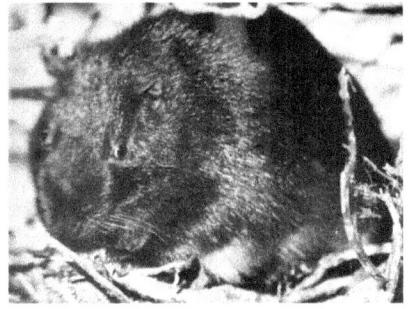

Figure 6.1 Jamaican *hutia* or coney. (Oliver 1983, 53.)

Birds

Over 200 species of birds are found in Jamaica, 113 species bred in Jamaica, and at least 25 species (possibly as many as 30) are endemic. Well-known endemic species include Jamaica's national bird, the streamertail hummingbird or doctor bird (*Trochilus polytmus*), the Jamaican woodpecker (*Melanerpes radiolatus*), and the Jamaican tody or robin redbreast (*Todus todus*). Endemic species that are endangered include the yellow-billed and black-billed parrots (genus *Amazona*), the ring-tailed pigeon (*Columba caribaea*) and the Jamaican blackbird (*Nesopsar nigerrimus*). There may have been an endemic Jamaican macaw that became extinct soon after the arrival of Columbus. The West Indian whistling-duck (*Dendrocygna arborea*) is a Caribbean endemic species that is considered endangered throughout its range.

Reptiles

Native reptile species include several small lizards (of which seven are endemic, including the green lizard); the endangered endemic Jamaican iguana; the American crocodile; nine snakes, including the large Jamaican boa (yellow snake); four species of sea turtles (see Figure 6.2), all of which are highly endangered worldwide; and the endemic pond turtle. The lizard-like galliwasps are also endemic. In all, there are thirty-three endemic reptiles.

Figure 6.2 Hawksbill turtle

Fishes

Of the many freshwater fishes found in Jamaica's rivers and streams, three species are endemic (minnows). Hundreds of marine species are found in Jamaican waters, but none are endemic.

Amphibians

Twenty-one endemic amphibian species are present in Jamaica. They include certain cave-dwelling species of frogs and bromeliad frogs.

Invertebrates

This broad group includes insects, molluscs and many other classes of animals without backbones. Unique in the world is the bromeliad crab, which lives in the water at the base of bromeliads in the limestone forests. The endangered endemic giant swallowtail butterfly is one of over one hundred butterfly species found here. It is found in only two areas, the Cockpit Country and the Blue and John Crow Mountains. With a wingspan of up to 15 cm, it is one of the world's largest butterflies. Jamaica has high levels of diversity in many insect groups, including fireflies (forty-eight species, of which forty-five are endemic).

Jamaica's mollusc fauna is among the most diverse in the world. There are about 550 species of land snails, of which 505 (92 per cent) are thought to be endemic. Of the 52 species of millipedes so far described from Jamaica, 48 (92 per cent) are endemic. There are thousands of species of marine invertebrates in Jamaican waters, including hard and soft corals, molluscs and crustaceans.

Table 6.4 Numbers of Endemic Species

Mammals	Birds	Reptiles	Amphibians	Fish
5	30	33	21	3

Source: Johnson 1988; Raffaele et al. 1998; Vogel, lecture, 1998.

Acknowledgements

Ann Haynes-Sutton reviewed these notes and provided valuable suggestions that have been incorporated into the document. Her assistance and contributions are gratefully acknowledged.

7  The Exploitation and Transformation of Jamaica's Natural Vegetation

Lesley-Gail Atkinson

Natural vegetation is influenced largely by topography, climate and precipitation. At present, forests occupy over 265,000 hectares or 24 per cent of Jamaica's total land mass (NRCA/NEPA/MLE 2001, 10). The island has an estimated 3,304 species of vascular plants, of which 923 (27.9 per cent) are endemic (ibid., 9). From an archaeological perspective, a limited amount of work has been done with regard to environmental studies of the island and the reconstruction of the natural vegetation.

The vegetation of Jamaica has undergone changes since the first human occupation of the island, more than thirteen centuries ago. All the major racial/ethnic groups that have inhabited the island have contributed to the island's present vegetation, as John Rashford (1991) discusses in his article "Arawak, Spanish and African Contributions to Jamaica's Settlement Vegetation". In it, Rashford applies the concept of human selective pressures to the Taínos. The Taínos were the first to have assisted in the transformation of the vegetation, whether deliberately or inadvertently. This chapter demonstrates the Taínos' impact on Jamaican vegetation and discusses the archaeological and ethnographic evidence for their utilization of endemic, indigenous and introduced flora, in particular the cassava (*Manihot esculenta*).

Evidence of Flora

Palaeoethnobotany refers to the analysis and interpretation of archaeobotanical remains to elucidate the interaction between human populations and plants (Hastorf and Popper 1988, ix). Colin Renfrew and Paul Bahn (2000) describe several different methods in which archaeologists derive information from plants, with the objectives of reconstructing the plant environment and determining subsistence and diet, evidence of trade and various ways in which societies utilize flora. Useful indicators for examination and analysis include macrobotanical remains, microbotanical remains, associated artefacts, art, and historical and ethnographic texts.

Macrobotanical Remains

The analysis of macrobotanical remains includes the study of seeds and fruits, plant residues and charcoal (Renfrew and Bahn 2000, 244–46). In Jamaica, faunal analysis has significantly overshadowed floral analysis. The excavations at White Marl, St Catherine, and Chancery Hall, St Andrew, highlight the importance of the recovery and analysis of faunal remains. The recovery of macrobotanical remains has been largely limited to the collection of charcoal, primarily for dating purposes. For example, a charcoal sample from Chancery Hall dated the site AD 1260 ± 50 (Lechler 2000, 11). The excavations conducted by Bill Keegan at Paradise Park, Westmoreland, have encouraged the recovery of macrobotanical remains from Taíno sites in an effort to reconstruct the natural environment.

Microbotanical Remains

The examination of microbotanical remains includes the analysis of pollen, phytoliths, fossil cuticles and plant DNA (Renfrew and Bahn 2000, 239–44). Unfortunately, to date there is no evidence that analysis of microbotanical remains has been conducted in the island.

Associated Artefacts

Tools associated with certain activities can be useful indicators of plant use. According to Renfrew and Bahn, tools can prove or at least suggest that plants were processed at a site, and on rare occasions may indicate the species and the use that was made of it (2000, 276). However, in the absence of supporting evidence, such as remains of domesticated plants, associated artefacts are inadequate indicators of such features (ibid.). Some artefacts are multifunctional, and without supporting evidence it is difficult to determine what function or activity was performed at the specific site. In Jamaica, there are many artefacts associated with plant use that have been found across the island, and these objects can at least be used as possible evidence.

Art

Art can be religious, functional, aesthetic or documentary (Atkinson 2002). Taíno art forms include idols, figurines, *duhos*, cave art and other items (Moure and Rivero de la Calle 1996). Prehistoric art can be useful in illustrating the importance of plants and how they were utilized by various societies. Jamaica has a number of examples of Taíno art; however, the motifs of Jamaican petroglyphs and pictographs are primarily zoomorphic and anthropomorphic (Atkinson 2002).

Texts

Most of our information on Taíno exploitation of plants and agricultural practices is derived from Hispanic ethnographic data. Gonzalo Fernández de Oviedo's *The Natural History of the West Indies* highlights some of the uses of plants by the Taínos of Hispaniola – and invites the reader to assume that similar techniques were used by the Jamaican Taínos: "All that I have said of the people and other things of Hispaniola applies in part to Cuba, Puerto Rico, and Jamaica" (1959, 19).

Because so little work has been done on macro- and microbotanical remains in the island, the arguments in this chapter rely on other evidence: associated artefacts, art and ethnographic texts.

Taíno Impact on the Natural Vegetation

The Jamaican Taínos and their predecessors, the Ostionoids (Ostionan and Meillacan), were the first to have an impact on the island's vegetation. According to Rashford, humans assist, directly or indirectly, in the transformation of natural environments. The intentional and unintentional selection of plants in the environment produces distinctive settlement vegetation that is an expression of the historical development of their way of life (1998, 37).

When the Ostionoids arrived in Jamaica around AD 650, they must have found incredibly rich natural resources:

> The West Indian forests contained an abundance of wild fruits and vegetables, including palms, guava berries, and *guáyiga*, a cycad with edible roots. Saltwater fish, shellfish, and waterfowl were available along the shores, especially in estuaries, mangrove swamps, and reefs, which provided shelter from the open sea. Manatees and turtles could also be hunted there. The food resources varied from island to island, making it possible for the natives to develop extensive trading networks. (Watters and Rouse 1989)

The Ostionoids undoubtedly sought to recreate a familiar environment in their new home. The Taínos assisted in the transformation of Jamaica's natural forests into settlement vegetation by two main human selective pressures: the impact on wild plants and the cultivation of domesticated and wild plants (Rashford 1991, 18).

According to Rashford, there are three human responses to wild plants: they are destroyed to make space, to remove interference and to create useful products; they are tolerated when they do not interfere with human activities; and when they are valued, they are protected and cultivated (ibid.). It is believed that the Taínos removed and altered the natural vegetation in order to establish settlements and areas for cultivation and to create useful products.

Settlements

When the Taínos' predecessors arrived, they must have required space for dwelling and other functions. It is logical to assume that the natural vegetation was altered first along the coasts. There is a consensus among archaeologists that the coast is generally settled first, and then expansions are made into the interior. Presumably, the natural vegetation was removed at areas where the newcomers wished to establish settlements.

The Ostionans – or, as they are locally known, the Redware culture – were the first known inhabitants of Jamaica. They settled primarily on the south coast, and in the interior of what is now the parish of St Ann (Lee 1980). Examples of Redware sites in the island are Alligator Pond or Bottom Bay, Manchester; Great Pedro Bay, St Elizabeth; Paradise Park, Westmoreland; and Little River, St Ann. All of these sites are located within the coastal plain.

The Meillacan occupation of the island commenced around AD 900 and continued to the point of European contact. The Meillacan distribution of sites ranges from coastal settlements such as Old Harbour Bay, St Catherine, to sites in the limestone hills and plateaus such as Mount Rosser, also in St Catherine. Certain areas of the island contained nuclei of Taíno settlements, as seen in the parishes of St Catherine, St Ann, St Mary and St James.

Cultivation

Agriculture was an important component of Taíno subsistence (and will be discussed later in the section "Cultivation of wild and domesticated plants"). Land would have been allocated for the cultivation of essential crops. Any disturbance of the natural vegetation cover provides growth opportunities for plants not normally dominant (Alexander 1969, 126). In "The Vascular Flora of Long Mountain", Andreas Oberli of the National Arboretum Foundation highlights the presence of invasive species such as woman's tongue (*Albizia lebbeck*), which is normally found on Taíno sites where land has been cleared for cultivation (Proctor and Oberli 2002). Mr Oberli had identified woman's tongue on the Long Mountain Taíno sites (ibid.). Another invasive species, logwood (*Haematoxylum campechianum*), despite being introduced in 1715, appears on Taíno sites across the island (Selvenious Walters, personal communication, 2002). The presence of logwood on Taíno sites could also be an indicator of land that had been cleared by the Taínos for cultivation.

The Creation of Useful Products

According to Bray and Trump (1982, 180), much of man's material equipment came and comes from vegetable matter – food, fibres for clothing, construction material for tools and houses, and so on. The Taínos were very resourceful, utilizing the endemic and indigenous plants to manufacture necessary commodities.

Housing

According to Fernández de Oviedo, the houses of the Taínos (see Figure 7.1)

> are made of substantial framing, with walls of canes tied with lianas, which are round vines or filaments that grow on large trees and interlaced with them. The lianas are all sizes and sometimes the natives cut and prepare those they need to tie the timber and supports of the house. The walls are made of canes placed close together, plastered over with earth four or five fingers thick, and extend to the top of the house. The houses are covered with straw or long grass which is well placed and lasts a long time. (1959, 39)

In Jamaica, an indigenous wild cane (*Gynerium sagittatum*) is readily accessible along the riverbanks. The blue mahoe (*Hibiscus elatus*) and red mangrove (*Rhizophora mangle*) (Adams 1972) are other species that would have been available for the construction of Taíno homes. The island has large lianas, *Tanaecium jaroba* and the endemic *Combretum robinsonii* (Clarke 1974), which could have been used to tie the canes together; the blue mahoe also was a source of good rope (Adams 1971). The varieties of Jamaican thatch – silver thatch (*Coccothrinax jamaicensis*), broad thatch (*Thrinax excelsa*) and long thatch (*Calyptronoma occidentalis*) – provide plentiful roofing material that is still used in contemporary Jamaica. At this point

Figure 7.1 Fernández de Oviedo's illustration of Taínan *caney*. (Rouse 1992, fig. 4.)

there is no direct material evidence to state that Taínos utilized these plants; however, ethnographic information and the present and historical functions of the plants suggest that they are likely to have been used.

Fishing

Fish was an important source of protein for the Jamaican Taínos. The Taínos built *canoas* and made poisons to assist in fishing. In Jamaica the Taínos were known for their majestic *canoas*. "Columbus later saw the biggest and best made Arawak canoes in Jamaica during his second voyage. Those belonging to the *caciques* of that island were elaborately decorated for they were the greatest symbols of their status" (Walker 1992, 58). Bernaldez wrote that "one Jamaican canoe measured later by Columbus proved to be no less than 96 feet in length and 8 feet wide" (ibid., 241). According to Viviene Wallace (1992, 88), there is evidence suggesting that the Taínan canoes were large and sturdy enough for deep-sea fishing, and analysis of fish bones recovered from kitchen middens revealed that some of the fish consumed by the Taínos were indeed deep-sea fish.

The West Indian cedar (*Cedrela odorata*) and the silk cotton tree (*Ceiba pentandra*) were durable sources of wood for the construction of *canoas*. The prow of a cedar canoe was found at the Halberstadt Cave, St Thomas. A full canoe found in 1993–94 in downtown Kingston consists of a single piece of wood (so far unidentified), is rounded at both ends and has a flat bottom with markings (presumably resulting from its construction) on both sides (Allsworth-Jones et al. 2001). Contemporary Jamaican fishermen still use the wood of the silk cotton tree for dugout canoes, whose construction is similar to those made by the Taínos (see Figure 7.2).

Wild cane (*Gynerium sagittatum*) is also used to make arrows and lances (William Keegan, personal communication, 2002; Figure 7.3). The firmness of the cane and the absence of nodes make it the perfect material for spears. In 1935, at Old Harbour, St Catherine, several stone projectile points were found, suggesting that the Taínos of Jamaica made arrows or spears (Lovén 1935).

Cotton

Cotton, from the cotton shrub (*Gossypium* spp.) (Adams 1972), was an essential, multifunctional product for Taínos. It was used for making hammocks, as described by

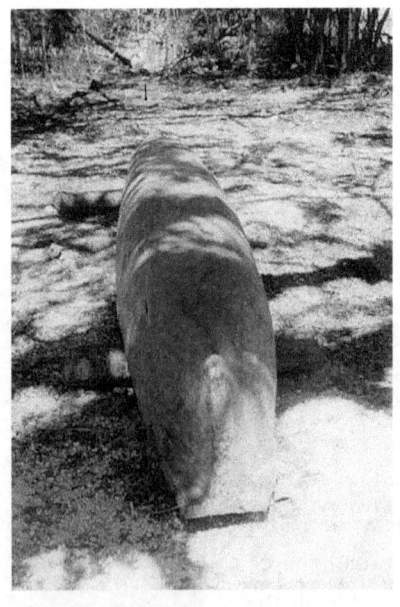

Figure 7.2 Dugout canoe from Black River, St Elizabeth

Figure 7.3 William Keegan explaining the use of the wild cane to participants at the Paradise Park 2002 excavations

Fernández de Oviedo (1959, 42): "The beds in which they sleep are called *hamacas* [hammocks], which are pieces of well-woven cotton cloth. . . . On the end they are covered with long cords made of *cabuya* (century plant) and of *henequén* (sisal hemp)." *Cabuya* and *henequén* belong to the *Agave* species.

Cotton was also used for making fishing nets and other articles of domestic use. A wooden spindle with a fishbone needle was found at Image Cave, Manchester, and spindle whorls were recovered from the sites at Chancery Hall, St Andrew, and Alligator Pond, St Elizabeth. These artefacts indicate that cotton or other fibres were being woven at these sites. The cotton was extracted from the pods and freed from the seeds; afterwards, it was pulled by hand into a long, uneven, loose band. One end of this was fastened to the hook or needle at the end of the spindle. Spindles were used in pairs and were held between the thumb and one finger of the left hand. A spinning and twisting motion produced cotton threads, which were then woven into cloth.

Sven Lovén (1935) reported that Jamaica furnished cotton cloth and hammocks to the islands of Cuba and Española [Hispaniola], which had been Spanish already for some time. It was also said that the Jamaican Taínos made sails for some Spanish ships (ibid.).

Abundant net sinkers were found across the island at Taíno sites such as Harbour View, Kingston and St Andrew; Seville, St Ann; and Rio Nuevo, St Mary (Figures 7.4 and 7.5). Net sinkers are inorganic evidence of fishing nets, to which they were previously attached as weights. These nets would have been made of cotton.

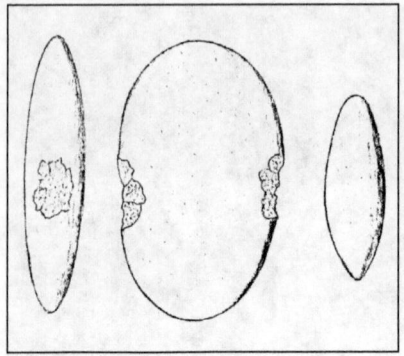
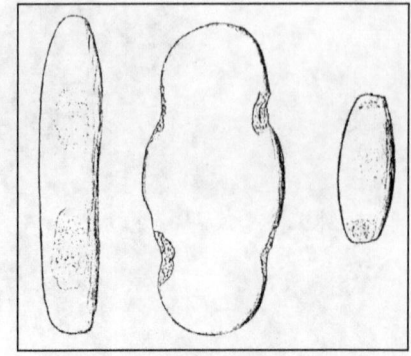

Figure 7.4 Two-notched net sinkers. (Illustration by James W. Lee, Archaeological Society of Jamaica.)

Figure 7.5 Four-notched net sinkers. (Illustration by James W. Lee, Archaeological Society of Jamaica.)

Dyes

According to Irving Rouse, Taíno married women wore short skirts called *naguas* (1992, 11). These skirts or aprons were made from cotton. Fernández de Oviedo adds that the Taínos used seeds, berries, leaves and bark to colour their cotton cloth: "They colour it black, tan, green, blue, yellow, and red, the colours being as vivid or as subdued as the Indians desire. After boiling the bark and leaves in a pot without changing the dye, they can produce all the distinct colours" (1959, 103).

Jamaica has various plants which can be used to make dyes. According to Rouse (1992, 11), red was a favoured colour. Three indigenous species that produce red dyes are the annatto (*Bixa orellana*) or, as the Taínos called it, *bija*, whose seeds/berries produce a reddish-orange dye (Figure 7.6); brazilwood or brasiletto wood (*Caesalpinia brasiliensis*); and red mangrove (*Rhizophora mangle*). Guava (*Psidium guajava*) is said to produce a black pigment.

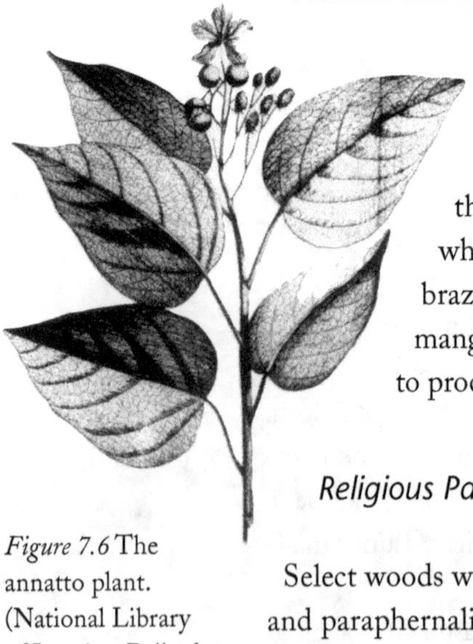

Religious Paraphernalia

Figure 7.6 The annatto plant. (National Library of Jamaica; Pollard 1983, 16.)

Select woods were used for the construction of wooden religious furniture and paraphernalia (Saunders and Gray 1996). The lignum vitae (*Guaiacum officinale*) or *guyacan* is referred to as "holy wood", "wood of life" or "holy Tree" (Fernández de Oviedo 1959; Adams 1972). *Zemís* and *duhos* were created from this wood. A small lignum vitae *duho* was recovered from the Cambridge Hill Burial Cave, St Thomas. Lignum vitae was also used for axe handles (Duerden 1897). West Indian mahogany (*Swietenia mahagoni*) or *caoba*, West Indian cedar (*Cedrela odorata*), santa maria (*Calophyllum calaba*) and blue mahoe (*Hibiscus elatus*) are examples of woods that were used for creating *zemís*.

The foregoing section illustrates the diverse ways in which the Jamaican Taínos responded to the natural environment and utilized it to meet their needs. The next section discusses the second type of human selective pressure: the cultivation of domesticated and wild plants.

Cultivation of Domesticated and Wild Plants

According to Colin Renfrew and Paul Bahn, subsistence – the ability to keep oneself alive – is the most basic of all necessities (2000, 269). The Jamaican Taíno subsistence consisted of agriculture, fishing and gathering (see Scudder, this volume). Agriculture was a very important component of the Taíno livelihood. It was a means of survival and regulated an organized system of labour.

Cultivation is simply the deliberate assistance given to plants, such as preparing the soil, fertilizing, irrigating, weeding and providing protection from predators. Whether grown from seeds or vegetatively, wild plants become domesticated when, through cultivation, they have been genetically modified to the point of dependence on human activity for their successful reproduction and dispersal (Rashford 1991).

The domestication of plants did not occur overnight but took thousands of years. According to Peter Ucko and G.W. Dimbleby, our record of manufactured tools goes back over one million years, but evidence of domesticated animals and plants starts much later, around the end of the European Ice Age, after *ca.* 10,000 BC (1969, xvii). They go on to say:

> Domestication was a process extending over several thousand years and that it [*sic*] had its own special characteristics in different areas of the ancient world. Domestication did not, of course, happen only once but has recurred time and time again in different parts of the world and at different times. Domestication as a process still continues. (Ucko and Dimbleby 1969, xx)

Agricultural Practices

The Slash-and-Burn Technique

The agricultural practices and techniques applied in Jamaica and the Greater Antilles were strongly influenced by the methods used in the Amazon region. Marcio Veloz Maggiolo states that rainforest farming and an agricultural system based on deforestation (forest-burning and ash-bedded sowing) reached the Caribbean around 400 BC. Slash-and-burn agriculture, as this system is called, requires that a population move to new land every ten to twelve years, soon after the soil has been exhausted (Veloz Maggiolo 1997, 34).

According to Veloz Maggiolo, the Ostionoid were the most important pre-Taíno society of the slash-and-burn agricultural period. Originally, they combined an attenuated approach to slash-and-burn agriculture with gathering, fishing and hunting (ibid., 36). He continues:

> In stark contrast to the vast expanses of rain forest on the mainland, the islands were small. So migrants had to shift away from slash-and-burn agriculture with its requirements of large tracts of land available for burning and constant mobility. Toward the first and second centuries AD, the island societies had adapted to the new environment They soon discovered a new technique: mound farming. Decomposed garbage and refuse accumulations, they found, were particularly fertile planting terrains, as nitrogen levels in these naturally fertilized mounds increased productivity. (ibid., 36)

Conucos

The Taínos cultivated their root crops, such as cassava (*Manihot esculenta*), in man-made earthen mound fields called *conucos*, or *monticulos* in Spanish. These *conucos* are what Veloz Maggiolo refers to as mound farming (1997). These mounds were 1 m high and some 3 m in circumference and were arranged in regular rows (Rouse 1992). The *conuco* was said to provide more room and fertile soil for the growth of the tuber; it maintained humidity longer, and thus the crops were not overly affected by seasonal variations in rainfall. The mature tuber could be stored in the ground for longer periods of time, and the mound's structure prevented soil erosion and improved drainage (ibid.). According to William Keegan, "the *Taino* name *conuco* refers to the fields in which their cultigens were planted". Keegan adds that "not all *conucos* had mounds; some had terraces, others were irrigated, and the majority had no significant modifications to the landscape" (personal communication, 2003).

Gonzalo Fernández de Oviedo in *The Natural History of the West Indies* infers that both techniques were used by the Taínos in specific circumstances, such as the cultivation of cassava:

> To propagate this plant, the Indians break a branch of it into pieces about 2 spans long. Some men make small hills of the earth at regular intervals. . . . In each hill they place 5 or 6 or more of the cuttings of the plant. Other Indians do not go to the trouble to make hills but simply level the soil and insert these cuttings at regular intervals in the earth. Before planting the yuca, the natives grub or cut over land and burn the brush just as they do in preparing the land for planting corn. . . . After a few days the cutting buds for then it takes root. (Fernández de Oviedo 1959, 16)

According to Rouse, the density of Jamaica's population suggests that its inhabitants practised the same advanced form of agriculture (*conuco*) as the Classic Taínos (1992, 18).

Introduction of Flora

Indigenous species are plants and animals that occur naturally in a particular country but may also be found elsewhere in the world. An endemic species is any plant or animal that is found only in a particular area (usually a country). For a small island, Jamaica has a high level of plant endemism; it been rated fifth among the world's islands in terms of plant endemism (NRCA/NEPA/MLE 2001, 9).

Veloz Maggiolo refers to the Taínos' use of the slash-and-burn technique. Since their ancestors brought their agricultural practices with them to the Caribbean, it is not far-fetched to assume that they, and the subsequent cultures, introduced domesticated flora into the islands. It is generally assumed that several species of plants which were of importance to the Taínos' ancestors were carried to the islands.

According to Rashford, the flora that the Taínos introduced into Jamaica was generally domesticated plants. This new flora was introduced by the Taínos to maintain their traditional lifestyles. The Taínos' ancestors are said to have originated in the Amazon basin of South America (Keegan 1992), where many species, such as the cassava or manioc (*Manihot esculenta*), were domesticated. South America was the probable centre of origin for the following cultivated plants: amaranth (*Amaranthus* spp.), peanut (*Arachis hypogaea*), common bean (*Phaseolus* spp.), manioc (*Manihot esculenta*), potato (*Ipomoea batatas*), cotton (*Gossypium* spp.), squash (*Cucurbita maxima*), bottle gourd (*Lagenaria siceraria*) and tobacco (*Nicotiana tabacum*) (Scarre 1999, 78).

The following is a list of flora introduced to Jamaica – these plants were neither endemic nor indigenous plants. Rashford states that these crops represent herbaceous plants, which require systematic cultivation (1991, 18).

1. Cassava (*Manihot esculenta*)
2. Sweet potato (*Ipomoea batatas*)
3. Yampi (*Colocasia* spp.)
4. Arrowroot (*Maranta arundinacea*)
5. Coco/Indian kale (*Xanthosoma sagittifolium*)
6. Maize (*Zea mays*)
7. Pineapple (*Ananas comosus*)
8. Peanuts (*Arachis hypogaea*)

9. Squashes (*Cucurbita maxima*)
10. Beans (*Phaseolus* spp.)
11. Tobacco (*Nicotiana rustica*)

According to ethnographic sources, the Taínos cultivated cassava, sweet potato, yampi, arrowroot, coco, maize, pineapple, peanuts, squash, beans and tobacco in their *conucos* or gardens. Fernández de Oviedo describes their cultivation of maize:

> In Hispaniola both the Indians and Spaniards have two kinds of bread, for the Christians eat the same bread as the Indians. One sort is made of *maiz* (maize), which is a grain, and the other is cassava, which is a root of the manioc. Corn is planted and harvested in the following manner.... The Indians first cut down the cane and trees where they wish to plant it. After the trees have been felled and the field grubbed, the land is burned and the ashes left as a dressing for the soil. An Indian takes in his hand a stick (*coa*) as tall as he is, and plunges the point into the earth, then he pulls it out, and in the hole he has made places with his other hand about seven or eight grains of corn. Then he takes another step forward and repeats the process. (1959, 13–14)

Fernández de Oviedo also states that when the Indians and Christians planted pineapples, they put them in regular rows like vine stalks in a vineyard (1959, 99). Cultivation of domesticated crops was clearly important to Taíno subsistence.

Evidence of Cultivation: The Cassava

Alexander (1969), in an article discussing evidence of plant domestication, states that the evidence can be divided into cultural and non-cultural. Direct cultural evidence includes precise literary references, drawings, paintings and carvings, specialized tools and cultivation systems. Indirect cultural evidence includes the actual remains of plant cultigens preserved by carbonization, matrix impressions, silica skeletons, and the bones, teeth, horns or antlers of animals (ibid.).

In determining evidence of the domestication and cultivation of species, Alexander suggests that the crop be assessed in terms of the following factors: clearing of the land; preparation of the land; planting or sowing; harvesting; processing and storing; and cooking and preparations for eating.

The Taínos' prized crop was *yuca*, the cassava or manioc (henceforth referred to as cassava). Cassava was not indigenous to Jamaica. Angulo Váldes states that roots and tubers dominated rainforest farming on the mainland, where the main staple was cassava, which began to be used for bread around 2000 BC (Veloz Maggiolo 1997). There are two species of cassava – sweet and bitter. The latter is poisonous and, according to Fernández de Oviedo (1959, 17), grows abundantly on the islands of San Juan (Puerto Rico), Cuba, Jamaica and Hispaniola.

The Taínos are believed to have used stone tools to fell trees for the clearing of land (Lovén 1935; Veloz Maggiolo 1997). The stone tool most commonly recovered in Jamaica is the celt (stone axe blade). Many of the celt specimens found are petal-shaped, hence the term *petaloid* celts (Porter 1990, 54). The celts were hafted into wooden handles. Most of the celts are almost symmetrical and highly polished (ibid.). Celts have been recovered from sites across the island including Norbrook, St Andrew; Rozelle, St Thomas; Liberty Hill, St Ann; California, St James; Salt River, Clarendon; and Port Henderson, St Catherine.

Celts served as knife, hammer and axe. As a general rule, the older, almost worn-out ones are triangular in shape, while others are double-ended, one end being a sharp cutting edge and the other a pointed butt. They can measure up to 25 cm in length (ibid.). The abundance of these celts and other stone implements suggests that they were used to clear land, carve canoes and possibly to cut manioc (Veloz Maggiolo 1997). Celts were used, along with fire, to fell selected trees and hack out the interior. This technique was used in the construction of dugout canoes, which, according to Ferdinand, were "hollowed like a tray" (Walker 1992, 58). Despite their distribution across the island, celts do not necessarily indicate agricultural activities, as they also served other functions; some highly polished ones were used in religious ceremonies.

Admittedly, it is difficult to prove archaeologically the details of cultivation, forcing reliance on ethnographic sources. A wooden *zemí* of Baibrama was found in Jamaica in 1757. Baibrama is said to have helped cassava to grow (Rouse 1992, 117); thus the presence of the *zemí* suggests the cultivation of cassava. Baibrama is generally depicted in a standing or squatting position with an erect penis, as if urinating to increase the growth of cassava. Baibrama is said to be one of the many alternative names for the Taíno supreme deity, Yocahu Bagua Maorocoti – the giver of the cassava and master of the sea. Yucahu is said to be the spirit of the cassava, who helped in the growing of cassava and cured people who were poisoned by the juice of the cassava. Three-pointed *zemís*, which represent Yocahu, are said to have mimicked the triad shape of the cassava tuber.

Cassava was essential to the Taínos, not just as a food staple but also in religious terms. According to Sven Lovén (1935, 563):

> Yocahu is identifiable as a Yuca god, "who gave and increased the natural food plants of the Antilleans". Fewkes agrees with this theory. It is probable that the compound part *yoca* is the same as *yuca*. Possibly the Taíno originally received yuca from *Yocahu*. But after they had received it, it grows through *zemí* co-operation.

After the cassava was harvested, it was processed and prepared for consumption. It is from this phase that additional evidence exists of the presence of the cassava. After the roots were grated, the poisonous juices were extracted by way of *cibucanes*, large woven baskets with a fastening on top and a ring at the bottom through which a stick would be inserted and turned to twist the basket, thus squeezing and straining the grated cassava inside (Veloz Maggiolo 1997, 39).

The resulting cassava flour was baked on a *burén*, a circular clay griddle, to make *casabe* – cassava bread. According to Fernández de Oviedo, this bread could be kept for a year or more (1959, 17). The poisonous juice was boiled to make *cassareep*, a preservative used in stews. Taíno *buréns* have been found island-wide, from Tower Hill, St Andrew, at Bengal, St Ann, Great Pedro Bay, St Elizabeth and Taylor's Hut Cave #2, Clarendon. The *burén* is believed to have been used solely for cooking cassava bread or cakes. According to James W. Lee:

> Jamaican Arawak *burén*s were essentially flat, more or less circular platters made of baked clay and were propped on stones above wood fires to cook cassava bread. The most typical style has a raised rim, bevelled outer edge, is more often than not poorly fired and has no decoration. The average thickness at the rim is 2.6 cm (about one inch), in the interior about 2.0 cm (0.78 inch) and in an annular zone a few centimetres from the rim 1.8 cm (0.71 inch); based on measurements of some 200 specimens of rim sherds in the author's collection. (Lee 1980a, 1–2)

No village site in Jamaica that has been carefully examined is without *burén* sherds, a fact that attests to the universal use of cassava as a dietary staple (ibid.).

In the text *Jamaica under the Spaniards* (1919), Frank Cundall and Joseph Pietersz refer to Jamaica as a food-producing country and offer evidence of the presence and production of cassava bread on the island:

> As early as that year (1512) it became evident that Jamaica, though possessing no gold of importance, would prove of value as a food producing country, and arrangements were made to send foodstuffs to the mainland. Two years later, Velasquez, the Governor of Cuba, sent a caravel to Jamaica for cassava bread as, owing to drought the natives in Trinidad (in Cuba) were suffering from famine. (Cundall and Pietersz 1919, 2)

In contemporary Jamaica, farmers use a mound-farming technique similar to the Taínan *conuco*. So-called cassava hills, generally 1 m wide and 50 cm high, are placed at regular intervals (Selvenious Walters, personal communication, 2002). Modern Jamaicans produce a cassava bread called bammy, which is also derived from the Taíno tradition.

Incidental Dispersal

The plant component of the Taíno diet included wild fruits and vegetables, such as sweetsop (*Annona muricata*), macca fat (*Acrocomia spinosa*) and papaya (*Carica papaya*). So far we have focused on deliberate means of transforming the natural vegetation; however, in some cases the Taínos accidentally encouraged the growth of flora not common to the specific terrain. Wild plants are incidentally dispersed in the settlement environment by humans and other animals and by wind, water and abiotic means. Human incidental dispersal results from three basic processes: harvesting, adhesion, and mediation (Rashford 1991, 18).

There are four ways in which incidental dispersal by harvesting can occur: rejection, loss, discard and defecation (ibid., 18–19). *Rejection* refers to the spreading of seeds as a result of humans spitting them out. The sweetsop (*Annona squamosa*) and soursop (*Annona sapota*) could have been spread this way. Incidental dispersal by *loss* occurs when collected fruits are dropped while being taken from one place to another. *Discard* is the intentional throwing away of seeds. Rashford suggests that the papaya and mammee (*Mammea americana*) were spread via discarded seeds. In the fourth method of incidental dispersal, the seeds are ingested with the rest of the fruit and later dispersed through *defecation*. Guava (*Psidium guajava*) may have been dispersed this way.

Rashford (ibid.) points out the complexity of incidental dispersal, as there are some plants – for instance, guava – which could have been spread by any or all of the methods. In any case, we know that incidental dispersal did take place: for example, in Jamaica there exists an endemic mountain guava (*Psidium montanum*) which is generally found in the Lower Montane Mist Forest between 375 m and 1,200 m above sea level (Adams 1972). The location of mountain guava at Taíno sites at lower elevations suggests human incidental dispersal.

The other methods of incidental dispersal are adhesion and mediation. *Adhesion* occurs when plants or seeds become attached to people, their equipment or their animals and are thus spread in the human environment. *Mediation* occurs as a result of human settlement, when a built environment, together with the activities associated with it, affects animals and other natural agents that in turn have an impact on plant dispersal (Rashford 1991, 19).

Generally, it is difficult to prove human incidental dispersal on an archaeological site. Knowledge of the processes of incidental dispersal, however, can provide clues to recognizing a Taíno site. For instance, at the Meillacan site at Paradise Park, Westmoreland, there is a very large silk cotton tree (*Ceiba pentandra*), 26 m tall. In Jamaica, the silk cotton tree is naturally found at elevations above 300 m (Adams 1972); yet the Paradise Park site was a coastal settlement.

The majority of known Taíno sites are located in the interior valleys and coastal plains (Atkinson 2002), which were the first places for human settlement. Many former Taíno sites were settled upon by the Spanish and subsequently by the British, and are now in built-up areas, as illustrated by Seville, St Ann, and Spanish Town, St Catherine. It is only in remote areas away from human disturbance that one could begin to search for evidence of incidental dispersal.

Conclusion

Traditionally, faunal analysis has predominated in archaeological investigation, and floral analysis has been sidelined. However, the development of the discipline of palaeoethnobotany is bringing about a change in attitude towards the importance of floral evidence. In Jamaica, a great deal of useful information can be obtained through the analysis of macro- and microbotanical remains. It has become obvious that we have barely scratched the surface of the evidence regarding the importance of flora to the Taíno, as plants had medicinal, subsistence and religious roles as well as food value. There is also the issue of the Taínos' impact on the natural environment, which was briefly discussed in this chapter. The Taínos' role in the introduction of new flora has been considered minimal in comparison with that of the Europeans; however, it is now recognized that the presence of cassava, maize and other non-indigenous plants indicate that they did contribute, directly or indirectly, to the present vegetation of Jamaica.

Figure 7.7 Members of the Paradise Park 2001 excavations measuring the *Ceiba* tree at the Meillacan site. From left: Bill Rogers, Dan Keegan, Bill Keegan, Ralph Pax, Mary Lou Pax, Bob Gezon, Nadia Manning and Lesley-Gail Atkinson. (Courtesy of William F. Keegan.)

8  Early Arawak Subsistence Strategies: The Rodney's House Site of Jamaica

Sylvia Scudder

ONE OF THE clearest links to past environments is the faunal material excavated from archaeological sites. Identification and analysis of vertebrate and invertebrate species sought as food by aboriginal peoples shed light on animal community structure, population dynamics, zoogeography, habitat use, food procurement techniques and food preferences. A careful scrutiny of faunal and botanical materials, taking into account losses due to taphonomy and other factors of deposition, sampling error and the bias of human choice, can eliminate subjective interpretations and provide a more complete picture of past settlement subsistence activity.

The Rodney's House site is designated S-5 and is located in the parish of St Catherine, Jamaica, in the limestone hills behind Port Henderson, at an elevation of 133 m above sea level. Four 1.5-m² units were excavated during two field seasons; the fauna material from those squares was analysed at the Environmental Archaeology Laboratory, Florida Museum of Natural History (FMNH). This report presents the results of that analysis, and then compares the Rodney's House fauna with analyses of faunal remains recovered at the sites Bellevue, St Andrew, and White Marl, St Catherine, also on Jamaica's south coast.

The Site and Its Environment

St Catherine is situated on the southeast coast of Jamaica at 17° 56' N latitude and 76° 53' W longitude. The southeastern portion of the parish, including

---

Originally published in *Archaeology Jamaica*, new ser., 6 (1992): 28–43.

the Hellshire Hills and Great Salt Pond area southwest of Kingston, is dry thorn scrub, receiving the least amount of rainfall of any area in Jamaica, approximately 508 mm per year (Collins and Longman 1978). Soils in the immediate vicinity of S-5 are predominantly shallow, somewhat excessively drained loams and clays formed on limestone, with numerous limestone outcroppings (Ministry of Agriculture 1987). South, towards Great Salt Pond, as the hill slope flattens to less than 1 per cent, the soils become very poorly drained, mottled, with weakly defined horizonation and high salt content. Within a few kilometres to the west a large area of deep alluvial soils is found. Within approximately 5 km of S-5 and encompassing the entire broad south coast of St Catherine parish, including the Hellshire Hills, is another area of shallow cambisols similar to those at the site (ibid.). Vegetation supported by these cambisols takes the form of dry limestone scrub forest (thorn woodland, according to the Holdridge system) and includes cactus, trees such as *Bursera*, *Acacia*, *Haematoxylon* and *Leucanea*, and a number of xerophytic climbing plants and epiphytes (Asprey and Robbins 1953). The coastal fringe of this dry forest is dominated by sclerophyllous dry limestone shrubs, cacti, halophytes and salt-tolerant trees such as *Chrysobalanus* and *Hippomane*. Sheltered bays may support a mangrove community. Seifriz (1943) aptly described this region: "The heat is intensive, the light blinding, every plant armed, no water, no shade, and no trail leading anywhere, as awe-inspiring, as fearful, as superb a picture of the eternal persistence of life under the most adverse conditions that nature can produce."

The site itself occupies about one-half a hectare of gently sloping land on the limestone hill behind Port Henderson. It is within 1 km of the coast at Green Bay and within 1.5 km of the mangrove swamps of Dawkins Pond and Great Salt Pond (Medhurst 1980). Six middens were identified, along with a flat area of cultivable land to the west. There is at present no permanent source of fresh water on the site. Medhurst and Clarke (1976a), in their report on the Bellevue site in the Manning Hills area of St Andrew Parish (approximately 18 km from S-5), mentions the presence of a recently dried-up pond and several springs within a 2-km radius of the site. He speculates that a possible cause of abandonment of S-5, with its ready access to food sources, may be that its water source dried up.

Excavation

Between February and July 1978, J.C. Wilman, in association with Colin Medhurst, excavated two 1.5-m² units (J1 and K2) in the centre of an apparent midden (Midden 2). Seven 20 cm levels were removed, the last reaching bedrock at 1.4 m. All material was screened (screen size was not indicated) and bagged by level. In April of 1979, Wilman and Medhurst excavated an additional unit of the same size at Midden 2 (K3), and another unit at Midden 3 (S17) using the same 20 cm vertical levels. Six levels resulted at unit K3 and two at S17 before sterile sand was reached. Mollusc remains were not saved from K3, but a sample from S17 was retained.

Methods

Faunal remains were analysed using standard zooarchaeological technique: identifications were made to the lowest possible taxon by comparison with known specimens in zooarchaeology collections, FMNH. Minimum numbers of individuals (MNI) were calculated by matching paired elements, taking size into consideration (Wing and Brown 1979, 123–26). Total number of fragments identified per taxon and weight of fragments per taxon were also determined. Reference was made to molluscs identified and presented in a previous report on Rodney's House by John Wilman (1978). Material from units J1 and K2 was combined for the analysis since each collection included complete samples of vertebrate, crab and molluscan material. Square K3, without molluscs, was treated separately, as was square S17 (representative mollusc sample taken but not defined). Of the three categories of data produced (fragment count, MNI and fragment weight) only fragment count was applied to the molluscan sample from J1 and K2 combined material. This is because, although the bivalves were counted as two valves per individual, it was not stated whether the valves were paired (left to right), so an accurate assessment of MNI could not be made. Also, no weights were taken on the molluscs. Molluscs from unit S17 were not included in the analysis since the manner in which they were sampled was not outlined. MNI of vertebrates and crabs were determined by level, in keeping with the method used for tabulation of numbers of molluscs. Regarding quantification of all molluscan material, both the sample taken in the field and incidentals found with the vertebrate material were retained in the raw data for each square but not included in the comparative analyses.

The faunal assemblage will be presented in two ways:

1. Vertebrate and crab material only, with all squares combined to give a picture of the site through time, and
2. Squares J1 and K2 combined, relating vertebrate, crab and mollusc components.

Results

Vertebrate and Crab Remains: All Units Combined

A total of 6,728 bone and crab fragments were identified to at least a family level, resulting in an MNI of 747. Mammal taxa were of five families, including five genera and four species. Birds were represented by four families, three genera and two species. Reptiles (no amphibians were found) yielded three families, three genera and three species; *Chondrichthyes* (sharks and rays) two families, two genera and two species; *Osteichthyes*, twenty-three families, twenty-five genera and sixteen species; and crabs and lobsters six families, seven genera, and one species. Table 8.1 summarizes the most abundant vertebrate and crab taxa in the assemblage (complete data and details of analysis can be obtained from the author). Table 8.3 (see appendix) presents a complete listing of all vertebrate and invertebrate taxa.

Mammals comprised 13.7 per cent of the total sample (considering MNI) and were dominated by *Geocapromys brownii*, the Jamaican *hutia* or coney, which constituted 87.2 per cent of mammalian species and 12.0 per cent of the total vertebrate/crab assemblage (see Table 8.1). One other rodent was found: *Oryzomys antillarum*, the Jamaican rice rat (7.4 per cent of the mammals and 1.0 per cent of the total).

Cyclura collei, the land iguana, was the most abundant reptile in the sample, with eleven individuals. The green sea turtle, *Chelonia mydas* and the sea turtle family Cheloniidae combined to yield four individuals. *Crocodylus acutus*, the saltwater crocodile, was represented by one individual.

Bony fish (with a few Chondrichthyes represented) constitute 53.4 per cent of the total sample (MNI = 365). The most abundant taxa are representatives of families that utilize both reef and open-bottom areas in shallow nearshore environments. The family Gerreidae, mojarras, and in particular the genus *Diapterus*, contributed 69 MNI of the fish sample and 10.1 per cent of the total. Lutjanidae, snappers, totalled 38 MNI. In decreasing order of abundance, other important taxa of fish included Sparidae, porgies, MNI 30; Haemulidae, grunts, MNI 29; Serranidae, groupers, MNI 27; Centropomidae, snook, MNI 25; Balistidae, triggerfish, MNI 21; and Carangidae, jacks, MNI 19. Carcharhinid sharks, requiem sharks, yielded eight individuals.

The contribution of crabs to the diet was second only to fish. The 172 individuals recorded constituted 25.1 per cent of the total sample. The large land crab, Cardisoma, was the most abundant genus recovered, yielding 98 individuals. The aquatic blue crab *Callinectes* was second in abundance (40 MNI). *Gecarcinus*, another large terrestrial crab, was represented by 17 individuals, and an unidentified member of the family Diogenidae the hermit crabs, con-

Table 8.1 Significant Vertebrate and Crab Remains from the Rodney's House Site

Taxon	Common Name	MNI	Per cent of Class	Per cent of Total
Mammals				13.7
Geocapromys brownii	*Hutia* or coney	28	87.2	12.0
Oryzomys antillarum	Jamaican rice rat	1	7.4	1.0
Reptiles				6.6
Cyclura collei	Land iguana	11	68.8	3.7
Chelonia mydas	Green sea turtle	4	25.0	1.6
Crocodylus acutus	Saltwater crocodile	1	6.2	0.8
Osteichthyes				53.4
Gerreidae	Mojarras	69	18.9	10.1
Lutjanidae	Snappers	38	10.4	5.6
Sparidae	Porgies	30	8.0	4.4
Haemulidae	Grunts	29	7.9	4.2
Serranidae	Groupers	27	7.4	3.9
Centropomidae	Snooks	25	6.8	3.7
Balistidae	Triggerfish	21	5.8	3.2
Carangidae	Jacks	19	5.2	2.8
Chondrichthyes				
Carcharchinidae	Requiem sharks	8	2.2	1.2
Crabs				25.1
Cardisoma	Land crabs	98	57.0	14.3
Diogenidae	Hermit crabs	18	7.6	1.9

tributed 18 individuals. Due to a lack of comparative crab material in the museum collections, the identification of the hermit crab remains incomplete. A large member of the family Diogenidae is the best possibility, the largest species, *Petrochirus diogenes*, being a denizen of mud- or sand-bottomed areas (Williams 1984). *Coenobita clypeatus*, in the family Coenobitidae, is another possibility. It is the largest terrestrial hermit crab in the area.

When presentation of MNI as total site percentage is broken down level by level, some interesting shifts in faunal exploitation emerge. Reptiles maintain a low and fairly stable percentage through time, from a high of 5.9 per cent in level 4 to a low of 2.7 per cent in level 3. Mammals start at 9.5 per cent in level 7, peak at 20.6 per cent in level 4, return to a low of 8.1 per cent in level 3, then increase slowly towards the surface levels. Of much greater interest is the interplay between fish and crabs. Both represent approximately 36 per cent of the level 7 sample. From this point they diverge dramatically, fish increasing to a maximum of 64.9 per cent in level 2 and crabs decreasing to a low of 10.4 per cent, also in level 2. There is a reversal and then recovery of both of these trends, between levels 4 and 5 for fish and between levels 3 and 4 for crabs. When mollusc fragment count is superimposed on the vertebrate MNI figures, it closely tracks the fish values, complete with reversal and recovery in levels 4 and 5.

Vertebrate and Complete Invertebrate Sample: Units J1 and K2

In the 1976 report on the Bellevue site, Medhurst and Clarke state: "In common with all Jamaican Arawak sites, vast quantities of molluscs were in the midden material" (1976a, 4). The mollusc sample taken from S-5 during the first field season represented an average of 43.6 per cent of the total fragment count in each level of squares J1 and K2 combined. As stated in the introduction, count was used instead of MNI in this comparison due to the question of valve pairing (or not) of molluscs in the original quantifications. Count and MNI will, of course be identical in the case of whole gastropods; the problem arises with the possibility of under-representation of bivalves.

Of a total of 9,418 identified vertebrate and invertebrate fragments, vertebrates contributed 4,063, crabs 1,245, and molluscs 4,110 fragments, or 43.6 per cent. Of these molluscs, 92 per cent were marine taxa and 8.4 per cent were terrestrial. The molluscan sample was dominated by two shallow-water bivalves: *Arca* spp., and *Donax denticulata*. *Arca* contributed 1,420 fragments and *Donax* totalled 1,149. One other nearshore bivalve contributed significantly: *Ostrea frons*, the leaf or coon oyster.

Minor contributors to the molluscan sample were *Chama* spp., the jewelbox shell, the family Neritidae, *Melongena* spp., the crown conchs, and *Cittarium pica*, the West Indian top shell. The only terrestrial molluscs occurring in abundance were *Pleurodonte* spp., and *Dentellaria peracutissima*. Both of these genera are found in leaf litter on the forest floor.

Discussion

Animal Habits and Habitats

In order to gain an understanding of the strategies and technologies needed to procure animals for food, one must have knowledge of their natural history and habitat preferences. Following are summaries of such information pertinent to the most significant species identified in the Rodney's House faunal material.

Geocapromys is a large (up to 2 kg) herbivorous rodent, once abundant in Jamaica and now nearly extinct. It is nocturnal and social, preferring areas that include exposed limestone outcrops, the crevices of which are used as refuges. Conies may breed throughout the year, usually producing one young per litter. They feed on leaves, bark and twigs of small shrubs, sometimes climbing up into the plants to reach forage (Walker 1975). *Oryzomys antillarum*, the Jamaican rice rat, was a small diurnal seedeater, also eating grass, fruit and invertebrates. It has not been seen in Jamaica since 1877, just five years after the mongoose was introduced to the island to help control the rat population in sugar-cane fields (Hall 1981).

The land iguana, or guana, is a large (approximately 4 to 5 kg) herbivorous lizard. It is diurnal, like the coney preferring limestone karst areas for protection among the natural crevices and tree roots. One clutch of eggs is laid per year, and data on the Turks and Caicos iguana (data not available on the Jamaican species) suggest that they are very long-lived, not reaching sexual maturity until the seventh year (Iverson 1979). The Jamaican iguana has been considered extinct on the island since the early 1940s, although a small population has maintained itself in the Hellshire Hills on the south coast (Carey 1975).

The green sea turtle, *Chelonia mydas*, is most easily caught as the females lay eggs on sandy beaches. Once nest digging commences, the females are completely vulnerable, being single-mindedly focused on the task at hand. Nest excavation and egg laying may take most of the night, providing ample opportunity for predation by hunters. The nesting season for the West Indies, according to Carr (1952), is May through October. *Crocodylus acutus*, the saltwater crocodile, occurs in mangrove swamps and marshes. It has been documented in archaeological sites on the south coast only (Wing 1972) and may never have occurred on the north coast.

Two of the most common families of bony fish, Sparidae and Gerreidae, are bottom-dwelling invertebrate feeders, preferring shallow, quiet waters with or without reefs. *Diapterus* may be found over muddy bottoms in brackish-water areas (Randall 1968). Haemulidae, the grunt family, forms dense aggregations on small patch reefs during the day, whereas at night individuals disperse to feed over sand and grass flats (Randall 1968). Some species of *Haemulon* exploit mud bottoms in brackish areas.

The fish genus most closely tied to the reef environment is *Balistes*, the triggerfish. The arrangement of interlocking dorsal spines on this fish is specifically adapted to offer protection from predators: when threatened, the fish swims into reef crevices, and its spines enable it to wedge itself in. Triggerfish occasionally venture out into clear sand areas. *Centropomus*, the snook, is most often encountered in freshwater or brackish areas of river mouths, or in mangrove swamps or salt marshes (Hoese and Moore 1977). They are occasionally found on inshore reefs near mangrove areas.

Lutjanidae (snappers) and Carangidae (jacks) are carnivorous predators. Snappers are usually nocturnal, feeding primarily over offshore reefs and banks (Randall 1968). The genus *Lutjanus* prefers the shallowest water of the group, and *L. griseus* actually spends most of its time inshore. Unfortunately, the faunal material was not well enough preserved to allow identification to the species level, so this zoogeographic information could not be accessed. Carangids are schooling predators that may use the reef as a foraging area but do not reside there. *Caranx hippos* are sometimes scavengers in areas of human use (Hoese and Moore 1977).

Cardisoma and *Gecarcinus* of the family Gecarcinidae are large terrestrial scavengers sometimes called soldier crabs. *Cardisoma* may reach maximum carapace length (posterior to anterior margins, at midline) of 90 mm, and *Gecarcinus* attains a maximum of 70 mm. *Cardisoma* inhabits the lower floodplains of rivers and other low-lying areas. Individuals construct burrows that penetrate the water table, and under threat, will plunge beneath the water to avoid danger. During daylight hours they rarely wander more than a metre from their burrows, though at night they roam considerable distances (Chace and Hobbs 1969). *Gecarcinus* occurs at higher elevations than *Cardisoma*, though the young of both species sympatrically inhabit the talus slopes at the bases of cliffs. Adults prefer cliffs and hills inland from the coastal lowlands. They emerge from their shallow burrows at night, especially after rain. *Callinectes*, the blue crab, is found in freshwater stream mouths, estuaries and shallow ocean settings. It is a diurnal scavenger that tolerates great extremes of salinity (ibid.). Some species are more tolerant than others of muddy or polluted conditions.

Both *Arca* and *Ostrea* can be found attached to hard substrates or mangrove roots in quiet-water areas (Emerson and Jacobson 1976). *Donax*, the coquina clam, inhabits wave-wash areas of sandy beaches, actively burrowing and being carried about the midtide line by wave action. They can be easily gathered in great quantities at certain localities. *Chama* may be found attached by the left valve to hard substrates below the tideline in warm, shallow waters. The right valve is often thrown onto shore during storm tides (Emerson and Jacobson 1976). *Cittarium* and the nerites cling to wave-washed rocks and may be found in dense groups. *Melongena* is an active predator and scavenger, usually frequenting sandy, shallow areas.

Changing Subsistence Strategies

The overall faunal assemblage depicts a localized exploitation of typical West Indian dry-coastal and shallow-water animal communities. S-5 is within a short distance of areas inhabited by the primary terrestrial and aquatic target species identified in the analysis. Limestone karst areas favoured by *Geocapromys* and *Cyclura* dominate the south-coast landscape. Marine edge, shallow bay and brackish water areas, inshore reefs and sand-bottomed shallow seas are all easily available and heavily exploited. The absence of the distant montane and pelagic species indicates a restricted catchment area, suggesting a highly supportive local environment and relative self-sufficiency.

The shift toward greater use of fish and marine molluscs and the concomitant decrease in abundance of crabs in later levels reveal an increased reliance on marine organisms over terrestrial ones. An interesting exception is *Callinectes*, the blue crab, whose representation in the sample decreases in concert with the terrestrial *Cardisoma* and *Gecarcinus*. Since these crabs are ubiquitous in stream mouths, estuaries and shallow embayments, their capture may be viewed as a simple extension of terrestrial gathering, explaining their disappearance along with that of the soldier crabs.

The dramatic shift in emphasis at Rodney's House from land to marine food species may indicate an over-exploitation of terrestrial habitats of low intrinsic productivity. Modern crab populations can be easily over-harvested and are jealously guarded in the Cayman Islands (R. Franz, Florida Museum of Natural History, personal communication). However, a brief examination of the occurrence of unfused long-bone epiphyses in the *Geocapromys* sample did not indicate a shift in age classes captured. In support of this, the fish vertebrate did not show a decrease in size through time, which would have suggested over-harvesting of the resource base.

Another explanation of the faunal shift may be cultural. A review of the ceramic chronology outlined by Wilman (1978) reveals that filleted rims on clay vessels begin appearing at the site in level 3, indicating a change in complexion of the human population and suggesting the possibility of disruption or alteration of subsistence activity. The seeming return to an earlier (or more terrestrial) pattern of faunal use may point to an influx of people unfamiliar with the local marine resources, or to a more general use of all habitats as a result of increased human population pressure. A third explanation may be that terrestrial animal population levels recovered in response to decreased hunting pressure as marine environments were increasingly utilized, and subsequently were re-exploited.

Effects of Geography and Location: A Comparison of Sites

Three important south-coast Jamaican sites – Rodney's House, White Marl and Bellevue – are located within an approximate 15-km radius of modern-day Kingston. Their positions along a continuum from coastal (Rodney's House) to inland (Bellevue) localities allow an interesting comparison of subsistence strategies and habitat exploitation within similar life zones.

The Bellevue site (K-13) in St Andrew, situated at an elevation of 412 m, lies approximately 10 km north of the coast at Kingston Harbour and 15 km north of Rodney's House. White Marl, in St Catherine, is approximately 5.5 km inland from Kingston Harbour to the west. Although the maximum elevation of White Marl is approximately 150 m, the greatest concentration of midden material is at 60 to 90 m. The Rio Cobre flows near the base of the hill, although its course was shifted to the west by the storm of 1722 (Silverberg, Vanderwal and Wing 1972). Extensive areas of fertile soil are found within the immediate vicinity of the site and suggest an excellent area for cassava production and other forms of gardening.

All three sites yielded griddle fragments and large numbers of staghorn coral *(Acropora prolifera)* fragments, indicating cassava utilization. According to Wilman (1978), the coral fragments were probably fitted into wooden frames that were used as scrapers to prepare the cassava. The proximity to all three sites of level, arable land suggests the importance of horticulture to these prehistoric people, but the absence of plant material in the recovered biological samples makes its contribution an unknown quantity as yet.

Silverberg et al. state in their 1972 report on the White Marl site that the most reliable ceramic chronological indicator in the Jamaican Meillacan Ostionoid subseries (Rouse 1986) is the replacement of plain rims by filleted rims. In that case, Rodney's House seems to pre-date both White Marl and Bellevue. Both Vanderwal at White Marl and Medhurst at Bellevue found filleted rims in even the earliest levels of those sites, whereas Rodney's House began yielding filleted rims only in level 3. Occupation of White Marl and Bellevue has been indicated by carbon dating to span a period from AD 900 to the beginning of the historical period or just before.

Fauna from the Bellevue site reflects a heavy dependence (89 per cent) on land species (Table 8.2). *Geocapromys, Oryzomys, Cyclura* and *Canis familiaris* (the domestic dog), are the most abundant taxa in the faunal assemblage. A preponderance of the remaining species are inshore mammals (*Trichechus manatus*, manatee), *Crocodylus* and fishes such as *Centropomus* (snook), Carangidae (jack), Sparidae (porgy) and *Aetobatis narinari*, spotted eagle ray. In addition, members of the families Serranidae (grouper), Lutjanidae (snap-

Table 8.2 Faunal Comparisons: Per cent of Site Total MNI

	Rodney's House	White Marl	Bellevue
Terrestrial	35	62	89
Inshore	26	25	8
Banks and reefs	26	10	2
Other: pelagic, beach	13	3	1

per) and Scombridae (tuna) – all active predators – are present in small numbers. The composition of this assemblage indicates a highly localized, mainly terrestrial subsistence strategy. Further, the virtually identical percentages of terrestrial species in both levels 3 and 2 (88 and 89 per cent, respectively) indicate a stable environment with no overt signs of over-exploitation or shift in faunal preference.

Wing's 1972 report on the White Marl site indicates that a total of 62 per cent of the MNI in the faunal sample analysed is composed of terrestrial species, with *Geocapromys* again dominating the sample. *Cyclura*, *Oryzomys* and a small number of *Canis familiaris* round out the land animals. Marine species make up the remaining 38 per cent of the MNI at White Marl. Twenty-two per cent of these species are inshore, estuarine taxa, 11 per cent are from banks and reefs and 3 per cent are from beach areas. The proportionate representation of these species accurately reflects the fact that the nearest water to White Marl is the large, shallow estuary of Kingston Harbour. The stability of the percentages through the levels of the site again indicates exploitation at or below carrying capacity of the environment. The inland location of the White Marl site explains the greater reliance of its inhabitants on terrestrial species than those at Rodney's House.

Summary and Conclusions

Analysis of the faunal material from the Rodney's House site, S-5, on the south coast of St Catherine, Jamaica, revealed subsistence strategies adapted to local conditions of dry thorn woodland and tropical marine edge environments. The communities of animals exploited derived exclusively from these areas; no montane or pelagic species appeared in the sample. A shift in proportional representation of two classes of animals, bony fish and crabs, indicates a disruption of, or voluntary change in, procurement patterns. Increasing use of fish through time, with a concomitant decrease in (mainly) terrestrial crabs, shows a growing reliance on marine resources.

A comparison of Rodney's House with the White Marl and Bellevue sites shows a clear continuum of coastal to inland localized adaptation, with Rodney's House (marine edge) yielding the highest proportion of marine fish, and Bellevue (inland hills) contrasting with a greater reliance on terrestrial species. White Marl, at a lower elevation than Bellevue and farther from the coast than Rodney's House, is intermediate in its ratio of terrestrial/marine taxa.

Future work on these sites – if it is possible, with urbanization taking place so rapidly in Jamaica, even on the south coast – should address the questions of plant remains and comparability of molluscan samples from within and among the sites. A refinement of crab identifications, as mentioned above, may reveal some choices in microhabitat exploitation that are elusive at this point.

Appendix

Table 8.3 Rodney's House Faunal List

Scientific Name	Common Name
Geocapromys brownii	Jamaican *hutia*
Oryzomys antillarum	Jamaican rice rat
Erophylla sezekorni	Buffy flower bat
cf. *Trichechus manatus*	West Indian manatee
Homo sapiens	Human
Unidentified mammal	
Egretta alba	Great egret
Ardeidie	Herons and egrets
Columba spp.	Doves
Columbidae	Doves and pigeons
Rallus longirostris	Clapper rail
Laridae	Seagulls
Unidentified bird	
Cyclura collei	Land iguana
Crocodylus acutus	Saltwater crocodile
Chelonia mydas	Green sea turtle
Cheloniidae	Sea turtles
Carcharhinus cf. *leucas*	Bull shark
Carcharhinus maculipinnis	Spinner shark
Carcharhinus spp.	Requiem shark
Caracharhinidae	Requiem sharks
Dasyatis spp.	Stingray
Chondrichthyes	Cartilaginous fish
Acanthurus spp.	Surgeon fish
Albula vulpes	Bonefish
Archosargus sp.	Sheepshead
Calamus sp.	Porgy
Sparidae	Porgies
Balistes cf. *vetula*	Queen triggerfish
Balistes spp.	Triggerfish
Balistidae	Triggerfish
Belonidae	Needlefish
Caranx hippos	Crevalle jack
Caranx latus	Horse-eye jack

Table 8.3 continues

Table 8.3 Rodney's House Faunal List *(cont'd)*

Scientific Name	Common Name
Caranx cf. rubber	Bar jack
Caranx sp.	Jack
Selene vomer	Lookdown
Carangidae	Jacks
Centropomus spp.	Snook
Chaetodipterus faber	Atlantic spadefish
Diapterus spp.	Mojarra
Diodon hystrix	Porcupine fish
Diodon spp.	Porcupine fish
Epinephelus morio	Red grouper
Epinephelus spp.	Grouper
Serranidae	Sea basses
Echeneidae	Remoras
Gerreidae	Mojarras
Gymnothorax sp.	Moray eel
cf. Muraenidae	Morays
Haemulon cf. album	Margate
Haemulon sciurus	Blue striped grunt
Haemulon spp.	Grunt
Haemulidae	Grunts
Lachnolaimus maximus	Hogfish
Lutjanus cf. analis	Mutton snapper
Lutjanus spp.	Snapper
Elops sp.	Ladyfish
Megalops atlanticus	Atlantic tarpon
Micropogonias furnieri	Croaker
Mugil sp.	Mullet
cf. Mugilidae	Mullets
Scarus sp.	Parrotfish
Sparisoma spp.	Parrotfish
cf. Scaridae	Parrot fishes
Sphyraena barracuda	Great barracuda
Sphyraena spp.	Barracuda
cf. Strongylura sp.	Needlefish
Scornberomorus sp.	Mackerel
Scombridae	Tunas and mackerels
Uid Osteichthyes	Bony fishes
Callinectes spp.	Blue crab
Cardisoma spp.	Soldier crab
Gecarcinus spp.	Land crab
cf. Diogenidae	Hermit crab

Table 8.3 continues

Table 8.3 Rodney's House Faunal List *(cont'd)*

Scientific Name	Common Name
Mithrax sp.	Coral crab
cf. Mithrax	Coral crab
Uca sp.	Fiddler crab
Uid crab	
Panulirus argus	Spiny lobster
Melongena melongena	Crown conch
Murex pomum	Apple mumex
Arca zebra	Turkey wing
Arca spp.	Arc shell
Neritina piratical	Nerite
Neritina virginina	Virgin nerite
Chama macerophylla	Leafy jewel
Chama spp.	Jewel box
Crassostrea sp.	Eastern oyster
Ostrea frons	Leafy oyster
Arca imbricate	Mossy arc
Chione cancellata	Cross-barred venus
Anomalocardia brasiliana	Venus clam
Asaphis deflorata	Sand clam
Codakia orbicularis	Tiger lucina
Anomia simplex	Jingle shell
Anadara brasiliana	Brazil arc
Neritina reclivata	Olive nerite
Neritina versicolor	Variegated nerite
Neritina tessellate	Tessellated nerite
Plicatula gibbosa	Kitten's paws
Brachidontes recurvus	Sea mussel
Cittarium pica	West Indian top shell
Donax denticulat	Coquina clam
Tectarius muricatus	Beaded periwinkle
Strombus pugilis	West Indian fighting conch
Strombus gigas	Queen conch
Neritina clenchi	Nerite
Phacoides pectinatus	Comb lucina
Strombus costatus	Milk conch
Astraea caelata	Engraved star shell
Chiamys ornate	Ornate scallop
Nerita peloranta	Bleeding tooth
Neritidae	Nerites
Petaloconchus McGintyi	Worm shell

Table 8.3 continues

Table 8.3 Rodney's House Faunal List *(cont'd)*

Scientific Name	Common Name
Petaloconchus irregularis	Worm shell
Lithophaga antillarum	Antillean date mussel
Anadara notabilis	Arc shell
Latirus McGintyi	Latirus
Cantharus auritulus	Lesser whelk
Oliva reticularis	Netted plive
Crepidula aculeate	Spiny slipper shell
Diodora listeri	List keyhole limpet
Natica cantrena	Colourful moon shell
Natica cayennensis	Moon shell
Tellina alternate	Alternate tellin
Charonia variegate	Trumpet triton
Vasum municatum	Caribbean vase shell
Littorina angulifera	Angulate periwinkle
Pteria sp.	Pearl oyster
Pleurodonte acuta	No common name
Pleurodonte jamaicensis	No common name
Pleurodonte sp.	No common name
Dentellaria peracutissima	No common name
Urocoptis sp.	Rock snails
Uid mollusc	
Cirripedia	Barnacles
Polyplacophora	Chitons

Section 3

Analysis of Taíno Archaeological Data

IN JAMAICA, THE most abundant artefacts recovered from Taíno sites are ceramics and, second, stone tools. This section analyses and highlights the importance of the data recovered from these sites, in particular the stone and ceramic artefacts.

Jamaican Taíno stone artefacts include celts, flint scrapers, *zemís* and pendants. Celts – petal-shaped axe blades made of either stone or shell, formally known as polished petaloid celts – are thought to be the most common stone tool. Celts, which Afro-Jamaicans call "thunderbolts", are said to have fallen from the sky, and are traditionally placed in yabba pots to cool water (Senior 1985). Thomas A. Joyce wrote that

> the petaloid celts of Jamaica, both for symmetry and polish, are unsurpassed by those of any locality in the world, and considering the fact that they are in most cases fashioned from a very hard variety of stone, the amount of patient labour involved in their preparation must been enormous. (1907, 234)

M.J. Roobol and J.W. Lee's paper, "Petrography and Source of Some Arawak Rock Artefacts from Jamaica" (1976, reprinted in this volume), reports on the first technical attempt since the nineteenth century to study these stone artefacts. The authors were able to identify and subdivide the artefacts into major rock types. Roobol and Lee analysed the artefacts according to colour, size and texture and were able to identify the source of the stones used to make them, thus providing evidence of intra- and inter-island trade.

The pottery of the Jamaican Taíno has been frequently described as "unique" or "simple". Lovén suggests that the pottery indicates "an endemic ceramic development" and adds that compared with the ceramics of other Taíno people, those of the Jamaican Taíno are much plainer. Many influences that affected the Taíno in Puerto Rico, Española and Cuba never reached

Jamaica (1935, 322). Originally, Jamaican pottery was classified as having sub-Taíno cultural traits; however, this terminology is no longer used. The term "Western Taíno" is now used by Rouse (1992) and other scholars to indicate a culture less developed than that of the Classic Taíno of Hispaniola and Puerto Rico.

The three other chapters in this section, by Norma Rodney-Harrack, J.W. Lee and Robyn Woodward, focus on Taíno ceramics. These chapters examine overlapping issues from different perspectives. Rodney-Harrack gives a general overview of Taíno ceramics, Lee discusses the Jamaican Redware culture, and Woodward assesses evidence of Taíno and Hispanic cultural contact.

Norma Rodney-Harrack's "Jamaican Taíno Pottery" examines the different Taíno ceramic cultures present in Jamaica – the Ostionoid and Meillacan – from a master potter's perspective. She discusses the Taíno techniques of fabricating and firing the clay and examines both the various vessel forms recovered from Taíno sites and their different surface decorations.

James W. Lee's study "Jamaican Redware" (1980c) was the first paper published on the Ostionoid culture of the island. It illustrates the history of Redware site discoveries. Lee describes the thirteen Redware sites that were located before 1980 and the types of ceramics and other artefacts associated with this cultural period. Since 1980, twelve additional Redware sites have been identified, including Paradise Park, Westmoreland; Mammee Bay, St Ann; and Porus and Anderson, both in Manchester (Atkinson 2003, 5).

Sevilla la Nueva, St Ann's Bay, is one of the most significant sites in Jamaica. The site of the first Spanish capital, it represents the point of cultural contact among the Taíno, Spanish, English and Africans. Robyn Woodward's study of the material culture from Seville identifies evidence of Taíno–Hispanic cultural contact. Woodward's research is essential in understanding the processes of cultural adaptation and the importance of Taíno labour in the establishment of the sixteenth-century Spanish capital.

9  Petrography and Source of Some Arawak Rock Artefacts from Jamaica

M. John Roobol
and
James W. Lee

The earth's crust comprises three main groups of rock:

1. *Sedimentary* – originating as sediments, pebbles, sand, silt and mud, which by the various processes of lithification become conglomerates, sandstones, shales and mudstones. Where the sediment is composed largely of the calcareous remains of organisms, limestone results.
2. *Igneous* – originating as a molten material which may be erupted onto the earth's surface to form lavas, domes or pyroclastic (fragmented by explosion) deposits, or remain within the crust and form coarser-grained intrusions.
3. *Metamorphic* – originating when either of the above groups are altered due to burial, where increased temperatures and pressures result in the formation of new minerals or recrystallization. Such rocks are exposed at the earth's surface by erosion.

If the geology of the Caribbean islands can be summarized in a few brief sentences, it might be said that the Greater Antilles are very similar to one another, being composed of an older (pre–60 million years) group of volcanic rocks inter-stratified with sediments. The latter are composed of fragments of the volcanic rocks and, as such, differ from their quartz-rich counterparts on the continents. These older volcanic and volcaniclastic sedimentary rocks have been affected to varying extents by metamorphism and also invaded by a belt of coarse-grained igneous intrusions. All of these are overlain by a group of younger sedimentary rocks (post–60 million years) where limestone predom-

---

Originally published in 1976, in *Proceedings of the Sixth International Congress for the Study of Pre-Columbian Cultures of the Lesser Antilles, Guadeloupe, 1975*: 304–13.

inates or is conspicuous. Volcanic rocks are sparsely present amongst these younger sedimentary rocks, many of which are unaffected by metamorphism. In contrast to the Greater Antilles, the Lesser Antilles – forming the arc from Saba in the north through Guadeloupe, Martinique and St Vincent to Grenada in the south – are built up almost entirely of volcanic rocks. These are all younger than 60 million years old and largely non-metamorphosed. This volcanic arc contains abundant active volcanoes and is continuing its growth today.

Thus volcanism was the major factor contributing to the growth of the Greater Antilles up until 60 million years ago, probably commencing around 130 million years ago. Around 60 million years ago, volcanism largely ceased along the Greater Antilles but began in the Eastern Caribbean, to build the Lesser Antilles. While these latter islands were building, the older, extinct volcanoes of the Greater Antilles were buried beneath sediments and partly metamorphosed. For further reading on this subject, one should consult Khudoley and Meyerhoff (1971) and Weyl (1966).

If the Caribbean archaeologist can have artefacts examined by a geologist in the light of the above variations, it may be possible to locate their sources within the Caribbean. In addition, the rocks of the Caribbean islands are very youthful and different from those of the earth's continents, so the geologist should be able to identify rocks that have been transported into the Caribbean. In Jamaica many such observations can be made. Fresh, white vesicular pumice occurs on the Pedro Cays. Those pumices in the Jamaican volcanic deposits have been altered by devitrification (as are many old bottles) and flattened by compaction, and the deposits lithified. The white pumice of the Pedro Cays is characterized by pipe vesicles (a structure found in pumice flow deposits) and most probably originated from one of the late-prehistoric pumice eruptions of Mt Pelee (Roobol, Pettijean Roget and Smith 1976) from which it drifted across. Boulders and pebbles of Precambrian gneisses and schist – some of the oldest metamorphic rocks on earth – can be found on the shores of the geologically youthful Jamaica. Some are scattered along the shore of Palisadoes, west of Plumb Point Lighthouse. Such rocks do not outcrop on any of the Greater or Lesser Antilles and probably originated in Scandinavia, coming to the Caribbean as ballast stones in ships. Those on Palisadoes mark the site of an early shipwreck close inshore, now largely destroyed by wave action. White Italian marble from Carrara abounds on the island in the form of early gravestones, and a fragment of a Carrara marble fountain was recently excavated at Kings House, Spanish Town. Around the ruined great houses of Jamaica, fragments of British roof slate can be found, some of which can be traced to particular quarries in North Wales, such as the purple slate with large white-green blebs from Penrhyn quarry.

The results discussed here were obtained from a study of Jamaican Arawak artefacts at the Institute of Jamaica, and others made available by members of the Archaeological Society of Jamaica. In the first instance, a collection of twenty-two broken petaloid tools was examined. As these proved to be extremely fine-grained, slices were cut from them and prepared for microscopic examination. Once the main rock types were identified with certainty, it was possible to identify further specimens without damage, by hand or binocular microscope examination of a wet surface. Many specimens required scrubbing before examination to remove surface encrustation.

The Geology of Jamaica

Unlike other islands of the Greater Antilles, most of the rocks outcropping at the surface are limestone (66.7 per cent of the area of Jamaica) containing abundant flints. The older volcanic and metamorphic rocks that underlie the limestone are exposed in a number of small inliers or erosional windows where the limestone has been removed. It is mainly these older metamorphic rocks that were used by the Jamaican Arawaks for the manufacture of their tools. Because of the distinctive nature of different inliers of oldest rocks, it is relatively easy in this case to trace the sources of the Arawak tools. In contrast, the other islands of the Greater Antilles have their ancient rocks exposed over greater areas (which also accounts for their greater mineral wealth, aside from bauxite), so that source areas cannot be pinpointed readily.

A simplified geological map of Jamaica (Figure 9.1) is based on the provisional geology map of Jamaica (1958). In keeping with the outline of the Greater Antilles given here, rocks are shown only as five groups. The younger series (post–60 million years) is divided between limestone and another group of mainly sedimentary rocks (Wagwater conglomerate and Richmond shale) containing some volcanic rocks (Newcastle keratophyres). The older series is divided as follows:

1. Sediments (of volcanic debris) found mainly in the inliers at the western end of the island.
2. A group of lavas and sediments with igneous intrusions which have not been so altered by burial that their original characteristics are now lost; for instance, lavas can still be distinguished from sediments. This group occurs in the central part of the island.
3. Metamorphic rocks occurring only in the large Blue Mountains Inlier and the tiny Green Bay inlier near Port Henderson.

The term *metamorphic* is used here in the sense that a sufficient portion of the rock has recrystallized so that the original characteristics cannot be seen

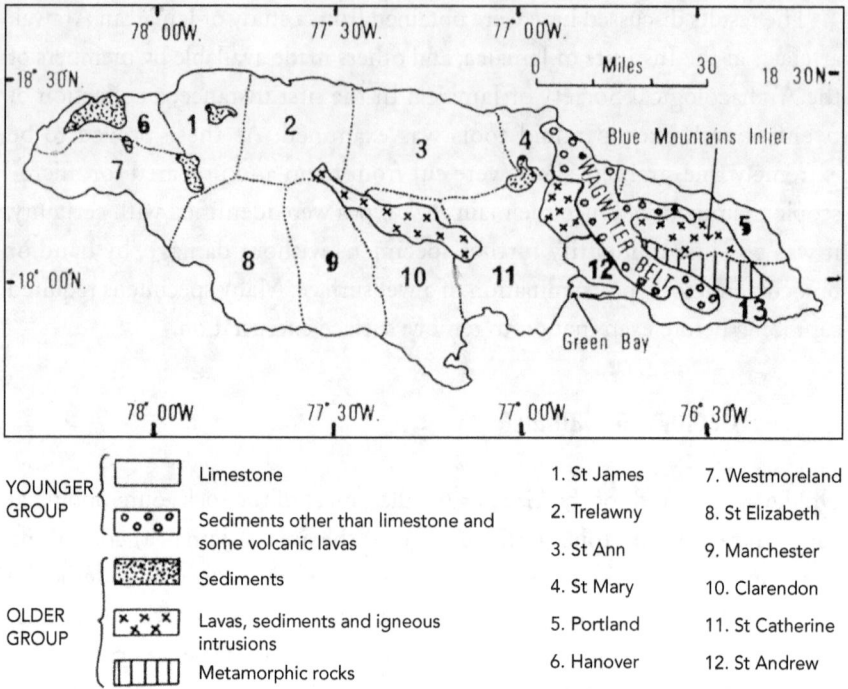

Figure 9.1 Simplified geological map of Jamaica showing parishes

in hand specimens. It is therefore not usually possible to say whether the original rock was, for instance, lava, a conglomerate or a sandstone before it was metamorphosed. Sometimes on a sawed section or under the microscope it may be possible to see a few relict structures or textures indicative of its origin. Most of the metamorphic rocks of Jamaica have not undergone a major alteration and can be considered to be only lightly metamorphosed. They appear as extremely fine-grained massive rocks lacking structure. Indeed, the crystals are so small that very often it is difficult to identify them under the microscope.

The most common of these rocks are coloured green, and the term "greenstone" seems as good as any. Less common is a black-coloured variety ("blackstone"), which occurs interlayered with the greenstone; where the two occur in cliff faces, they are usually strongly folded. Marble (metamorphosed limestone) also occurs interlayered with the greenstone – for example, at the quarry at Serge Island Estate in the east arm of the Morant River, southern Blue Mountains. A higher degree of metamorphism results in a coarser-grained rock which shows a foliation of crystals. Such a rock is called a schist and tends to split easily.

Petaloid Axes of Arawak Origin from Jamaica

During the present study, 456 specimens of smooth-ground petaloid axe were examined. Eight different rock types were recognized; the numbers and percentages of each are listed in Table 9.1. Each of the rock groups is described and their probable sources within Jamaica discussed below.

Greenstone

This is by far the most common rock used for the celts (78.3 per cent). Greenstone celts vary in texture and colour. Most are extremely fine-grained, others coarser, so that individual crystals can be seen in the hand specimen. They generally lack structures, although a few show sparse, well-shaped, large feldspar crystals on polished surfaces, indicating that the particular specimen was a lava before metamorphism. All are green-coloured, although the shade varies: some are black-green due to a predominance of the mineral chlorite, others are vegetable-green due to actinolite, and still others are yellow-green due to epidote. Some are mottled due to a patchy distribution of these minerals. The three green minerals all form during the relatively low-

Table 9.1 Lithology of Arawak Petaloid Celts from Jamaica

Collection	Green-stone*	Black-stone*	White Schist*	Blue Schist*	Lava	Sediment-ary Rock	Conch Shell	Mineral
1. J. Lee, Pres., ASJ	260	37	5	1	17	8	8	1
2. Bond coll., IOJ	59	–	1	1	–	5	–	–
3. Mannings Hill coll. of Senior, Medhurst, Clarke and Hart	19	3	–	1	4	–	–	–
4. Alligator Pond coll. S. Hart	1	–	–	–	1	–	–	–
5. Naggo Head coll. G. Senior	1	–	–	–	1	–	–	–
6. Lee coll., 22 celts microscope study	17	2	–	–	1	1	–	1
Totals	357	42	6	3	24	14	8	2
Percentages	78.3	9.2	1.3	0.7	5.3	3.1	1.7	0.4

*Metamorphic rocks as found in the Blue Mountain Inlier

pressure, low-temperature, hydrous burial metamorphism of older rocks. The small crystals are interlocking so that the rock is extremely tough. Their hardness is similar to that of steel, with some harder and some softer. Where the greenstones of Jamaica outcrop, they usually show a good jointing or parting; however, by the time the fragments have been transported some distance by river, all joint planes have been opened, and the resulting pebbles are extremely tough. It is probable that river pebbles were the principal source. Greenstones occur in the Blue Mountain Inlier where they form the core of the mountains, especially on the south side of the ridge. They also occur in the tiny inlier behind the beach at Green Bay, Port Henderson. At the latter locality the rocks are schistose and probably unsuitable for the manufacture of tools.

The term "greenstone" as used here would also include the hydrous silicate mineral nephrite, which is the most common variety of jade. Although the latter has not yet been identified in Jamaica, it is interesting to note that this particular variety of greenstone was similarly used for stone implements in Mexico, at the Swiss Lake Habitations and by the Maori of New Zealand, whose term for nephrite was *punamu* – axe stone.

Blackstone

This variety of low-grade metamorphic rock contains similar minerals to the greenstone but also an abundance of tiny granules of the black iron oxide magnetite. Axes made from this type of stone retain a high degree of polish. Blackstone occurs only in the Blue Mountain Inlier of Jamaica, where it interleaves with the greenstone but is far less common in occurrence.

White Schist

Also restricted to the Blue Mountain Inlier are small areas of white schist. These are coarser-grained than the greenstone and usually have a poor schistosity. They are composed of the white or colourless minerals quartz, feldspar and muscovite (white mica). White schist represents a higher degree of metamorphism than the greenstone and blackstone. A small number of axes are made of this rock type, which has an unfortunate tendency to split readily because of the parallelism of muscovite flakes. The white schist occurs only in the Blue Mountains of Jamaica in close proximity to the greenstone and blackstone – all having been faulted up from great depths to form the mountains. White-schist pebbles occur in the same riverbeds as the greenstones. They are, however, far from common, as white schist occurs only sparsely.

Blue Schist

The story of Jamaican blue schist is particularly interesting. The rock has a striking blue colour caused by the mineral glaucophane. This rock currently has great geological significance as it forms under conditions of low-temperature, high-pressure metamorphism, thought to exist only at the margins of lithospheric plates (in terms of current plate tectonic theory). It was previously known in the Caribbean only in southeast Cuba and the Dominican Republic but was discovered in Jamaica in 1972 on Union Hill, St Thomas, on the south flanks of the Blue Mountain Inlier (Draper and Horsfield 1973). This prominent hill forms the divide between the eastern and western arms of the Morant River, and sparse pebbles of blue schist occur in the riverbed. They are very rare on the south-coast beaches. Three celts are composed of this rock, which almost certainly originated in Union Hill.

Lava

A number of celts are composed of relatively unaltered lava – mostly andesites, readily recognized by their porphyritic texture of large, well-shaped crystals of white feldspar and black pyroxene or amphibole, set in a finer-grained ground-mass. It is not possible to identify the source of the lava as such rocks are found in all of the inliers of older rocks in Jamaica. They occur either as ancient lava flows or as pebbles and boulders of lava in the sedimentary rocks, where they were derived by erosion of the ancient lavas many millions of years ago. Lava boulders are also abundant in the younger sedimentary rocks of Jamaica and have a similar origin. It is possible, however, that one day archaeologists may find a tool with such striking and unusual texture that it can be matched with its parent lava flow. Several such flows exist; for example, in the Wagwater River there are pebbles of an andesite lava with abundant feldspar phenocrysts around 3 cm long. The Swift River in Portland provides the north-coast beaches with pebbles of another striking andesite, notable for an abundance of cube-shaped, plagioclase phenocrysts.

Sedimentary Rock

A few axes are composed of the sedimentary rocks sandstone and shale. These are khaki- or yellow-coloured, and their source cannot be located as they occur as both younger and older sedimentary rocks across the island. It is surprising to see tools manufactured from these rocks, for although the coarser sedimentary grains are composed of lava or hard minerals found in lava, the grains are cemented by calcite. This mineral breaks very easily, so such tools are inferior to those of low-grade metamorphic rock.

Mineral

Only two specimens were found which were manufactured from samples of what might be called mineral rather than rock, as they are largely mono-minerallic. One of these is composed of white calcite crystals. Layers of this mineral occur as cavity linings in limestone. The cavity forms by solution of the limestone in percolating underground water, and the coarsely crystalline calcite is a later partial infilling caused by reprecipitation from the circulating water. The second specimen (A277, site A-14 – Tobolski, St Ann) is an altered iron ore (mainly the mineral magnetite). Such a mineral deposit is best known at Mavis Bank, St Andrew, near Kingston. Boulders of similar material have been found derived from unexplored mineral deposits in the headwaters of the east arm of the Morant River on the south side of the Blue Mountains and in the Swift River on the north side.

Conch Shell

A small number of celts were manufactured from the shell of the common conch (*Strombus*), which can be found today all around the island, browsing on seagrass (*Thallasia*) in shallow water. Similar celts were described from Jamaica by Duerden (1897).

Other Rock Artefacts from Arawak Sites

A small number of other artefacts were examined and found to be manufactured from rocks and minerals common to Jamaica.

Flint Scrapers

A fine set of about twenty elongate flakes or scrapers of flint was recently gathered (H.R. Clarke collection) at site K-13, Bellevue, St Andrew. A few others are present in the collections at the Institute of Jamaica. Many are mentioned by Duerden (1897). The Lee collection contains numerous flint specimens, chiefly from north-coast sites in the Montego Bay area (sites J-1, Mammee Hill; J-3, Fairfield; and J-11, Mount Salem) and in St Mary (Y-4, Rio Nuevo; Y-14, Iter Boreale; Y-15, Nonsuch; Y-17, Tweedside; and Y-19,

Coleraine) but also from other major sites in Trelawny and St Ann (T-1, New Forest; T-3, Spring; and A-19, Windsor). Secondary working of flakes is extremely rare. These flints originate in the white limestone group, which covers two-thirds of Jamaica; some can be traced to particular horizons as they contain an abundance of silicified fossils. The flints are concentrated in the rivers and on beaches around the island.

Beads

Eight small (1 cm diameter) cylindrical beads perforated by a central hole were examined (Lee and Clarke collections). Three are from site K-13, Bellevue, St Andrew; three from C-7, Harmony Hall, Clarendon; one from Y-21, Fort Haldane, St Mary, and one from E-5, Alligator Pond, St Elizabeth. All are composed of white chalcedony containing small green crystals of the minerals epidote and chlorite. The rock can be matched only with chalcedony pods present in the greenstones of the southern Blue Mountains Inlier. Lee obtained spherical beads of limestone from S-8, Marlie Mount, and S-12, Naggo Head, both in St Catherine.

Pendants

Seven pendants were examined and found to be composed of rocks that can be readily matched in Jamaica. Four (Lee collection), from Y-19, Coleraine, St Mary; Pepper, St Elizabeth; S-12, Naggo Head, St Catherine; and C-12, Logie Green, Clarendon, are composed of polished clear keratophyre. A fifth pendant of this rock has just been found by James Godfrey of Mandeville at E-2, Fort Charles, St Elizabeth. Keratophyre is a rare altered igneous rock in Jamaica, and the clear, non-weathered variety is found only in the Stony River Valley in the southern Blue Mountains Inlier, although extensive outcrops of its weathered equivalent occur along the Wagwater Belt (see Figure 9.1). Pendants found by Lee at Runaway Bay, St Ann, and at T-1, New Forest, Trelawny, are of calcite and limestone, respectively. Two other pendants (G. Senior collection) found at K-13, Bellevue, St Andrew, are composed of porphyritic lava, which cannot be traced to a particular locality.

Pebbles and Boulders

Numbers of unworked pebbles and boulders have been found in Jamaican middens. These too, like the petaloid celts, can often be demonstrated as being alien to the midden area. Most common are pebbles of greenstone. One very unusual specimen (Medhurst collection) was found at Mannings Hill. It is a white, garnet-bearing rock, which occurs only as inclusions in the serpentinite in the vicinity of the Stony River, southern Blue Mountains.

Artefacts of Rocks Alien to Jamaica

All of the artefacts so far described were manufactured from rocks and minerals common to Jamaica. This does not prove that they originated in Jamaica, as the geology of this island is very similar to that of Hispaniola and Puerto Rico. Only two of the artefacts found were composed of rock that can be proven to have originated outside of Jamaica. A small, well-shaped pendant from K-13, Bellevue, St Andrew (H.R. Clarke collection), is composed of granular quartzite. A similar but broken pendant was found at C-8, Wallman Town, Clarendon, by Lee (specimen no. 368). These two small artefacts are of great interest, as quartzite does not occur in either the Greater or the Lesser Antilles. The rock quartzite forms from sands composed almost entirely of quartz grains which either are metamorphosed and recrystallized or are cemented in a sedimentary environment by silica. Quartz does not form a common detrital grain in the Greater Antilles. More than 60 million years ago, a number of large bodies or intrusions of quartz-bearing igneous material (granodiorite and tonalite) were emplaced along the Greater Antilles. Their subsequent deroofing and erosion provided more detrital quartz in the younger sediments. Quartzite occurs in areas where the most ancient recrystallized parts of the Earth's crust are being eroded – the nearest place being northern South America. It is therefore concluded that these two artefacts were transported to Jamaica via the Lesser Antilles from South America.

Subdivision of Greenstone Group

The next step in the petrographic study is the subdivision of the greenstone group. This at present covers a wide variety of rock types differing in grain size, texture, structure, composition, mineral assemblage and ability to take a polish. Separation of at least the most striking types could provide an estimate of inter-island trade or migration within the Greater Antilles (a particularly striking study could be made in Puerto Rico, near the eastern end of the greenstone belt, southeast of which only lavas and rare cherts or jaspers are available on the volcanic Lesser Antilles). A preliminary attempt at such a study was made when eight stone celts and one pestle from Haiti were compared with their Jamaican counterparts in Lee's collection. Three Haitian specimens of distinctive rock types matched exactly (by hand lens) the rock from which several Jamaican artefacts were made. In every instance, there were four or more Jamaican specimens corresponding to the Haitian celt. Although lacking absolute certainty of comparison, this evidence points strongly to an origin in one or the other island and to the existence of pre-Columbian inter-island trade. Another celt from Lee's collection (no. 197) compares exactly in shape and rock colour, type and texture with a specimen in the museum at Roseau, Dominica, which was found in that island. Because the rock is a flow-textured young volcanic type, it appears that the Jamaican specimen is an import from the Lesser Antilles.

Discussion

The percentages of rock types for the celts, together with the artefacts described above, indicate that by far the greater part of the Jamaican Arawak rock and mineral artefacts are composed of metamorphic rocks similar to those occurring either in the southern part of the Blue Mountain Inlier or at Green Bay, Port Henderson. Their presence across the entire island suggests that they were transported there. Some of this transportation occurred naturally by rivers and longshore drift along the coast. A check was made on all rivers draining the Blue Mountains to assess their content of greenstone pebbles and boulders. The Wagwater River, Rio Nuevo and Rio Grande lack them. There are a few pebbles of greenstone in the Swift River, more in the Yallahs River, but it is only in the lower reaches of the Morant River on the south flanks of the Blue Mountains that such pebbles are abundant. Greenstone pebbles are therefore being added to the beaches in some quantity only along the south shore of the Blue Mountains. Here the longshore drift is from east to west, and it is surprising how sparse the content of pebbles has become on the Palisadoes beach bar, south of Kingston. It must therefore be concluded that greenstone pebbles can be collected, with patience, from the beaches south of the Blue Mountains, and readily only from the Morant River.

In 1972, blue schist – an extremely rare rock in the Caribbean – was discovered for the first time in Jamaica on Union Hill, separating the east and west arms of the Morant River. Three celts were found to be composed of this rock, which can be traced to Union Hill or – as extremely sparse pebbles – in the Morant River. The five pendants of keratophyre lava, together with the garnetiferous boulder mentioned previously, can be matched only with rocks outcropping between the Stony River and Cedar Valley on the south flanks of the Blue Mountains Inlier, immediately west of the Morant River. It is therefore concluded that the Arawak Indians of Jamaica did not make many of their rock tools and decorations from rock and pebbles in the vicinity of the middens; rather, they obtained mainly fine-grained metamorphic rocks from the rivers and shores of the southern Blue Mountains. This indicates that domestic trade must have existed within the island.

Although the data are not really sufficient, a start has been made on cataloguing the lithologies of the petaloid tools parish by parish (Table 9.2). The ultimate aim must be to catalogue midden by midden, where the percentages of the different rock types used will reflect movement across the island; this may vary by stratigraphic level. For the seven parishes where there is a fair number of samples, the percentages of tools composed of non-metamorphic rocks (that is, those that could be collected from areas other than the southern Blue Mountains) have been determined. It is tempting to look at this sparse data and to see yet another correlation with the geology of Jamaica. The percentages of non-metamorphic rocks appear to be greatest for south-coast parishes, suggesting that the wide gravel plains of the south coast provided a small percentage of non-metamorphic pebbles suitable for tool making. The presence of only limestone and flints along the north coast of Jamaica results

Table 9.2 Lithology of Petaloid Celts from Some Parishes of Jamaica

Parish	Metamorphic				Non-metamorphic				Per cent Non-metamorphic
	Greenstone	Blackstone	White Schist	Blue Schist	Lava	Sedimentary Rock	Conch Shell	Mineral	
Trelawny	60	6	–	–	1	1	–	–	3.0
N. Coast	88.2%	8.8%	–	–	1.5%	1.5%	–	–	–
St Ann	57	12	2	–	1	1	1	2	6.5
N. Coast	75.0%	15.8%	2.6%	–	–	1.3%	1.3%	1.3%	2.6%
St Elizabeth	52	4	1	1	4	4	3	–	15.9
S. Coast	75.4%	6.0%	1.5%	1.5%	6.0%	6.0%	4.3%	–	–
Manchester	33	7	–	–	2	–	–	–	4.8
S. Coast	78.6%	–	16.7%	–	–	4.8%	–	–	–
Clarendon	15	3	–	–	2	1	–	–	14.3
S. Coast	71.4%	14.3%	–	–	9.5%	4.8%	–	–	–
St Catherine	23	5	2	–	5	–	–	–	14.3
S. Coast	65.7%	14.3%	5.7%	–	14.3%	–	–	–	–
St Andrew	23	3	–	1	5	–	–	–	15.6
S. Coast	71.9%	9.4%	–	3.1%	15.6%	–	–	–	–

Note: Whole numbers corresponding to individual parishes represent numbers of celts found there.

in a lack of suitable rocks, so that imported Blue Mountains metamorphic rock predominates there.

Comments on the 1895 Display of Arawak Material

In November 1895, Mr J.E. Duerden, curator of the museum of the Institute of Jamaica, assembled a large collection of Arawak artefacts and described them in his excellent publication of 1897. Although at that time far less was known than today of the geology of Jamaica and of the other Caribbean islands, it is of particular interest, in the light of the present work, to requite Duerden's observations on the lithologies of the collection of almost four hundred celts that he assembled. He wrote of the celts:

> The material of which the implements are composed varies considerably, examples of most of the types of the sedimentary, metamorphic, and igneous rocks being met with. The most abundant material undoubtedly belongs to the trappean series of rocks, including the trachytes, felsites, rhyolites, and basalts, so prominent in various part of the island. Dolerite is rather common, as well as a greenish schist, and others graduating between quartzites and gneisses. A metamorphic siliceous green rock resembling jade, and taking a high polish, is met with, sometimes with light and dark bands. Most of the material is such as occurs in the island. The flint is the same as is derived from various districts. (1897, 37)

There is a discrepancy here between Duerden's observations and those presented here. His trappean group are here grouped as lava. His identification refers to hand specimens, and the term would not be used today in the light of chemical analyses. Duerden's trachyte is probably a flow-banded andesite, the felsite and rhyolite are keratophyre, and the basalt either black vitrophyric andesite or spilite. Nonetheless, his point that the lava group predominates differs from the present study, where lava makes up only 5.3 per cent. The greenish schist and metamorphic jade-like rock undoubtedly refer to the present greenstone group and the gneiss to the present white schist group. His observation of quartzite is very interesting in the light of the two pendants described here, but may refer to sandstones. The problem is raised, however, as to why, in a collection of almost 400 celts, lava should predominate, whereas in the present study of 450, metamorphic rocks predominate. Duerden listed the ownership of the celts he described, and none of them were available during the present study. Apart from the Bond collection of sixty-six celts from the Institute, all of the remainder examined during the present study were collected by members of the Archaeological Society of Jamaica during the past two decades. There are several possible explanations for the difference in predominant rock type between the two collections.

1. The study made by Duerden was not primarily aimed at the petrography, and he examined only a small, non-representative group. His terminology, however, is such that anyone familiar with Jamaican rocks can recognize his groupings, except perhaps for "dolerite".
2. Perhaps neither of the two collections is representative of the island, and further study is required of larger numbers of samples. We do not favour this solution. Over a two-year period, while increasing numbers of celts were being examined, the proportions of the different groups did not change appreciably from that established in the initial set of twenty-two celts (see Table 9.1).
3. There is a stratigraphic variation in the proportion of rock types. Many of the celts available to Duerden were complete and were collected from off the surface of the earth. These presumably represented the youngest material. After these had been collected and removed from circulation, erosion and cuts for foundations and roads would have revealed a generally older set of celts in which broken specimens from middens were more frequent. It is possible that in the older celts greenstones predominate, while in the younger group volcanic rocks (perhaps even imported from other islands) predominate.

There seems no immediate way of settling this problem other than by further examination of more celts, both in Jamaica and in the early collections now on other Caribbean islands or on the North, Central and South American mainland.

Conclusions

The petrographic study of Arawak rock artefacts from Jamaica has provided an answer to the question of source material. Nearly all rock artefacts can be matched with rocks outcropping in Jamaica, where the geology is similar to that of the Greater Antilles as a whole. Around 90 per cent of the artefacts are manufactured from low-grade metamorphic rocks, of which greenstone predominates. To a much lesser extent, ancient lava was used. Rarely, friable sedimentary and mineral specimens were used. Only two small, well-shaped pendants can be shown to be composed of rock alien to the Antilles, and these, significantly, are small pendants, bored and carried attached to the body. However, a preliminary attempt at subdivision of the greenstones for a comparison of Haitian and Jamaican samples reveals varieties common to both islands. This suggests that within the Greater Antilles there were common origins and consequently transport between the islands.

A surprising conclusion of the present petrographic study is that most of the rocks used, if derived from Jamaica, must have a source in the southern Blue Mountains. The fissile greenstone of the tiny Green Bay Inlier is unsuitable for working. The present degree of understanding of Caribbean geology is such that the conclusion about the utilization of metamorphic rock in the Greater Antilles raises another question. In the Lesser Antilles the active volcanic islands lack metamorphic rocks, which are thus not available for tool manufacture. What then did the people of these islands use to make tools? Furthermore, any artefacts manufactured from low-grade metamorphic rock in the Lesser Antilles must have been transported there from either northern Venezuela or the Greater Antilles. With this unanswered question in mind, it is interesting to note that one of us was recently shown a broken Arawak celt in Martinique (collection of the president of the Society of History), which was composed of greenstone. On this island its "unusual" colour had attracted attention.

Acknowledgements

We wish to thank members of the Archaeological Society of Jamaica for making available their collections and Mr Bernard Lewis and Mr Neville Dawes for permission to examine the collections at the Institute of Jamaica. The study was made between 1972 and 1974 while one of us (MJR) lectured at the University of the West Indies,

10 Jamaican Taíno Pottery

Norma Rodney-Harrack

Kingston, Jamaica.

Early Jamaican pottery designs, in terms of their form and decorative elements, can be traced to the indigenous Taíno people. Two Taíno pottery phases have been identified for Jamaica, the Ostionoid culture and the Meillacan culture (Rouse 1992, 107).

Ostionoid/Ostionan Culture

The Ostionan were Jamaica's earliest inhabitants, from AD 600 to 900 (ibid.), and the first ceramic culture to arrive in the island. Ostionan pottery is often referred to as Redware, reflective of the red slip or gilt that was painted, smudged or banded on in areas of the pot's shoulder. Redware sites are generally found on Jamaica's southern coasts, with exceptions in the parish of St Ann (see Lee 1980c). Their pottery is characterized by a fine-grained red bauxite clay "body". Taíno pottery is frequently burnished to a high, lustrous sheen and decorated with zoomorphic designs of turtles, manatees, fish and crocodiles.

Meillacan Culture

The Meillacan culture appeared after AD 900 (Rouse 1992, 107). Meillacan pottery is also locally known as White Marl, after its type-site at White Marl, Central Village, in St Catherine. This type of pottery is formulated from a non-lustrous brown clay paste and has a thinner clay wall than Redware pottery (Figure 10.1). These potters incorporated various decorative motifs that were impressed, incised and modelled. The Meillacan people occupied the entire island – coasts, plains, low-lying hills and highland interior – and con-

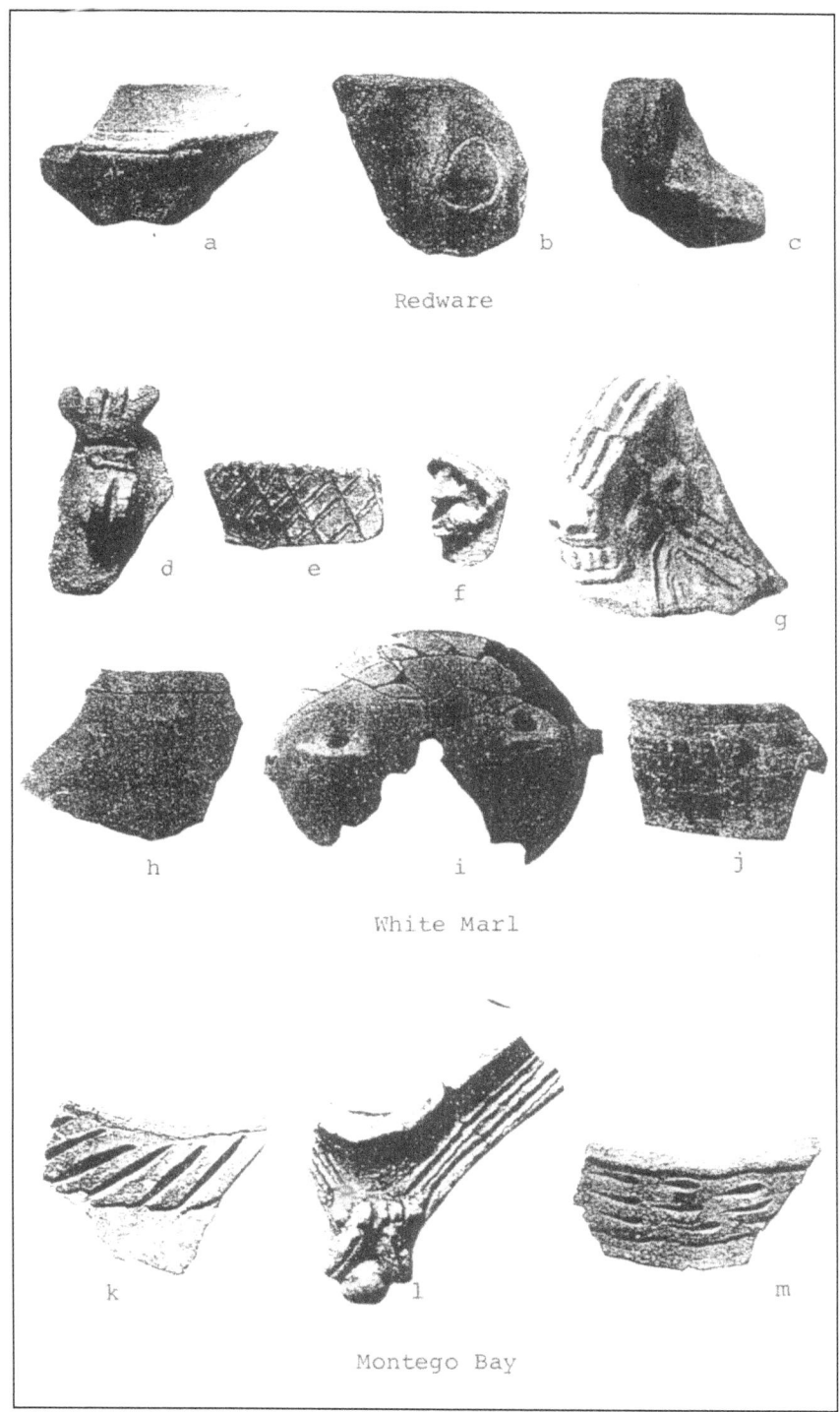

Figure 10.1 Redware, White Marl and Montego Bay styles. (Vanderwal 1968a.)

sequently, their pottery is found virtually everywhere on the island.

These two types form the main origins of early Jamaican pottery. A subphase known as the Montego Bay style (see Figure 10.1) is said to be less striking in its deviation from the main Jamaican pottery tradition, particularly in its use of incision. This ceramic substyle is found in the western section of the island – for instance, at Fairfield, St James.

Fabrication Method

Taíno hand-coiled pottery reached an aesthetic level comparable to that of more advanced ceramic cultures. Taíno potters are documented as having had good knowledge of local clays, which they used extensively to fashion a wide range of shapes for varying uses. To strengthen the fabric of the fired pottery, they first tempered the clays with substances such as sand, ash, crushed shell or vegetable fibres. The Taíno, it is presumed, would lay out coils vertically, in concentric circles, for bowls and jars, and horizontally for plates and flat-bottomed vessels, such as *buréns*. Modelling with their hands, they smoothed and fused the coils together. They also employed the paddle-and-anvil technique to thin and compress the clay walls of their pots: the anvil is held inside the pot while the paddle is used on the outside. This process resulted in thin-walled, lightweight pots, some of which can be seen in our heritage museums.

Pottery Forms

A large percentage of Taíno pottery exhibits a low lustre on both exterior and interior surfaces as a result of burnishing without a gilt or slip. Burnishing is a process of smoothing leather-hard clay with a hard object, like a smooth pebble, for decorative purposes and to give a hard, dense coating to unglazed ware.

Figure 10.2 Normal boat-shaped vessel. (Institute of Jamaica Collection.)

The corpus of Taíno pottery included bowls for cooking and serving, effigy vessels, *buréns* (cassava griddles), body stamps and other forms of human and zoomorphic designs for ancestral worship. But the two basic shapes that remained intrinsic to Jamaican Taíno pottery are the round and boat-shaped bowls. The boat, or oval, shape is the more common of the two (Figure 10.2). These vessels usually have both ends elevated and often terminate in cylindrical or flat handles that flare at the tips. An alternative design has only one end elevated, resulting in a calabash shape. When the boat-shaped vessel is devoid of terminal handles, the stems or projecting ends are modelled to form thickened triangular ridges. It is thought that the shape of the turtle may have inspired the oval or boat-shaped vessels; the Taíno esteemed the turtle and used turtle motifs extensively as adornment on their pottery.

In contrast, the round bowls were modelled in a form similar to the calabash, sometimes with only one end elevated (Figure 10.3). Often when terminal handles are absent, the stems of the vessels, like those of the boat-shaped bowls, are worked into slightly thickened triangular ridges. Both round and oval bowls have symmetrically rounded bottoms and frequently have distinctive shoulders. With or without a shoulder, the sides of these bowls invariably curve inwards towards the rim so that the opening is smaller than the greatest diameter. A vessel of this shape is commonly referred to as a carinated bowl. Carination is an angular bending used to turn pots sharply inwards or create a constricted mouth with inward-curving shoulders.

Figure 10.3 Round vessel. (Institute of Jamaica Collection.)

The bowls were made for several purposes: some were used for cooking and serving and others as eating vessels. Others were specifically made for sniffing during *zemí* worship. Some bore complex designs and are thought to have been used for preparation of food during a ritual or as a burial offering. Other pottery items include bottles, effigy vessels, carafes, funerary urns and *buréns* for baking cassava bread. The functions of these vessels, however, do not appear to have a strict morphological correlation. Many types of vessels were smoothed on the outside, indicating their use as cooking pots. Variations in depth suggest possible differences in function. Taíno potters also made body stamps. The Taínos did not wear much clothing; instead they decorated their bodies with designs using pottery stamps coated with red, white and black pigments obtained from plants and coloured clays.

We believe that the most intricate objects were made by women who were receptive to new ideas, drawing on traditions from their own society and fusing them with elements of Jamaican life into something unique. The autochthonous Taíno people sought out influences from the environment that would lead them through to their own creative trajectory.

Surface Decoration

The most distinguishing feature of Taíno pottery is its surface decoration, which incorporated incising, punctuation, modelling and other techniques to produce designs of parallel and curved lines, spirals, cross-hatching and circles. These decorative motifs, undoubtedly the hallmark of Taíno pottery, have long aroused interest among scholars, archaeologists and historians.

Taínos customarily incorporated modelled heads of human and animal forms on lugs and handles of their vessels (Figure 10.4). Several such adornments can be identified with certainty as turtle and snake heads, whereas others portrayed spiritual *zemí* symbols as well as objects of power that represented gods and ancestors.

Figure 10.4 Handled Taíno bowl. (Institute of Jamaica Collection.)

Lugs and handles show the greatest variation and are the most frequently decorated features of Taíno pottery. There are four main types of handles (Figure 10.5): cylindrical knob-like handles, hourglass-shaped flaring handles

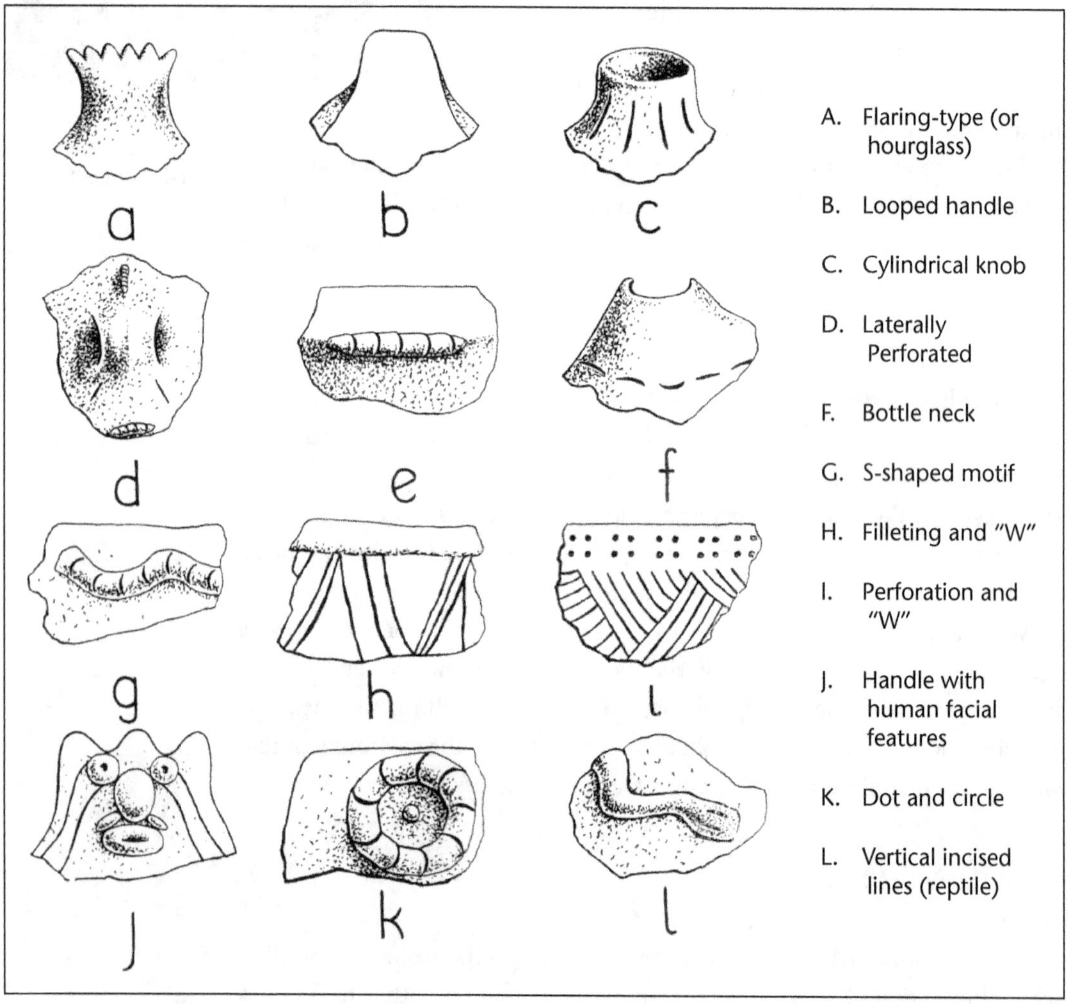

A. Flaring-type (or hourglass)
B. Looped handle
C. Cylindrical knob
D. Laterally Perforated
F. Bottle neck
G. S-shaped motif
H. Filleting and "W"
I. Perforation and "W"
J. Handle with human facial features
K. Dot and circle
L. Vertical incised lines (reptile)

Figure 10.5 Handles, lugs and decorative motifs. (Howard 1950.)

(also see Figure 10.6), loop handles, and raised, laterally perforated knob handles (also see Figure 10.7).

The looped handle is the least frequently encountered, while the hourglass type, usually placed at both ends of boat-shaped vessels, is the most frequently seen. Cylindrical knobs were often placed at either end of a vessel, at the apex or just below the rim. There may be one such knob or groups of two or three smaller ones. The laterally perforated knob handle, which resembles a crude face with perforations representing the eye and the ridge of the mouth, is said to be unique to Jamaica. Their large size would indicate their probable use on large bowls and jars (Figure 10.7). The most common type of lug is wedge-shaped; these were customarily placed on the shoulder or rim and at the end of a vessel.

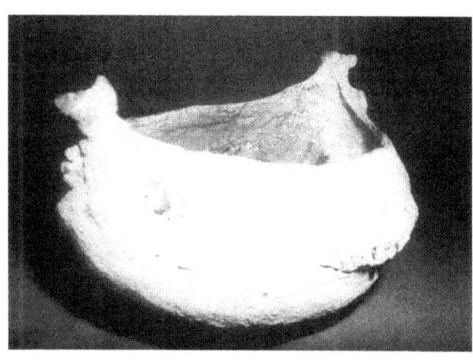

Figure 10.6 Taíno bowl with hourglass-type handle. (Institute of Jamaica Collection).

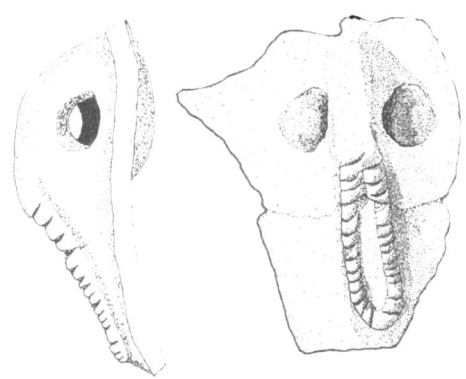

Figure 10.7 Laterally perforated handle. (Illustration by Audrey Wiles, James W. Lee collection. Courtesy of the Jamaica Bauxite Institute.)

Incised linear designs appear to have been a favourite with Taíno potters. Curved lines, also referred to as ribboning (Figure 10.8), and parallel lines occurred on only a few potsherds. Spirals and circles were also used. Cross-hatching was a common decorative motif around the vessel (Figure 10.9). There are several variations of these basic patterns.

The favoured areas for incised decorations were the vessels' shoulders, handles and lugs. Rims and edges only rarely received ornamentation. Rims, however, are known for the significant feature of filleting, in which the edge of the wall was turned outwards and flattened against itself, or a strip or small coil of clay was added to the outside of the vessel against the rim and then smoothed into the wall.

According to James W. Lee, "The favourite motif [of Taíno potters] was the turtle, with head and foreflippers at one end of a bowl and tail and hind-

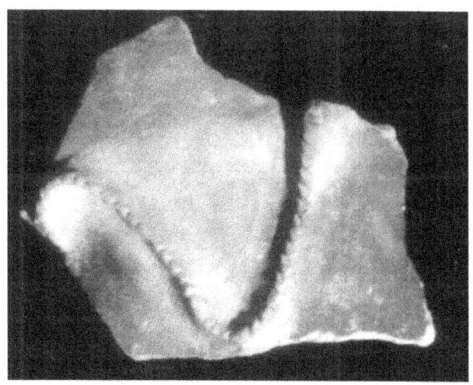

Figure 10.8 Ribbon decoration. (Norma Rodney-Harrack collection.)

JAMAICAN TAÍNO POTTERY

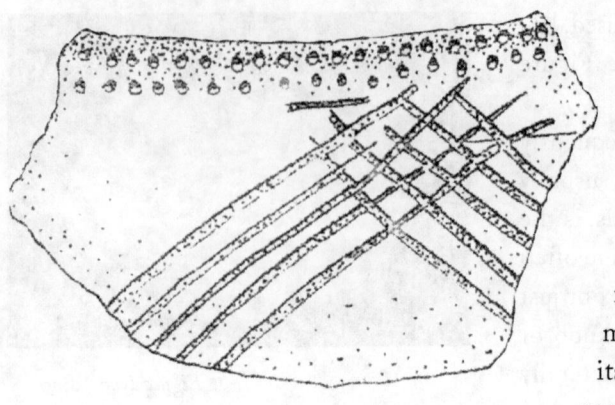

Figure 10.9 Crosshatch decoration. (Illustration by Audrey Wiles, James W. Lee collection. Courtesy of the Jamaica Bauxite Institute.)

flippers at the opposite end. Incision was used to create the impression of scales, particularly on the flippers" (Lee 1980b, 600). It was also customary for the sides of bowls to have extended turtle fins modelled onto them. Bowls were the preferred items for adornment: moulded and sculpted elements were attached to them for either utilitarian or purely decorative purposes, or a combination of both. It is not unusual for Taíno enthusiasts to employ the Spanish word *adorno* in reference to pottery adornment. Primarily, *adornos* are either zoomorphic or anthropomorphic. The eye, moulded in pairs, is a significant adornment feature.

Firing

The process of transforming the clay body into pottery by exposing it to heat is called firing. Indigenous societies practised simple firing in the open using wood, dung and grass. Taíno potters used this type of firing; they packed their dry pots atop one another in the open and stacked potsherds, wood, grass and twigs around them. As the firing took place, this fuel became a body of hot embers that retained the heat directly around the pots.

The Taíno population is said to have dwindled before the impact of the aggressive Spanish colonizers and European diseases to which they had no immunity. According to J. H. Parry and Philip Sherlock, "within less than 100 years they were extinct" (1971, v). However, this matter is debatable, as individuals and groups of Indians managed to survive and integrate with the Jamaican maroons (Agorsah 1994; Wilson 1997a). What is apparent is that many of their cultural traditions had been passed on through domestic unions, social interaction and cultural fusion throughout the centuries.

11 Jamaican Redware

JAMES W. LEE

A DISTINCTIVE ABORIGINAL pottery style found in eleven Jamaican occupation sites has been named Redware because of the characteristic red slip applied to parts of some vessels. Lieutenant Commander J.S. Tyndale-Biscoe, an English surveyor and amateur archaeologist, had noticed, long before 1933, that many potsherds from the dry southern coastal areas of St Elizabeth parish showed an unmistakable red slip, but he had no occasion to write about his discovery, nor did he realize until much later (1962) that this was a separate culture both in style and time from other Arawak settlements in Jamaica.

Howard (1956) described in some detail the ceramics of the "Little River style" and agreed with De Wolf (1953) that, chronologically, it belonged to Rouse's period IIIa (Rouse 1951, 1964). Ronald L. Vanderwal, then government archaeologist, had charcoal from the Alligator Pond site (M-4) tested in 1965 and gave the date as AD 650 ± 120 (Vanderwal 1968a). By comparison, the earliest date so far determined for White Marl type-sites in Jamaica is AD 900. Recent work at the Rodney's House site (S-5) by John Wilman (1978) suggests the possibility of an age at that location pre-dating the White Marl site but with the same style of pottery.

Lee (1976a) summarized the Redware status as of that date and later (1978c) reviewed the overall picture of this culture in a paper submitted to the Ponce conference in August 1978.

Redware Sites

Except for the two most recently discovered occupation sites (which are both about 1 km inland), all the Redware settlements were directly on the seashore

---

Originally published in 1980, in *Proceedings of the Eighth International Congress for the Study of Pre-Columbian Cultures of the Lesser Antilles, St Kitts, 1979*: 597–609.

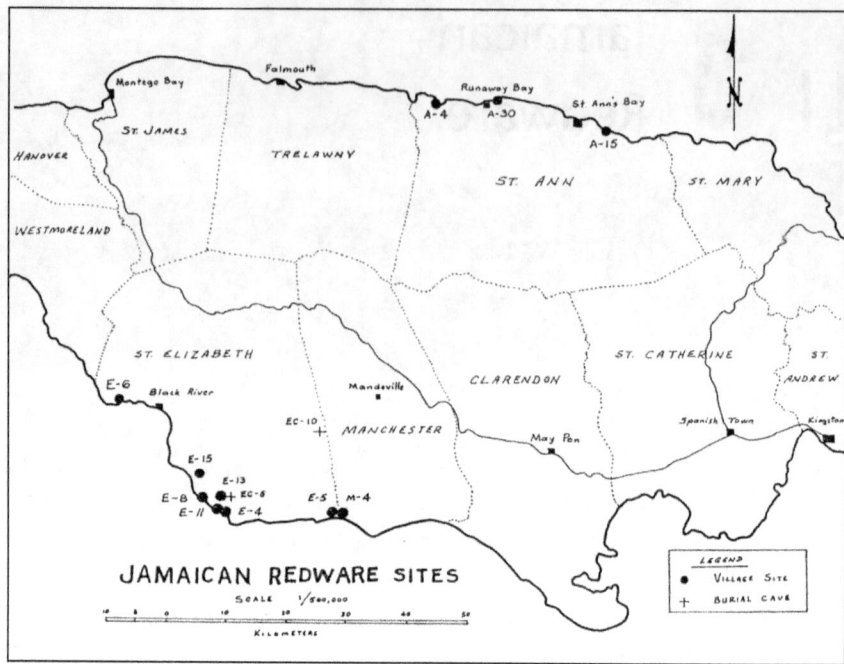

Figure 11.1 Map of Jamaican Redware sites (prior to 1980)

(Figure 11.1). Midden material in sites usually commences at the high-water mark and extends at most only a few hundred metres inland. Other features common to most Redware sites are that they are on or very near a sandy beach; that midden deposits are shallow, generally less than 10 cm; that middens are surrounded by a wide "halo" of small potsherds; and that the sites are close to a supply of fresh water.

The choice of village locations at or near sea level contrasts with the later White Marl people's preference for hilltops. Although many White Marl–type middens are also shallow, the major sites contain deposits 2 m or more thick, indicative of either long or repeated periods of occupation. The shallow depth of midden accumulation points to a relatively short term of activity at every Redware site.

The maximum midden thickness personally observed is about 25 cm. In the majority of cases, modern cultivation by small farmers has disturbed practically the entire stratum of original midden material. The hot, dry climate of the Alligator Pond–Black River area (St Elizabeth) obviously appealed to the Redware people, for along this 40-km belt are eight of eleven occupation sites. Rainfall of 35 to 50 cm annually is poorly distributed seasonally and, consequently, the area does not produce food crops readily – cassava being the one exception able to withstand the long droughts. A few vegetables will mature only if planted at exactly the correct time in relation to the infrequent rains.

When considering the relatively brief sojourn of these people in Jamaica, one wonders what made them leave their former homeland in the first place? Were they lured away by curiosity to explore new islands? Or did they flee from some danger? Were they chased? Then, having reached Jamaica, why were they here for such a short time? Did they, perhaps, send scouts ahead to some other location and then pack up to go off to a new and better area? There is no evidence to show that this happened, so perhaps our Redware people were themselves an exploratory group checking out Jamaica on behalf of others who decided not to follow. Or is the answer simply that a severe hurricane demolished their coastal villages and crippled the colony so badly it never recovered? This could be the reason for the halos of potsherds scattered inland from the seaside middens, but such scattering could as easily have occurred at any time since the sites were last occupied.

Ceramics

De Wolf's description of the Redware pottery is still the most concise:

> . . . curvatures of the surface; simplicity of decoration; ware, medium fine grained but poorly fired; colour, reds, tans and greys; average thickness 0.5 cm; shape, open bowls with some flat bottoms; shoulder, straight or incurving; rim, tapered to the lip; lip, rounded or flat; D-shaped handles, amorphous and tab lugs; some painting and rubbing of restricted area. (1953, 233)

The graceful, sleek appearance and other characteristics as detailed above by De Wolf and by Howard (1956) compare most closely to late Cuevas and to earliest Ostiones of Puerto Rico. Paradoxically, the handsome, artistic Redware pre-dates the rough but sturdy White Marl pottery. The first impression, when viewing the two types, is that the more crudely worked White Marl ought to be the older, with the smooth, shapely, red-painted vessels following as a final stage of evolution, but this is a wrong conception. In all probability, the two peoples did not co-exist in Jamaica, as the 250-year difference in the radiocarbon dates of their artefacts seems far longer than the time span necessary to produce the very shallow midden deposits.

Painting

Judging from the relative numbers of sherds with and without the diagnostic red slip, probably fewer than 20 per cent of all pottery objects had this type of finish, which was restricted to the exterior of the bowl above the line where the line turns under to form the bottom. Handles are always included in the painted zone. Bowls with zoomorphic handles are almost always painted, while only the smallest of those with loop or "D" handles are.

One possible example of a black-painted handle has been found, and another specimen contains what appears to be white pigment imbedded in the incision of a design.

Red-painted sherds were generally poorly fired, resulting in black cores and such brittleness that the majority of fragments are only a few centimetres in size. On the other hand, vessels with "D" handles were fired usually to a uniform tan colour and were relatively stronger, as reflected in the much greater size of sherds.

Thickness and Temper

The vessels range from 3 to 8 mm in thickness, and the average is between 4 and 5 mm. Generally the bottom is thicker than the sides, and there is commonly a gentle taper toward the rounded rim. The most common temper is a sandy grit, apparently obtained locally from dark beach sand, and identified by black magnetic grains of ilmenite and magnetite.

Cassava griddles vary from 1 or 2 cm thick in central parts to over 4 cm at the rims (Figure 11.2).

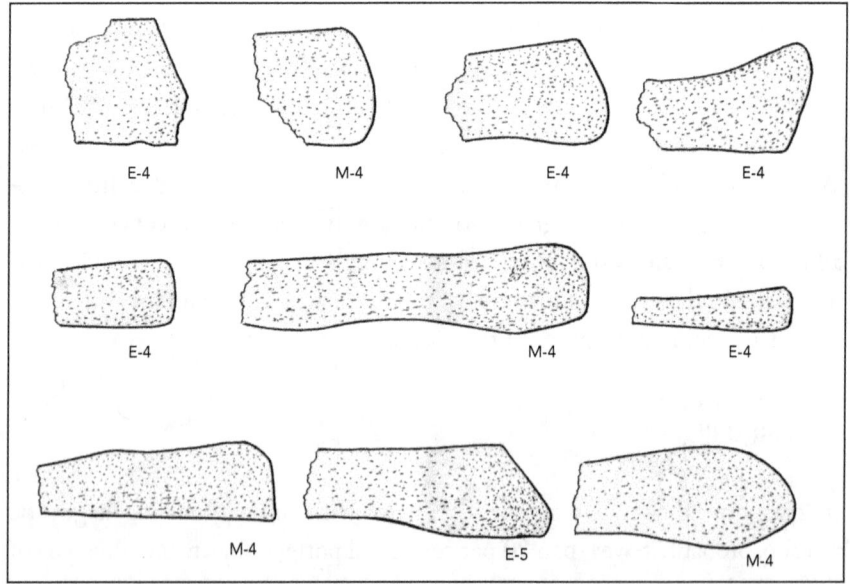

Figure 11.2 Burén rim profiles

Handles

Handles may be classified in the following groups: "D", loop, zoomorphic, geometric and amorphous tabs or lugs.

"D" handles (Figure 11.3) are the most common. Their flat straps range from 1 to 3.6 cm in width and from 0.5 to 1 cm in thickness. Ratios of width to thickness average 3.5 but vary from 2 to 8. This group can be subdivided into several types: Types I, II and III have a simple strap whose upper end melds smoothly into the rim of the vessel, and Types Ia and IIIa have bowl rims distinctly higher than the top of the "D". Type I straps have lower ends or bases which form a continuous graceful sweep into the side of the bowl. In Type II, the strap bases flare out to join the body of the bowl in a symmetrical pair of lifting lugs. Type III handles have flared bases like Type II and, in addition, have a spur or tab fixed to the strap itself. These three main and two subsidiary types are illustrated in Figures 11.3 to 11.6.

Only one complete specimen is known of a horizontal loop handle (Figure 11.6). The strip making the loop has an oval cross-section, 0.75 × 1.0 cm, and the space between the vessel wall and the loop is about 0.3 × 1.5 cm. This handle and the area above it (towards the rim) are red-painted, the loop being affixed at the line where the side of the bowl turns under. One end of the loop has three short horizontal incisions. A second example, also painted and incised, is lacking one end of the loop.

Zoomorphic handles were almost always used for red-painted vessels, and the handles themselves were also painted. The favourite motif was the turtle, with head and foreflippers at one end of the bowl and a tail and hindflippers at the opposite end. Incision was used to create the impression of scales, particularly on the flippers.

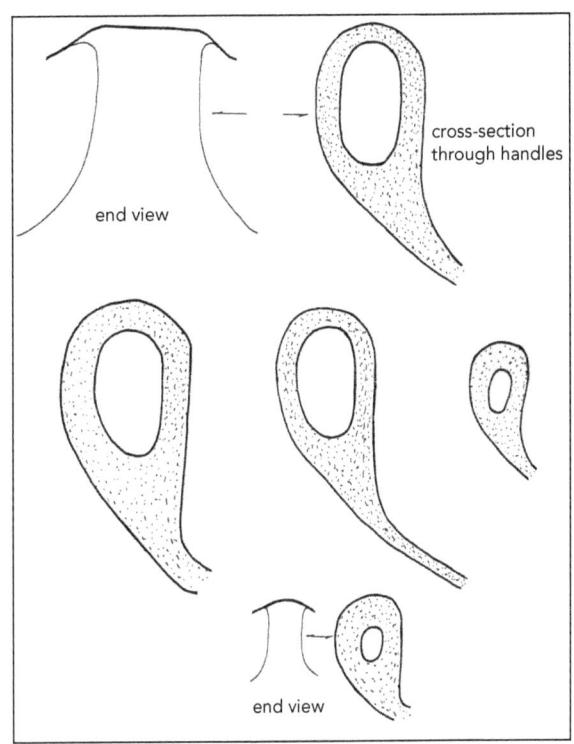

Figure 11.3 Type I handles – plain "D" handles

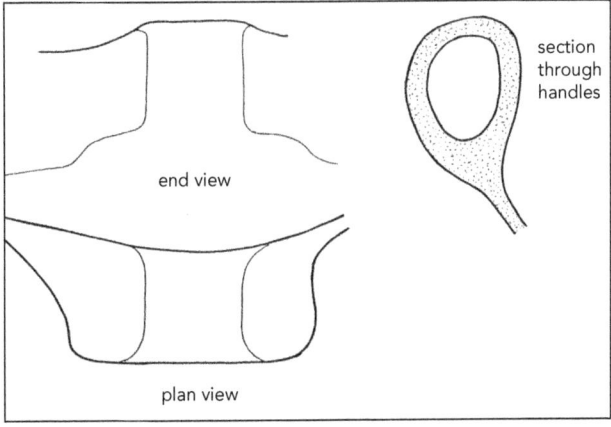

Figure 11.4 Type II handles – similar to Type I but with flared base to strap

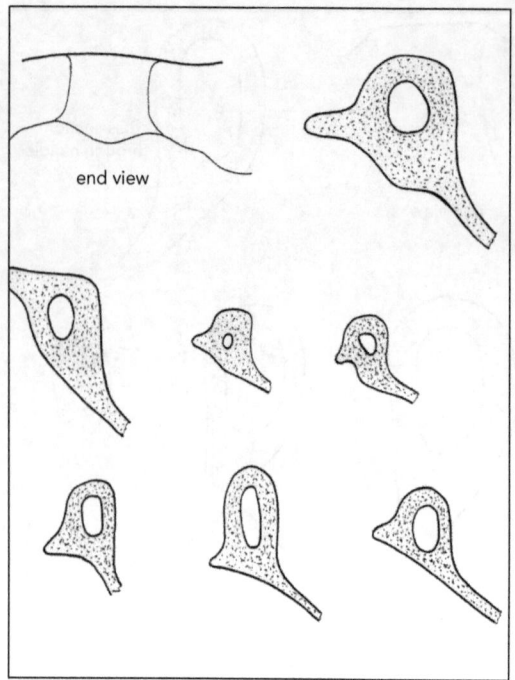

Figure 11.5 Type III handles – similar to Types I and II but with flared base and tabular spur

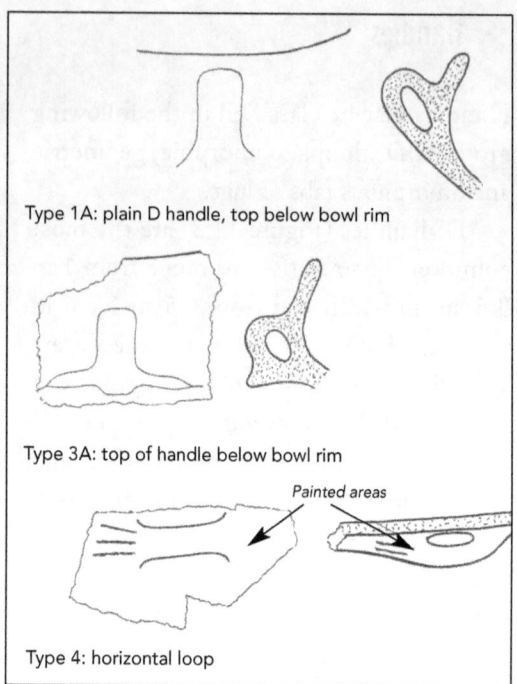

Figure 11.6 Other handle variations

Other recognizable forms depicted in Redware handles are heads of crocodiles, snakes, birds (parrot, duck) and various fish. Often the artist accentuated the eyes, mouth, gills and fins by incised lines.

The geometric class includes cylindrical to flattened oval knobs and miniatures of the bow or stern of canoes. There are indentations to produce crescentic ridges and slightly raised V-shaped patterns, which merge over into the amorphous tabs and lugs.

Miscellaneous Features of Pottery

Piercing at or just above the handle is fairly common, the holes being typically 2 to 3 mm in diameter. Some vessels had feet, and one of these has an incised pattern on its sole. One vessel has a circular incision on the inside wall directly over the foot. In addition to its chief use for zoomorphic features, incision occasionally forms abstract designs such as concentric triangles or polygons. Unexplained single or doubles lines occur on some sherds.

The author's collection contains two examples of spouts, both bluntly conical, slightly curved and with inside diameters of 5 mm at the tips. The interior of the spout of one is funnel-shaped with walls 1 cm thick. The other spout is solid except for the constant-diameter 5-mm hole.

Two more or less spheroidal pottery beads have been found in Redware sites – 1 cm and 2 cm in size – each pierced by a hole 2 mm in diameter. The larger one may possibly be a spindle whorl.

Other Artefacts

Polished petaloid greenstone celts or broken pieces of them have been found in several sites. Brother Michael excavated one 23 cm long in 1966 at Long Acre Point (E-6). A perfect specimen 5.5 cm long was collected at Alligator Pond (E-5) by the author, and three fragments were found by his daughter at the E-4 and M-4 sites.

Two off-white chalcedony beads from the E-5 site are cylindrical, about 1 cm in each dimension, and pierced longitudinally by holes 2.5 mm in diameter. An elliptical bead of milky agate found at M-4 is also pierced longitudinally. Two small pendants, or perhaps beads, from Calabash Bay (E-11) were made from a distinctive coarsely crystalline white metamorphic rock with occasional speckles of a jet-black mineral strongly resembling a rock used in the extreme southeastern Caribbean for the manufacture of similar small ornamental trinkets. Such rock is unknown in Jamaica, so there must have been trade or travel to transport these two pieces to our island. Likewise, a small figurine or *zemí* of white quartzite found at Great Pedro (E-4) is made from a type of rock that does not occur in Jamaica. Pieces of white and grey-flaked flint abound but only rarely do any show evidence of wear. Some may have been scrapers, knives or awls, while others are obviously cores from which useful flakes were struck. All have a heavy whitish patina.

Three specimens of *Oliva reticularis* with spire truncated and outer lip pierced were probably once part of either an anklet or wristlet to be shaken during dances. Other possible shell artefacts include cores of various *Strombus*, which may have been used as crude gouges, and portions of outer lips that resemble spoons or ladles. Thick conch lip fragments may have been intended as clubs. No conch celts, ceramic *zemís* or large polished stone pendants have been found yet on Redware sites.

Food

The presence of griddle fragments indicates that cassava was cultivated. Based only on casual examination of midden material, it appears that about a dozen varieties of shellfish provided the bulk of the protein consumed. These are *Strombus pugilis, S. raninus, S. gigas, Melongena melongena, Arcopagia fausta, Anadara brasiliana, A. chemmitzi, A. ovalis, Arca imbricate, A. zebra* and *Donax denticulatus*.

Burials

No midden burials have been found yet, but two caves are known to have had human bones in close association with Redware potsherds, suggesting that secondary burial in caves was practised at least to a limited degree. There is no evidence that Redware people were responsible for any of the Jamaican petroglyphs or pictographs.

Conclusion

Having recognized that this early Arawak culture is so different from the later White Marl period, we should identify topics for future study that will enable us to clarify parts of the overall picture that are today still hazy. We should, for instance, obtain more radiocarbon dates to reinforce the single date we now have and to determine the span of occupation by checking ages for several sites. There is no published report of a systematic excavation of a Jamaican Redware site.

Limestone areas surrounding the south-coast Redware sites could be explored for burial caves to see whether the practice of secondary burial was rare or common. Most important, there should be exchange of information among the researchers of the Greater Antilles to establish migration routes and comparisons of this culture in its several locations.

12 Taíno Ceramics from Post-Contact Jamaica

Robyn P. Woodward

The expanding economies of renaissance Europe created a demand for luxury goods, especially spices to make food edible, and precious metals. The objective of the fifteenth- and early sixteenth-century voyages of reconnaissance, sponsored first by the Portuguese Crown and later by the other western European powers, was not discovery for its own sake but rather the opening of oceanic routes to the rich markets of the east: India, China and Japan. The heroic accomplishments of these early explorers, however, obscure the true effects of European colonialism on local ecologies and the cultural structures and practices of indigenous people. These effects occurred as a consequence of the sustained contact between the Old World and New which began on 12 October 1492 – the day Christopher Columbus arrived in the Caribbean.

The discovery of gold, and the Spanish need for labour to exploit this resource, dominated the initial Caribbean phase of the conquest. Consideration of settlement and structured colonization were subordinate to the desire of amassing a quick profit from the labours of Indian slaves (Hennessy 1993, 9). The comparative dearth of archival records for this initial phase of Hispanic–Indian contact in the Caribbean means that the material culture – of both Europeans and Indians – recovered from archaeological excavations is essential to enable our understanding of cultural adaptation, state formation and dissolution, labour arrangements, race, class and gender – all of which shaped this period of momentous historical change (Paynter 2000, 170). The analysis of the aboriginal ceramics and faunal remains from the fortress at the Spanish town site of Sevilla la Nueva in Jamaica provides an understanding of how some of these processes worked to shape the colonial society of a primarily agricultural settlement during the first decades of the sixteenth century (Figure 12.1).

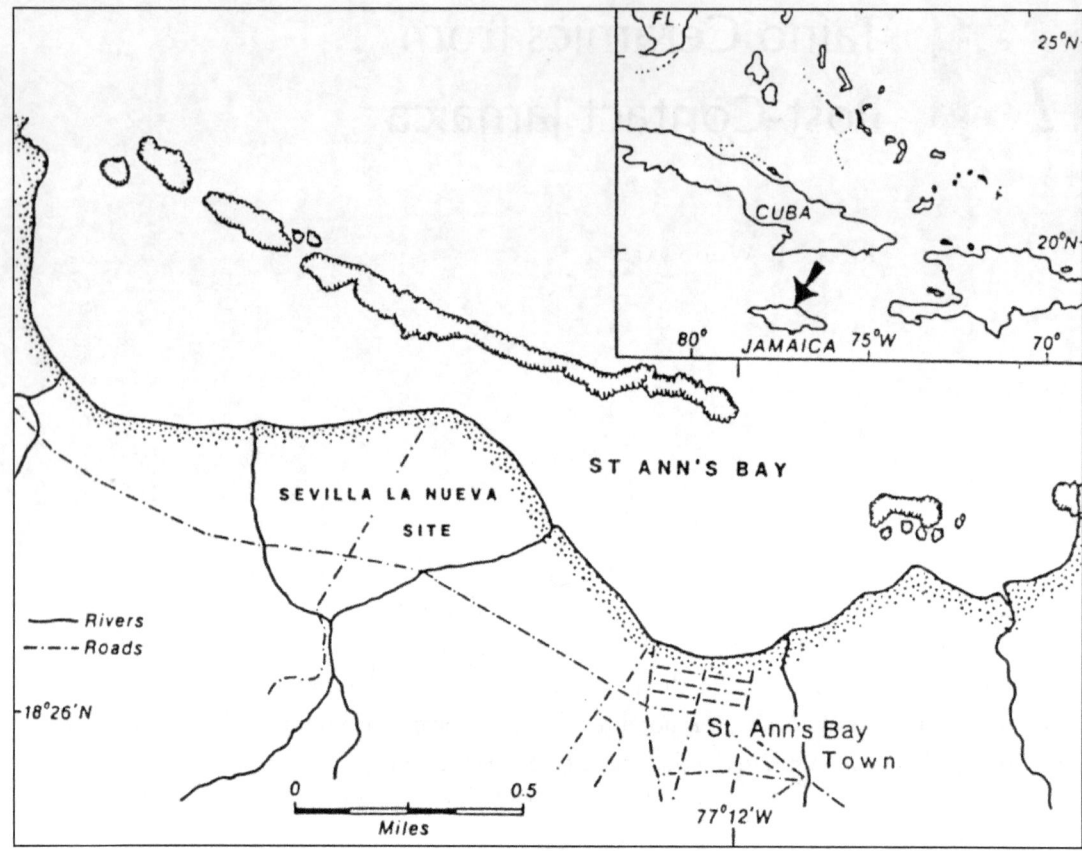

Figure 12.1 Map of St Ann's Bay, Jamaica

A major part of the initial Spanish colonial enterprise was concerned with the organization and exploitation of mineral and human resources of the Greater Antilles. The strategies and policies that were developed to achieve these objectives not only had a profound impact on the peoples of the Caribbean but ultimately shaped Spanish attitudes and colonial institutions, which were subsequently implemented throughout their empire (Deagan 1988, 188). No single institution was to have a more profound impact than that of the *encomienda*, a policy of forced labour, in which the Crown granted certain Spanish settlers a restricted set of property rights over a specified number of local Indians for use as labourers for mining, construction, transportation and, later, farming. The Spanish were entitled to extract tribute from their Indian labourers in the form of goods, precious metals or direct labour services in exchange for "protection" and instruction in the Catholic religion and civilization (Yeager 1990, 843). These entitlements could not be sold or rented, nor could they be inherited past a second generation or relocated from the geographical area in which they were originally granted (ibid.). When and wherever peaceful relations existed between the two groups, the organization and distribution of native labour was effected through the *caciques* – native chiefs (Deagan 1988, 198). Resistance to these forced labour arrangements was frequent, resulting in outright enslavement or massacres of whole villages (Rouse 1992, 154). The absence of young males and females from the villages disrupted the traditional social hierarchy and lifeways of the various indigenous peoples, and this, combined with exposure to European disease, caused a precipitous decline in the indigenous population, first on the island of Hispaniola and later throughout the region. The need for additional slaves to mine gold on Hispaniola was the major impetus for the exploratory expeditions to Cuba, Puerto Rico, Florida and Central America.

Spanish Settlement in Jamaica

The history of Jamaica and of the first Spanish settlement on the island, Sevilla la Nueva, is elaborately entwined with that of Christopher Columbus and his heirs (Woodward 1988, 9). He discovered the north coast of the island on his second voyage to the New World. Entering the present-day St Ann's Bay, which he named Santa Gloria, on 5 May 1494, the admiral declared that the island was the "fairest that eyes had beheld, mountainous and heavily populated" (Morison 1974, 126). In 1503, nearing the end of his fourth and final voyage to the Caribbean, Columbus was forced to return to this bay and remained there for more than a year due to the waterlogged condition of his two remaining ships. Columbus returned to Spain in late 1504 and died within a year.

In 1508, Diego Colon, Columbus's eldest son, was appointed governor of the Indies. In an effort to forestall any further erosion of his family's claims in the New World, he charged Juan de Esquivel with the responsibility of colonizing Jamaica. Esquivel had been on Hispaniola for some years and was a battle-hardened lieutenant of Nicolás de Ovando, the former governor of the Indies and Diego Colon's immediate predecessor (Rouse 1992). Esquivel landed on the island in 1510 with eighty settlers and established the settlement of Sevilla la Nueva, in the bay of Santa Gloria, which was known to have both a sheltered harbour and a large, peaceful Indian populace (Cotter 1970, 15).

Shortly after their arrival in 1509, the Spanish discovered that Jamaica lacked the rich alluvial gold resources of Hispaniola. The Crown encouraged the settlers to turn their efforts to raising food crops and European livestock to support other expeditions to Central and South America (Wright 1921, 71). Columbus and Peter Martyr (the first Abbot of Jamaica, albeit he actually never visited the island) wrote extensively about Jamaica's fertile soil, large native population and finely fashioned canoes (Sauer 1966, 179). However, reports of the brutal atrocities carried out by Esquivel and his men against rebellious Taíno Indians resulted in the appointment of Francisco de Garay as Esquivel's replacement in 1513.

Garay did not arrive on the island from Spain until May 1515, bringing with him skilled farmers and livestock for the two estates that he was to own in partnership with King Ferdinand. The period of Garay's governorship appears to have been a relatively prosperous one for Jamaica. There was a steady build-up of Spanish settlers, agricultural resources and livestock, the establishment of a second town and the development of sugar estates and two mills owned by the governor himself (Wright 1921, 76). Garay left the island with a number of the island's Spanish residents in June 1523 to lead an expedition of conquest in Northern New Spain (Cundall and Pietersz 1919, 6). The subsequent discovery of the rich mineral resources of Central and South America, given the depletion of human and mineral resources in the Antilles, diverted the attention of the Spanish Crown away from the Caribbean.

By 1524 the fortunes of Jamaica had entered a period of drastic decline, and in 1528 the king's estates were dissolved, with the livestock and land divided among the remaining residents (Wright 1921). Sevilla la Nueva was abandoned in 1534 when the island's administrative centre moved to Ville de la Vega, on the south coast, near the sugar estate of Pedro de Mazuelo, the island's treasurer.

The driving force behind the early colonial economy in the sixteenth-century Caribbean was aboriginal labour; without it, the Spanish could not have mined the alluvial gold beds, established agricultural estates or built towns. Many contemporary historians believe that Jamaica, like many other islands of the region, was exploited for its human resources, and this, combined with disease, resulted in the virtual extinction of the indigenous Taíno Indians by 1520 (Sauer 1966, 181). A closer examination of archival records for Jamaica, however, details Indian slaves at work on the abbey in Sevilla la Nueva in 1526. In 1533 there were two censuses of Indians, slaves and cattle, and as late as 1597 authorities were discussing how to settle the remaining Indians (Cundall and Pietersz 1919, 7–8, 20). The archaeological record from Sevilla la Nueva supports these archival sources, in that it appears that the local Taíno Indians were present at the site throughout its short occupation.

Archaeological Investigation of Sevilla la Nueva

The fortress at Sevilla la Nueva (Figure 12.2) was excavated by Charles Cotter between 1953 and 1964. It yielded a large collection of carved limestone blocks, Spanish bricks, tiles, ceramic vessels, beads, Taíno ceramics and mixed faunal materials. The structure had substantial stone and brick foundations, brick floors, and a brick-lined cellar and vaulted cistern. Horizontal spatial

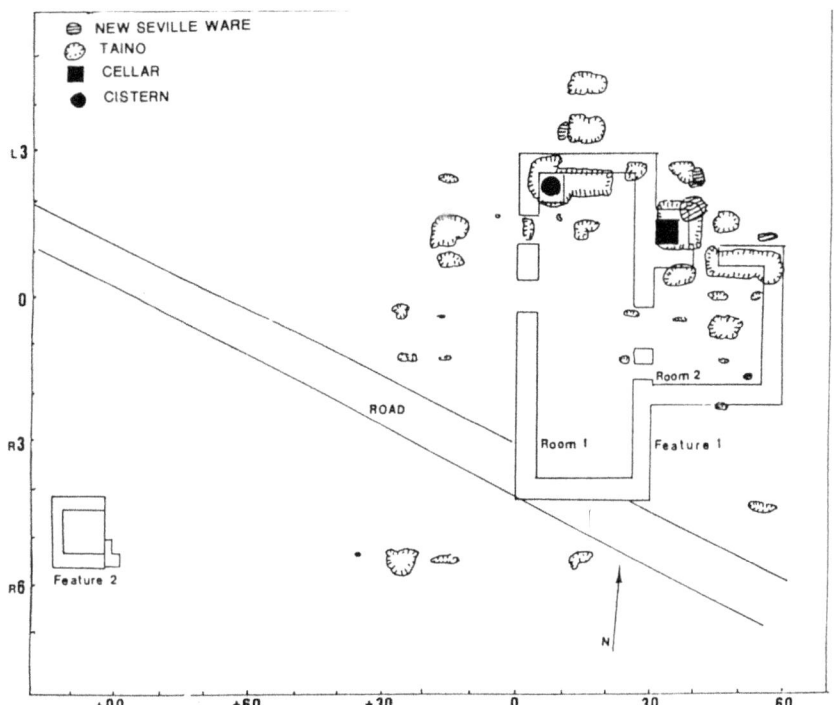

Figure 12.2 Distribution of New Seville and Taíno ceramics

control was maintained during this investigation, but because of the relatively short occupancy of the town and the fact that this land was used only for agriculture in later historical times, Cotter did not document temporal distinctions. Upon his death, Cotter's unpublished collection of artefacts and field notes were left to the Institute of Jamaica, and I subsequently studied them as part of my research for my master's thesis. It should be noted that this fortress was investigated by Dr Lorenzo López y Sebastián between 1981 and 1986, but materials recovered during this later project have not been published or made available for study.

Taíno Ceramics

Ceramics manufactured by the local indigenous people were the most common ceramic type in the assemblage from the fortress area. Based on the documented material discovered by Cotter, 63.3 per cent of the vessel-form ceramics from the fortress were Taíno, and 1.3 per cent of the total was New Seville ware, a locally manufactured Hispanic–Taíno Indian colonoware. Spanish tin-glazed majolica tableware accounts for just 6.7 per cent of the total, and Spanish lead-glazed and unglazed storage- and tableware make up the remaining 28.7 per cent of the assemblage (Woodward 1988, 50). The intrusive European ceramics from the seventeenth, eighteenth and nineteenth centuries that Cotter collected from across the whole lower estate were not factored into this analysis.

The Casimiroid peoples began human occupation of the West Indies around 4000 BC (Rouse 1992, 51). The first settlers of Jamaica were the Ostionoids, who expanded south and west through the island of Hispaniola and across the Jamaica Channel to the south coast of Jamaica by AD 650 (Atkinson 2003, 1). The Meillacan Ostionoids, who would evolve into the Western Taínos of Jamaica and parts of Cuba, were present in Jamaica by 880 BC (Rouse 1992, 96). The White Marl style of the Meillacan subseries of pottery is characteristic of all Meillacan and Western Taíno sites in Jamaica, and St Ann's Bay in particular (ibid., 52). This ware is characterized by coil-constructed vessels, the coils being set and then shaped by an anvil-and-paddle technique rather than by scraping (Howard 1950, 140). The pottery varies in colour from brick-red through dull brown and even black. A dull polish was applied to the exterior surfaces of most vessels. Temper was not normally added to the clays; the sand or marl particles that are in evidence appear to have been part of the original clay. The paste of the Taíno sherds found in Cotter's collection from the fortress conforms to this tradition.

The shapes of the White Marl–style vessels are limited to thin-walled (averaging 8 mm) carinated boat-shaped or round bowls (ibid., 141). Both these bowl forms have symmetrically rounded bottoms and frequently have distinctive shoulders (Figure 12.3). Regardless of whether the bowls have a shoulder or not, the sides of these vessels invariably curve inward towards the rim so that the opening of the bowl is smaller than the greatest diameter of the vessel (ibid., 138).

The rims of the White Marl–style vessels are predominantly rounded or slightly rectangular in shape (Figure 12.4a–e). The second variant is a filleted rim, which has a strip or thin fillet of clay applied along the exterior edge (Figure 12.4f–h) or, less frequently, along the interior edge (Figure 12.4i). Decorated rims are rare, but when they are encountered, they are more elaborate than on contemporaneous vessels from elsewhere in the Caribbean. Decorative devices include incised designs (Figure 12.5a), cross-hatching (Figure 12.5c), and closely spaced parallel incisions placed along the top edge of the

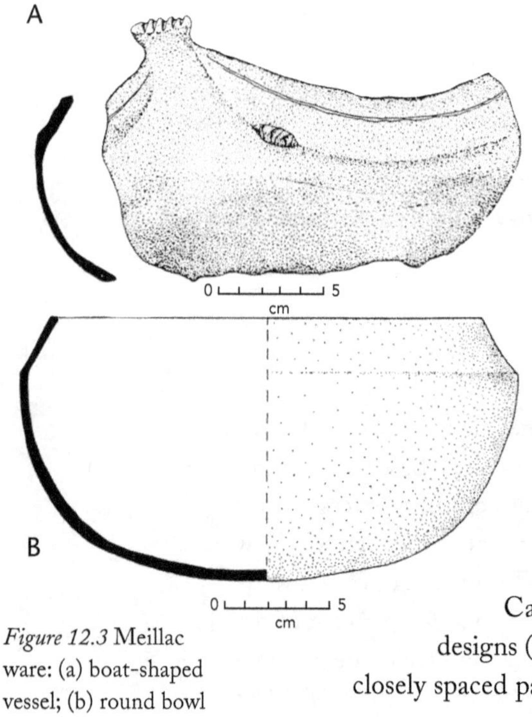

Figure 12.3 Meillac ware: (a) boat-shaped vessel; (b) round bowl

rim to create a serrated effect (Figure 12.5b, d). The collection also contains one example of a thicker, more massive decorated rim, characteristic of the variant Montego Bay style (Howard 1950, 144–45). It has incised oblique parallel lines running down from the rim to the shoulder. Finally, there is one sherd that has a perforation between the appliquéd shoulder ridges below the rim (Figure 12.5f). This perforation appears to be utilitarian in nature, permitting the bowl to be suspended (ibid., 151).

Excavations at other Taíno sites on Jamaica have demonstrated that although plain rounded rims are always present in greater numbers, there is a tendency in the later levels towards an increase in the number of filleted rims (James W. Lee, personal communication, 1984). Of the rims from Sevilla la Nueva, 56.14 per cent are plain, 36.84 per cent are filleted and 7.02 per cent are decorated (Woodward 1988, 103). Based on this collection of Taíno ceramics excavated by Cotter from the fortress, there is no evidence that the indigenous ceramic style went through a phase of simplification in form or degradation of quality, as has been documented at contact-period colonial sites in Cuba, Haiti and Nueva Cadiz (Willis 1976, 143; Deagan 1983, 295).

The Cotter collection includes three round, plain-rimmed bowls, two of which have distinct shoulders and polished exteriors. These bowls (the largest of which is illustrated in Figure 12.3b) have diameters of 16.5 cm, 23 cm and 32 cm. The bottom of the smallest bowl has been blackened from use over a fire. The large fragment belonging to a boat-shaped bowl (Figure 12.3a) has a filleted rim and an upraised prow at the remaining end. The incised wedge knobs on either side of this prow are its only form of decoration. The presence of smoke patches on the lower regions of this bowl indicates that it was also used for cooking.

The collection contains one round, single-spouted inhaling bowl (Figure 12.6) that is a unique

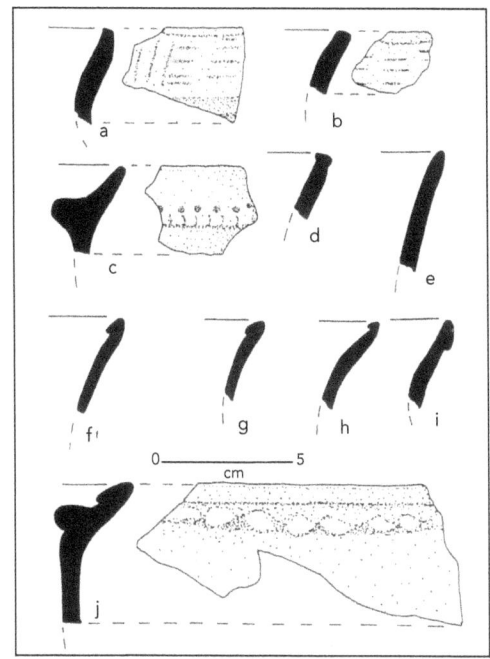

Figure 12.4 Rim profiles

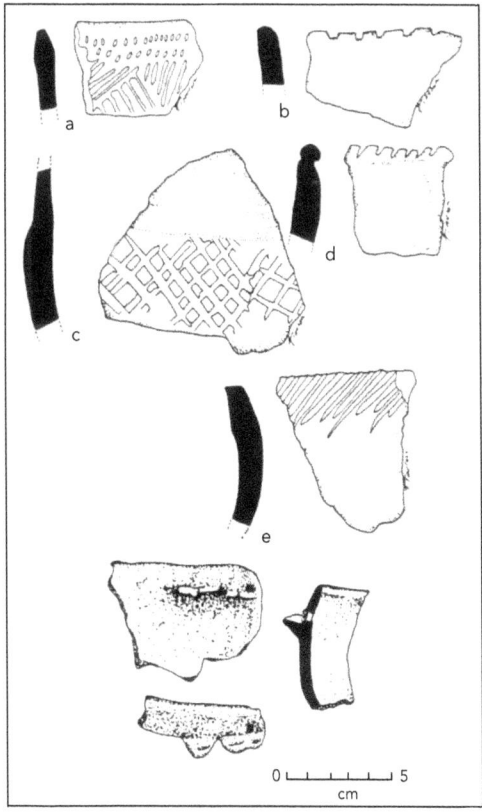

Figure 12.5 Decorated rim sherds

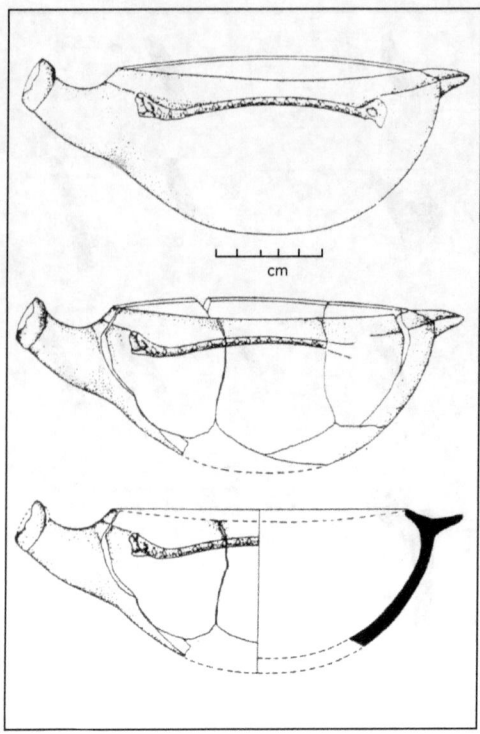

Figure 12.6 Spouted bowl

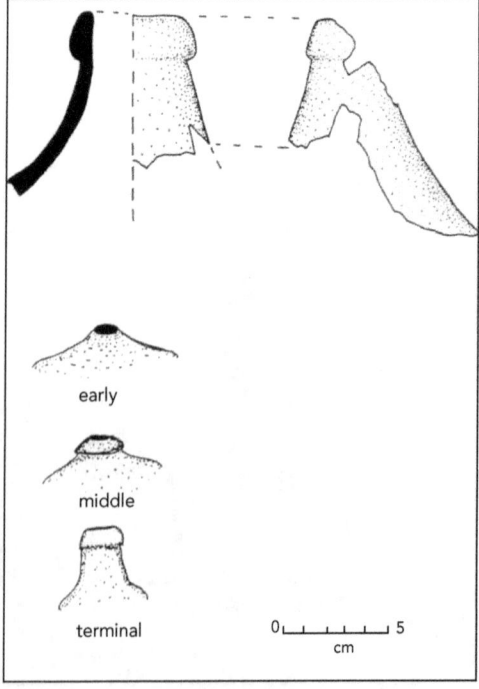

Figure 12.7 Taíno water bottle

example of this vessel form in Jamaica (Lee, personal communication, 1984). It is generally accepted that the spout would have acted as an inhaling device and that these bowls were used in the ritual inhaling of *cohobas*, hallucinogenic powders (Kaye, 1999, 59). Taíno ritual paraphernalia is commonly decorated with anthropomorphic or zoomorphic imagery, and in the inverted position this small bowl resembles a turtle. Turtles feature prominently in the creation myths of the Taíno (ibid., 65). Other ceremonial Taíno artefacts such as *zemís* (statuettes), *duhos* (ceremonial chairs) and vomitive spatulas are commonly found in ritual settings, such as cave burials, where access is controlled and limited to those of high social standing in the community. Inhaling bowls, however, have most frequently been found in domestic midden burials, perhaps demonstrating a wider participation in ritual activity than previously believed (ibid., 61).

Figure 12.7 depicts the well-defined neck and spout of a Taíno water bottle found at the Spanish fortress. Although no precise chronological sequence has been developed for these bottles, it is thought that the neck and spout became more pronounced during this terminal period (Lee, personal communication, 1984). Water bottles were typically well fired on the outside, but due to their small aperture, their interior surfaces were poorly finished.

Sixteen fragments of Taíno cassava griddles, or *buréns*, were present in the assemblage. These are flat, circular platters, 30 to 60 cm in diameter, made of very coarse tempered earthenware. These clay platters are typically suspended on rocks above a fire. The Jamaican *buréns* usually have a smooth upper surface that at times may have been burnished, and a rough, heavily pitted underside. The griddle fragments ranged from 12.2 to 22.5 cm in thickness. Owing to the fact that these thick *buréns* were fired at a low temperature, they are frequently friable (Lee, personal communication, 1984). The single griddle-rim sherd has a slightly upturned or bevelled outer edge, which is a common feature of Jamaican *buréns*.

The Spanish called cassava "the bread of the Indies", and these *buréns* have been reported from all Taíno sites in the Caribbean, attesting to the universal use of cassava as a dietary staple in the region (Lee 1980a, 1). As wheat did not grow well on the Caribbean islands and shipments of grain from Spain were sporadic, cassava bread was somewhat reluctantly adopted into the Spanish diet early in the conquest period (Faerron 1985, 2). Not only was cassava readily available, it also had the advantage over traditional grain-based breads of being able to be stored for months without spoiling (Lee 1980a, 2).

Cotter's notes indicate that the majority of the Taíno ceramics were found in the area of the cellar and on the floor in the northern end of Room 2 in the Spanish fortress. There was a second major concentration of this material around the well and in the two refuse dumps north of the fortress (see Figure 12.2). Obviously these vessels played an integral role in food preparation by the Spanish inhabitants, and the presence of cassava *buréns* further suggests the adoption by the Spanish of some of the aboriginal subsistence traditions.

New Seville Ware

From the time Esquivel arrived in Jamaica in 1509, the Spanish, under the policy of the *encomienda*, had a large aboriginal work force under their command. While locally produced Taíno ceramics were widely used by the Spanish for cookware, it is evident from the presence of a unique style of colonoware in the Cotter collection that native potters were also being organized to work at craft production in this colony. Thirty-two sherds and seven vessels can be identified as belonging to a category of pottery now designated as "New Seville ware". The presence of this style of syncretic Hispanic–Indian ware demonstrates a degree of cultural adaptation at the domestic level that has only been found at a few sixteenth-century Spanish contact sites, and never in this form. Hispanic–Indian colonoware was found at Concepción de la Vega on Hispaniola. That pottery, however, exhibits characteristics of the ceramics of the South American Arawaks as opposed to those of the Western Taíno (Deagan 1988, 210). Archaeologists have suggested that the

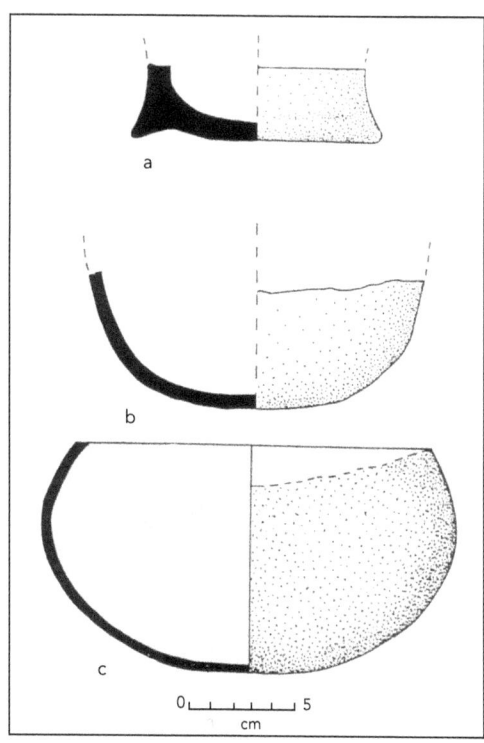

Figure 12.8 New Seville ware bowls

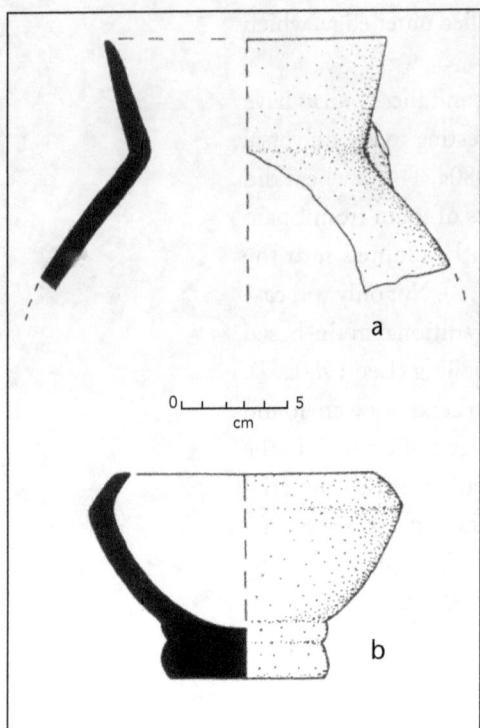

Figure 12.9 New Seville ware: (a) pitcher; (b) pedestal cup

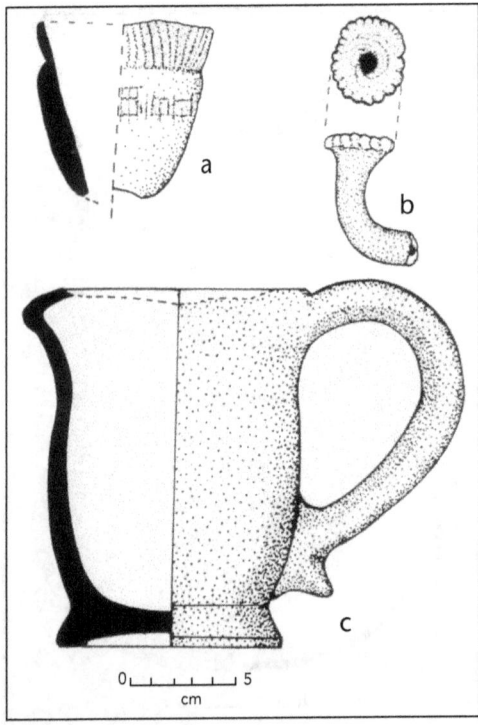

Figure 12.10 New Seville ware (a) cup; (b) spout; (c) jug

presence of this colonoware in Hispaniola represents the importation of non-Taíno Indians as slaves. Various examples of colonoware have also been found at a number of Western Taíno sites in Cuba (most notably Yalal) as well as a few Taíno sites on Hispaniola (ibid., 204). Colonowares were also encountered in late-sixteenth-century deposits at St Augustine, Florida (Deagan 1978, 33).

The vast majority of the New Seville ware sherds have sandy, pale brown to yellowish-brown paste. Like the Taíno ceramics, these pottery vessels are constructed of hand-formed coils, in contrast to the wheel-thrown tradition of European ceramics. Included in this group are six base sherds from small bowls that either have a triangular wedge pushed onto the rounded base as a crudely formed ring-foot (Figure 12.8a) or show clearly where this wedge has been sheared off. Figure 12.8b depicts the most complete example of these bowls. It has a diameter of 11 cm, and two others have a diameter of 16 cm. These bowls are similar in size to the Columbia Plain majolica *escudillas* found at the site and invariably served as substitutes for this form of Spanish tableware. There are also two rims/shoulder fragments of small open-mouthed jars or pitchers. One of these fragments is the neck and round shoulder of a jug (Figure 12.9a). Finally, there are eighteen fragments of small round handles, a device not used on any White Marl–style vessel.

Two examples of New Seville ware in the Cotter collection are complete vessels: a small jug and a pedestal cup. The coil-constructed pedestal cup (Figures 12.9b, 12.12) appears to have the same paste as the majority of the Taíno sherds in the collection: dark brown to black, with a dull polish on the exterior surface. The interior is more highly polished than the exterior, and the cup has a solid ribbed pedestal and base.

The handmade jug (Figures 12.10c, 12.11) has the same paste as the cup, and finger indentations are clearly visible on the interior of this 6-mm-thick

Figure 12.11 New Seville ware: jug   *Figure 12.12* New Seville pedestal cup

vessel. The handle is not completely round but is similar in shape and thickness to the other handle fragments of New Seville ware mentioned above. The base of the jug has a flat outer rim and a slightly concave centre. Both these vessels were found in Room 1 of the fortress and were obviously used as Spanish tableware (Cotter n.d., 39).

The other two New Seville ware vessels in this collection were a small cup decorated with parallel, incised lines around the rim (Figure 12.10a), and a spout from an unknown type of vessel (Figure 12.10b). The decoration of both these vessels is consistent with the decorated rims of White Marl style bowls; their European forms, however, indicate that they were locally crafted copies of Spanish wares.

Faunal Remains

Faunal evidence from the fortress at Sevilla la Nueva indicates that European domestic animals account for 95 per cent of the biomass. Pig was the most commonly occurring species, accounting for 33 per cent of the total biomass, while local marine fish and molluscs accounted for just 3 per cent. Nearly half of the mammalian bones from the site belonged to medium- to large-sized animals that were unidentifiable but are believed to be pig (McEwan 1982).

As was first observed at St Augustine, Florida, and subsequently at many other sixteenth-century Spanish-contact sites in the Caribbean, Spanish settlers preferred and attempted to maintain Iberian lifeways, especially in the more visible areas such as tableware, diet, ornamentation and architecture (Deagan 1983; Ewan 1991; McEwan 1995). Those households with the highest socioeconomic status were expected to have greater access to scarce imported goods. The reliance of the inhabitants of the fortress at Sevilla la Nueva on imported domestic mammals would therefore be expected. The faunal assemblage is highly fragmented, and very few bones exhibit any sign of being charred, suggesting that the meat was boiled rather than roasted. Traditional Iberian food-preparation techniques emphasized boiling versus roasting (McEwan 1982, 6), and pork dishes were preferred by the upper classes (ibid.). The faunal assemblage of the Cotter collection conforms to the pattern of upper-class Iberian food preferences. The almost total absence of fish in the diet of the fortress inhabitants could also be predicted, as fish was the common food of the lower-status Spanish peasants and the indigenous peoples of the region.

Discussion

The Spanish settlers at Sevilla la Nueva, as elsewhere in the Caribbean, held the dominant political position over the local Indian inhabitants and controlled them through the auspices of the hierarchical structure of the local Amerindian societies. Within the Spanish contingent there were also social distinctions: the *conquistadors* and high government officials of the Crown formed the upper social class and held the economic power, while the rest of the settlers, who were tradesmen and commoners, tended to be less exclusivist and were normally in more direct contact with the non-Hispanic people. These commoners tended toward more exchange and racial mixing with the local Amerindian population and also were the social class most influenced by the process of acculturation with the Indians (Esteva-Fabregat 1995, 19).

> *Acculturation*: is a phenomenon resulting from the addition to an already existent cultural system of one or various elements of another, or other systems. These additions appear in the form of isolated traits or of complexes that, upon joining the system, modify the ingredients of social action and thus the cultural system without necessarily transforming its political or social structure. (ibid., 5)

In the early decades of the sixteenth century, the majority of Spanish immigrants were young, unmarried men from the lower ranks of the nobility or from the working class, seeking fortunes to better their social positions at home (Pérez-Mallaína 1998, 35). As only 6 per cent of the Spanish immigrants were women, unions between Spanish men and Indian women were common (Hennessy 1993, 17). The church naturally encouraged formal marriages, especially unions with either female *caciques* (local chiefs) or the daughters of the *caciques*. These politically motivated unions were thought to ensure the cooperation and even subservience of the local Indians. However, multiple unions of an informal, polygynous nature, between Spanish men of every social class and Indian women, were more frequently the case in the early decades of the conquest (Esteva-Fabregat 1995, 34). Whereas family migration was common among English settlers along the eastern seaboard of North America in the seventeenth century, the widespread incorporation of Amerindian women into domestic unions with Spanish settlers gave rise to a distinct "Spanish Colonial pattern" that is reflected in the archaeological remains of all contact-period sites (Deagan 1983; McEwan 1995).

By the second decade of the sixteenth century, Santo Domingo, on the southeast end of the island of Hispaniola, was the main port of call for supply ships from Spain. Since the prevailing trade winds in the Caribbean come from the southeast, Jamaica is downwind of Hispaniola. As the island lacked lucrative mineral resources, there was little reason for trading vessels to visit the island unless they were already bound for the Central American coast or were in need of foodstuffs. With the exception of European domestic animals (which were raised on the island in great numbers) and a small quantity of Iberian ceramics, Cotter did not recover any glassware, candleholders, clothing and sewing accessories, personal items, weapons, hooks or ornaments during his excavation of the fortress. This seems to support the premise that this isolated colony on the Spanish frontier not only was less well supplied with European merchandise than other contact-period sites such as Nueva Cadiz, Puerto Real or even the later settlement of St Augustine (Woodward 1988, 113; McEwan 1995, 216–17), but also had few Hispanic women. As such, the upper-class inhabitants of the fortress at Sevilla la Nueva were forced to adapt more fully to their new environment than those residing closer to the major colonial centres on Hispaniola or even to the rich pearl-fishing colony of Nueva Cadiz, off the coast of Venezuela (McEwan 1995; Willis 1976).

Conclusion

The high social standing of the inhabitants of the fortress at Sevilla la Nueva is reflected in their diet and in the presence of majolica tableware and elaborate architectural ornamentation. The presence of aboriginal ceramics and the evidence of some aboriginal food-preparation techniques indicate that local Taíno women were employed in daily domestic activities. It appears that both the remoteness of this colony and the lack of Spanish women forced even the highest-status Hispanic settlers to engage in some degree of cultural mixing.

Lack of access to Iberian tableware and drinking vessels caused the residents of Sevilla la Nueva to organize a craft industry to produce locally manufactured equivalents. In so doing, the Spanish settlers resisted the outright adoption of aboriginal vessel forms in the visible arena of dining, in an attempt to maintain their traditional Iberian cultural norms.

Despite the predominance of European domestic animals in the diet of the fortress's residents, the presence of cassava *buréns* suggests that the inhabitants also adopted cassava bread as a substitute for their grain-based breads.

The degree to which the lower-class Spanish settlers at Sevilla la Nueva were able to maintain their traditional lifeways has yet to be determined, as no other residential features have been identified or investigated. Based on the archaeological evidence from St Augustine and Puerto Real, one might expect to see varying patterns of acculturation based on social status (McEwan 1995).

Examining the Cotter collection material from the perspective of the Taíno women, one could suggest that the lack of Spanish domestic materials at Sevilla la Nueva enabled them to maintain a small degree of cultural autonomy within a totally Hispanic setting. Archaeological evidence demonstrates that they used their traditional cooking wares to prepare food, even if they were forced to adopt some Hispanic food-preparation techniques, such as boiling rather than roasting meats. While Spanish materials have shown up in surface collections at White Marl, the large Taíno site on the south coast of Jamaica, the degree to which the indigenous population of St Ann's Bay incorporated Hispanic food or materials into their traditional lifeways during the first decades of contact has yet to be determined (Goggin 1968, 36). Likewise, it has been noted that the degradation of local ceramic traditions is not immediately apparent from the materials found in the domestic assemblage of the Spanish fortress. The effects of the Spanish colonization on the indigenous social structures, farming techniques and craft industries will truly be determined only through controlled excavations of the several Taíno sites on the hills surrounding the site of Sevilla la Nueva.

As at all other Spanish colonial sites in the Caribbean, the Spanish colonial pattern is evident at Sevilla la Nueva; however, the diversity in cultural patterning and the degree to which any individual or culture is forced to integrate were clearly influenced by the processes of economic and political domination, the degree of remoteness of specific colonies, race, social status and gender. The examination of Taíno ceramics and faunal materials from the fortress at Sevilla la Nueva demonstrates that even in the narrow domestic arena, a variety of cultural syncretisms evolved in response to the differing economic and natural environment of frontier communities, as well as social spheres of the individual inhabitants.

ART IS A CRITICAL and continual aspect of the human experience. Art, regardless of chronology and geographic locale, has been used to express thoughts,

Section 4

Taíno Art Forms

emotions, beliefs and events. It can be religious, functional, aesthetic or documentary. Ramón Dacal Moure and Manuel Rivero de la Calle, in *Art and Archaeology of Pre-Columbian Cuba* (1996), categorize the art of the Taíno into *idolillos,* wooden idols, figurines, *duhos* and cave art. Caves were used by the Taínos as shrines, burial sites, temporary shelters, water sources and rock art sites. Since the eighteenth century, caves in Jamaica have provided invaluable evidence of Taíno culture and art forms.

Cave art can be broken down into two main categories: *mobiliary art* and *cave art proper*. In Jamaica, there is evidence of both categories. Mobiliary art consists of small objects found inside caves; examples include the wooden *zemís* found in Carpenter's Mountain, Manchester (1799), and Aboukir, St Ann (1992).

Cave art proper consists of petroglyphs – carvings – and pictographs – paintings – found inside caves. Petroglyphs can be located on almost every Caribbean island, in both the Greater and the Lesser Antilles (Bullen 1974). In Jamaica, the earliest known petroglyph site was the Dryland Cave, St Mary, from 1820. This site is now known as One Bubby Susan, found in Woodside, St Mary. The Mountain River Cave, St Catherine, is the earliest known pictograph site, discovered in 1896 (Duerden 1897).

The two chapters in this section discuss the Taíno art forms found in Jamaica. James W. Lee's paper "The Petroglyphs of Jamaica" was published in 1990. It highlights the discovery of cave art sites before 1952 and sites discovered between 1952 and 1985. Lee discusses the motifs of the petroglyphs and pictographs, and identifies a spatial relationship between cave art sites and occupation sites. Lee identified twenty-four cave art sites; since then an additional eleven sites have been discovered. The highest concentration of cave art sites in Jamaica is found in the southern parishes of Clarendon, St Elizabeth,

St Catherine and Manchester.

Ethnographic data reveal that Jamaican Taínos are renowned for several things – cotton, cassava bread, celts and, most important, wooden idols. After he assessed the three wooden sculptures from Carpenter's Mountain in 1792, William Faggs said:

> It is remarkable, since rather few figures in wood have been found in the Americas, that this one tribe, the Arawak, has produced so many works of supreme sculptural merit, fit to be compared with the best tribal works of the other continents, and, so far as the surviving works allow us to judge, probably the finest works of wood sculpture produced in the Americas before or since Columbus. (National Gallery of Jamaica 1992, 4)

Cave art sites in Jamaica are not as common as burial caves, and wooden *zemís* found in caves are considered rare treasures. Nicholas Saunders and Dorrick Gray, in their chapter "*Zemís*, Trees and Symbolic Landscapes: Three Taíno Carvings from Jamaica", discuss the most important Taíno find in Jamaica since the eighteenth century – the Aboukir *zemís* recovered in 1992. The Aboukir finds include a ceremonial staff, a bird figure and a small ceremonial ladle or spoon, which are now housed in the National Gallery of Jamaica.

Saunders and Gray re-examine the place of wooden *zemís* in Taíno religion. They highlight the importance of the *zemís*, the selection of the wood used in their creation and the Taíno perception of the natural world. The authors then demonstrate similarities between the Taíno view of the natural world and that of the lowland Amazon societies.

Since the discovery of the Aboukir *zemís*, a wooden *duho* has been recovered from the Hellshire Hills, St Catherine. This *duho*, dated AD 1000–1170, is currently housed in the National Gallery of Jamaica. Thus an estimated thirteen wooden objects have been obtained from Jamaican caves, located in the parishes of Manchester, St Thomas, St Ann and St Catherine.

TWENTY-FOUR PETROGLYPH and pictograph sites have been mapped in Jamaica, and reports of several others remain to be verified. All

13  The Petroglyphs of Jamaica

James W. Lee

occur in limestone terrain and have been worked in soft dripstone of rock shelters or cave entrances. By far the most common motif is a simple oval face, incised by a continuous line and three circular depressions to represent eyes and mouth. Three-dimensional figures on stalagmites or pillars are rare.

Distribution of sites suggests a spatial relationship to the White Marl (later) phase of Arawak settlement, and this is corroborated by ceramics associated with cave burials at or near several of the petroglyphs. All sites are particularly susceptible to vandalism, and only Mountain River Cave has so far been provided with permanent protection and placed in the care of the Jamaica National Trust Commission.

History of Site Reports

Early Period

Four petroglyph sites were known in Jamaica before the beginning of the twentieth century (Duerden 1897). By 1952, three of these locations had been "lost" to the scientific community as a result of inadequate descriptions in the early reports and subsequent lack of public interest. The lone exception was Pantrepant, Trelawny, owned until recently by Mr Frank Roxburgh, whose wife was the sister of the well-known amateur archaeologist Captain Charles Cotter. Cotter's frequent visits to his sister and brother-in-law allowed him to check the original Pantrepant East site from time to time and led to his discovery of the second group of carvings on the west side of the same property.

Originally published in 1990, in *Proceedings of the Eleventh International Congress for Caribbean Archaeology, Puerto Rico, 1985*: 153–61.

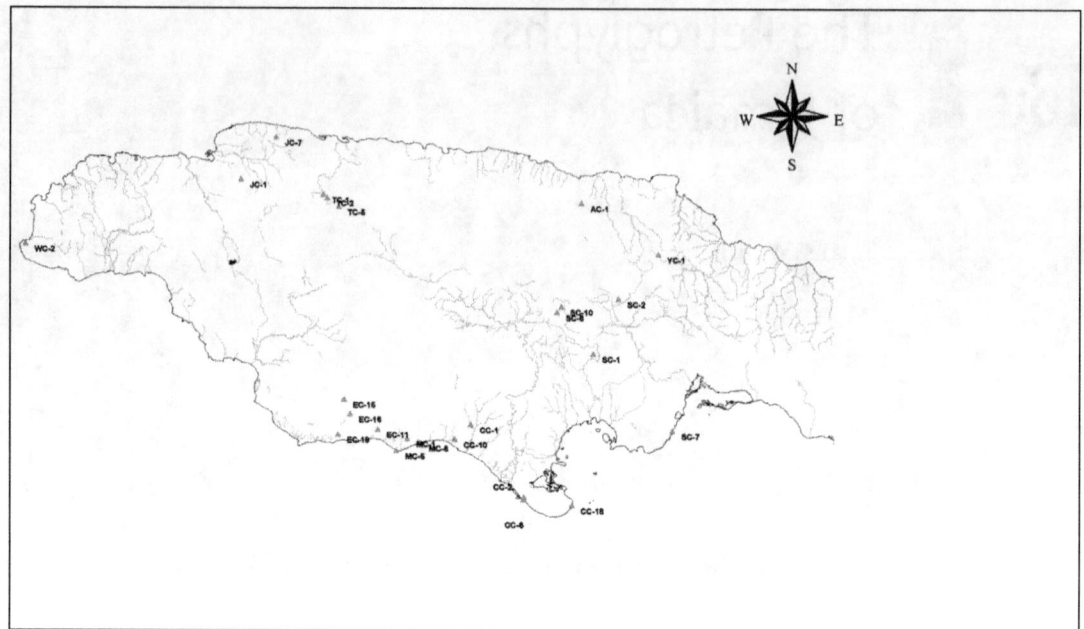

Figure 13.1 Map of cave art sites

These two sites, fortunately, have suffered minimal wear and tear compared with the damage to other petroglyphs by vandals, who chop and hack for no reason at all.

The other three sites described by Duerden are at Dryland, St Mary, known from about 1820, though not then officially reported; Kempshot, St James, seen by the property owner, Mr Maxwell Hall, from about 1872 but not recognized as aboriginal until the mid-1890s; and the Mountain River Cave, discovered shortly before the publication of Duerden's article in the *Journal of the Institute of Jamaica*.

Second Period

During the years 1897–1939, four more petroglyph sites were observed (Sherlock 1939). These comprise caves at Coventry, St Ann, reported by Miss Lily Perkins in 1913; Windsor, Trelawny, found by H.D. LaCaille in 1925; Byndloss Mountain, St Catherine, discovered by Archibald Campbell in 1931; and the Canoe Valley petroglyph cluster, first noted in 1916 by Martin and MacCormack.

Recent Period

No new petroglyph sites were identified in literature published between 1939 and 1967, but since the formation of the Archaeological Society of Jamaica, **reports** by its members have confirmed a further fifteen sites. In addition, all previously described petroglyphs except LaCaille's Windsor site have been relocated. Data for these sites are tabulated below in Table 13.1.

General Description of Sites

Brief descriptions of Jamaican petroglyphs are included in articles published by Duerden (1897, 48) and Lee (1974, 2). These writers stated that Jamaican petroglyphs are executed in limestone, a tertiary age rock that forms the western two-thirds of the island. Many, if not most, of the carvings are incised in the soft dripstone deposits coating the walls of caves or rock shelters or on pulpits, pillars, stalactites or stalagmites of the same material. Few petroglyphs are actually inside caves but rather are found at cave entrances or on the surface of massive blocks of limestone broken from sinkhole or cave walls.

The most common motif by far is the human face, portrayed by simple oval-shaped lines 1 to 2 cm wide, incised to a depth generally less than 1 cm (Figures 13.2a, c, d). Three shallow circular or oval depressions represent eyes and mouth. Variations on this basic theme include elongate-oval or straight-line incisions for the mouth (Figure 13.2b), lines running from the eyes as tears, one or more "haloes" above the head (Figures 13.3b, 13.4a), raising the eyeballs in high relief within the depression (Figure 13.3c), and steeply slanted, narrow incisions for the eyes (Figure 13.4d).

Table 13.1 New Petroglyph/Pictograph Sites, 1952–1985

Site	Parish Reference	Date	Reporter*
Spot Valley (JC-7)	St James	1970	David Fletcher 70/4
Worthy Park No. 1 (SC-6)	St Catherine	1963	Marjorie Sweeting 70/4
Two Sisters Cave (SC-7)	St Catherine	1968	Alan Teulon 88/1
Worthy Park No. 2 (SC-10)	St Catherine	1973	George Clarke 73/1
Milk River (CC-1)	Clarendon	1964	R.E. Anderson
Jackson Bay Cave (CC-2)	Clarendon	1953	C.B. Lewis
East of Jackson Bay Cave (CC-6)	Clarendon	1968	R.L. Vanderwal 68/2
God's Well (CC-10)	Clarendon	1969	J.W. Lee 69/1
Little Miller's Bay (CC-18)	Clarendon	1970	C.B. Lewis
Cuckold Point (MC-5)	Manchester	1968	Mrs Lee Hart 68/3
Gut River (MC-6)	Manchester	1969	J.W. Lee 69/1
Duff House (EC-11)	St Elizabeth	1980	Wendy A. Lee 80/1
Warminister (EC-15)	St Elizabeth	1969	J.W. Lee 80/1
Red Bank (EC-16)	St Elizabeth	1969	J.W. Lee 69/1
Reynold Bent (EC-19)	St Elizabeth	1970	J.W. Lee 70/1
Negril (WC-2)	Westmoreland	1969	E.S. Harvey 67/3

*Numbers refer to *Archaeology Jamaica* newsletters.

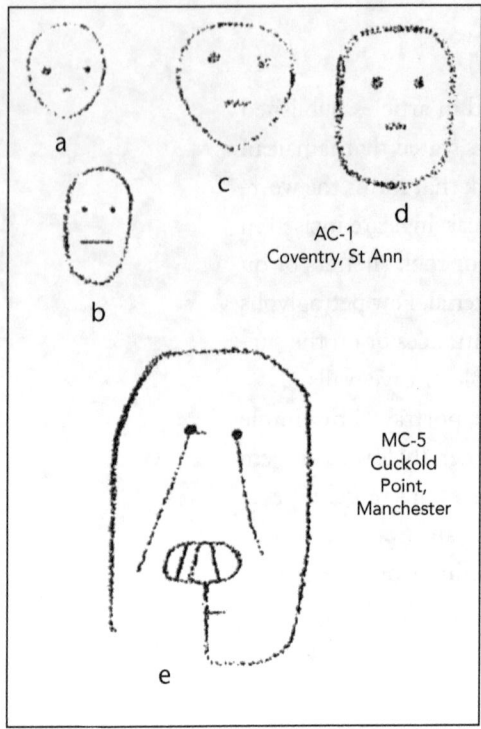

Figure 13.2 Petroglyphs from Coventry and Cuckold Point

Pillars or other vertical cave formations are often adapted to create a three-dimensional appearance for the carvings. Abstract or geometric patterns also occur but rarely.

Table 13.2 (see appendix) gives details of petroglyph locations and their proximity to known occupation sites. Figure 13.1 shows petroglyphs in relation to the principal Arawak settlements. Apart from WC-2, AC-1 and YC-1, which are relatively isolated from either settlements or other petroglyphs, the remaining occurrences comprise a central cluster of four in St Catherine; a south-coast group of thirteen, ranging from St Catherine to St Elizabeth; and another group of four in St James and Trelawny. The very dry south-coast climate may be responsible for the better survival of petroglyphs in that belt, as the geologic processes of solution and re-deposition of limestone are less active. The wetter north-coast zone probably has lost some aboriginal sculptures in limestone because of either more rapid solution by rainwater or faster build-up

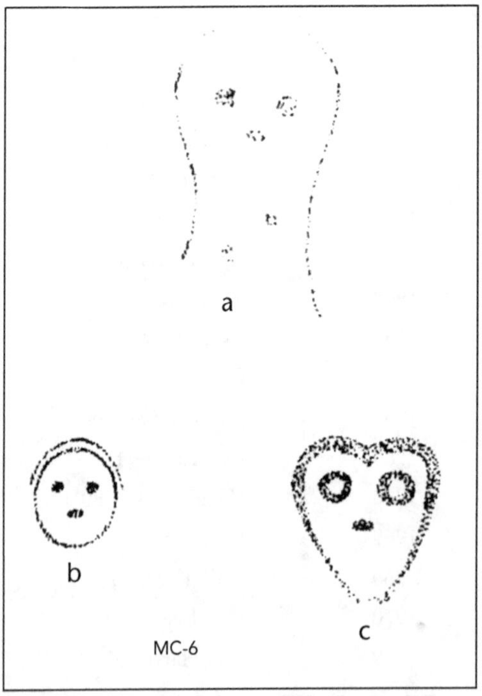

Figure 13.3 Petroglyphs from Gut River No. 1

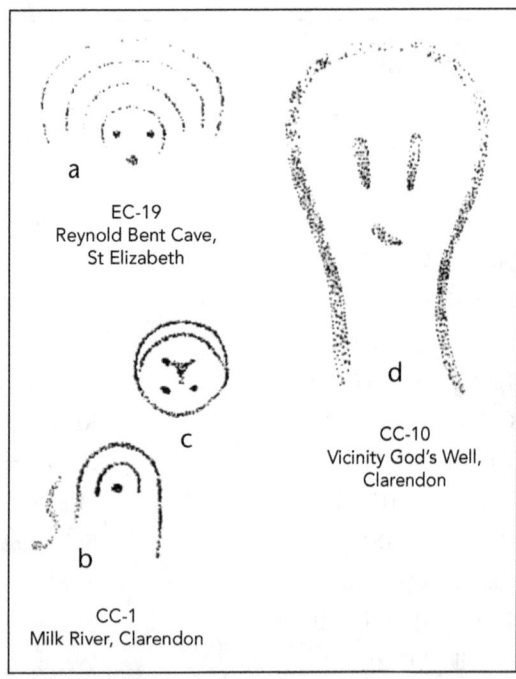

Figure 13.4 Petroglyphs from Reynold Bent, Milk River and near God's Well

of the dripstone, which tends to mask earlier features. In exceptional circumstances, such objects as modern Coca-Cola bottles have become completely imbedded in travertine precipitated from dripping or splashing water over a period of fifteen to twenty years.

Details of Sites

The twenty-four sites mapped by the author include several where only one glyph was observed or where only one carving had originally been reported and was no longer visible, as a result of either defacing or removal. Examples of these are Dryland, Byndloss Mountain, Two Sisters Cave, Cuckold Point, Red Bank, Reynold Bent and Negril. Others boast one principal carving and a few smaller or less well-executed efforts that may be so widely spaced as to give the impression of single glyphs. In this category are the sites at Coventry Cave, Pantrepant East, Little Miller's Bay, Gut River No. 1 and Duff House. Finally, there are locations where the petroglyphs occur in clusters. Until 1970, by far the best example of Jamaican petroglyphs was the group at Canoe Valley (Figures 13.5 and 13.6). But several misguided people, who claimed afterward that they believed construction work for a new road would shortly demolish the site, and who attempted to "save" the petroglyphs by sawing them from the outcrop, succeeded in almost totally destroying this once prime site. Not

Figure 13.5
Petroglyphs at Canoe Valley

Figure 13.6
Petroglyphs at Canoe Valley

one of the "saved" pieces has had the good fortune to find its way into the Institute of Jamaica's Museum.

The Canoe Valley site is only a few metres away from the road between Alligator Pond and Milk River, near Mile Post 48. It formerly had about thirty petroglyphs. Perhaps two-thirds of these were the basic oval face outline enclosing eye and mouth depressions. Others were loops and curves that may have been incomplete drawing or may have represented some concept that we cannot understand. Haloes appear on several heads, and one even has its face line completely encircled by another, outer line. The largest are barely life-size, and the smaller ones start at about 7 cm in width. All are carved into several steeply sloping to vertical limestone surfaces at the base of a precipitous ridge forming part of the south edge of the Manchester Plateau.

At the nearby occupation sites, White Marl–style pottery (AD 900–1500) suggests that the artists were Arawaks of the later period.

Other "cluster"-type sites are simple, smooth circular or oval depressions. Rarely, the artist produces an annular depression with a raised centre, like an eyeball in its socket. Gut River No. 1 (see Figure 13.3c) and the Two Sisters Cave are examples. The sloping, narrow eye shape, similar to the mask motifs on pottery handles, occurs in several sites – Warminister, God's Well and Worthy Park No. 1. Tear lines streaming from the eyes are discernible in one of the Canoe Valley carvings and at Cuckold Point.

Two figures portray the nose quite distinctly at the Two Sisters Cave and at Worthy Park No. 1, but all the others accentuate only eyes and mouth. Perhaps the haloes represent hair or headdresses, features that are often included as part of face-handles decorating Jamaican bowls. But whereas the potters occasionally showed ears on faces, the petroglyph sculptors never did.

The petroglyph at Cuckold Point differs from the normal style in that the outline of the face is almost rectangular, the eye depressions are disproportionately smaller and more close-set than usual and the mouth is accentuated by lines that may represent large teeth. There is always the possibility that it may be a fake, but the sculpting appears to be at the very least fifty to one hundred years old, and at that time there was virtually no human traffic in that area because of the difficulty in traversing the honeycomb limestone through nearly impenetrable thornbush and cactus. Moreover, in the same sinkhole, a few metres from the petroglyph, there is a freshwater pool, and around it were numerous sherds of White Marl–style earthenware water bottles, presumably broken while transporting water for the village at M-5, about 400 m away.

Another carving that is unique is the principal one at Little Miller's Bay. It is carved into waist-high stalagmite in a small, low cave with a wide mouth, within 50 m of the rocky coast forming the west side of Old Harbour Bay. This glyph has bolding eyes, which have small, round central depressions. The face has a forehead, eyes and flattish nose. The absence of a mouth suggests that the nose might be a beak and the whole figure might be intended as an owl.

The few abstract designs seem to be purely whimsical, and repetition of any pattern has not been recognized.

Pictographs

Aboriginal paintings have been observed at three sites in Jamaica – Mountain River Cave and Worthy Park in St Catherine and Spot Valley in St James. At the first two sites, petroglyphs and sparse White Marl–style earthenware potsherds corroborate an Arawak origin for both types of primitive art. At Spot Valley, the paintings (Figure 13.7), partly obscured by dirt, dust or smoke, are on one wall of a small cave whose single chamber measures about 8 m by 12 m and contains evidence of Arawak burials in the floor, White Marl–style potsherds and human skeletal material.

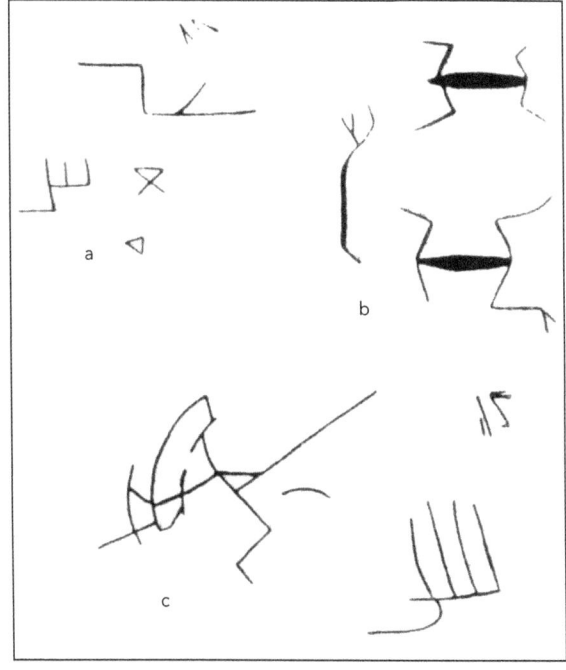

The Mountain River site was first mentioned by Duerden (1897) and again when the title for the two-acre parcel of land was handed over to the Jamaica National Trust Commission by the Archaeological Society (Lee 1982; Morbán Laucer 1982). The cave, which is really a limestone rock shelter, is situated in rugged terrain near Guanaboa Valley. The paintings are black silhouette figures applied to the ceiling of the shelter, whose 5-m by 15-m area is now secured behind metal grillwork and protected by National Trust monument guards.

The artist's emphasis was on birds, turtles, lizards, fishes, frogs and humans. There are also some abstract patterns whose significance has not been deciphered. With so many of the paintings dealing with food sources and consumers, it seems likely that the "cave" was used for religious purposes intended to ensure successful hunts. Morbán Laucer sees some of the figures as participants in the *cohoba* rite of smoking tobacco, whereas the bird masks of these same figures suggest that they may be catching food birds by a method similar to the one described in the text accompanying Tommaso Porcacchi's 1576 map of Jamaica (said to have been taken verbatim from Gonzalez Fernando

Figure 13.7 Pictographs at Spot Valley

de Oviedo's *Historia General y Natural de las Indias* [1519]). We are fortunate that this excellent group of paintings has been preserved from further damage, as it is without doubt the best example of its kind in Jamaica, if not the entire Caribbean.

Associated Ceramics

For many years, there was uncertainty as to whether the petroglyphs were the work of the earlier Redware or the later White Marl Indians. It now seems fairly clear that both the rock carvings and the rock painting were produced in the White Marl period. We have the close association of petroglyphs, pictographs and pottery at Mountain River Cave and Worthy Park and the burial and painting site at Spot Valley. In addition, there are three instances where White Marl potsherds occur within a few metres of petroglyphs: at Jackson Bay Cave, Cuckold Point and Duff House. Finally, the Pantrepant East petroglyphs are located a mere 200 m from a small village site (T-7) whose middens contain Montego Bay–substyle potsherds. I recently illustrated one adorno handle (Lee 1983b).

Conclusion

We may be reasonably sure that the majority of Jamaica petroglyphs belong to the later period of Arawak occupation, inasmuch as all pottery so far found closely associated with these rock carvings is in the White Marl style. The spatial distribution of petroglyph sites also supports this view. Of the twenty-four locations listed in Table 13.2, thirteen are much farther from the coast than any known Redware site, and White Marl–type villages are the nearest occupation sites in every case.

Appendix

IN 1495, DURING his second voyage to the Caribbean, Christopher Columbus was one of a handful of Europeans to observe a religious rite of the indigenous Taíno (Arawak) inhabitants of Hispaniola (Bourne 1906, 171–72; Columbus 1969, 192). Central to this ritual was the

Table 13.2 Jamaican Petroglyph Sites by Parish

Parish	Site	Elevation (m)	Island Grid Coordinates (ft)	Nearest Occupation Site	Distance (km)
St James	Kempshot (JC-1)*	503	547,100 N 248,800 E	Upper Retirement (J-17)	3.05
	Spot Valley (JC-7)	290	576,250 N 279,800 E	Spot Valley (J-15)	1.22
Trelawny	Pantrepant West (TC-1)	91	536,600 N 308,450 E	Pantrepant (T-7)	1.49
	Pantrepant East (TC-2)	91	535,950 N 313,900 E	Pantrepant (T-7)	0.20
	Windsor-LaCaille (TC-5)†				
St Ann	Coventry (AC-1)	427	528,000 N 513,300 E	Friendship (A-22)	3.14
St Mary	Dryland (YC-1)	390	489,900 N 572,950 E	Nonsuch (T-15)	5.58
St Catherine	Mountain River Cave (SC-1)	290	422,800 N 522,150 E	Dover (S-2)	6.64
	Byndloss Mountain (SC-2)*	198	455,150 N 522,850 E	Mt. Rosser (S-3)	4.33
	Worthy Park #1 (SC-6)	381	447,100 N 494,100 E	Oakes (C-15)	8.66
	Two Sisters Cave (SC-7)	15	357,000 N 489,000 E	Salt Pond (S-11)	5.00
	Worthy Park #2 (SC-10)	457	458,500 N 489,000 E	E Mt. Rosser (S-3)	9.45
Clarendon	Milk River (CC-1)	83	44,300 N 421,150 E	Round Hill (C-1)	2.41
	Jackson Bay (CC-2)*	8	302,350 N 472,650 E	Harmony Hall (C-7)	3.26
	East of Jackson Bay (CC-6)	30	303,200 N 471,850 E	Harmony Hall (C-7)	3.05

Table 13.2 continues

Table 13.2 Jamaican Petroglyph Sites by Parish *(cont'd)*

Parish	Site	Elevation (m)	Island Grid Coordinates (ft)	Nearest Occupation Site	Distance (km)
Clarendon (Cont'd)	God's Well (CC-10)	23	351,250 N 414,000 E	Round Hill–NW Ridge (C-11)	0.76
	Little Miller's Bay (CC-18)	8	303,000 N 505,950 E	Holmes Bay (C-5)	1.52
Manchester	Canoe Valley (MC-1)*	8	351,050 N 393,950 E	Bossue (M-10)	3.44
	Cuckold Point (MC-5)	8	342,650 N 370,000 E	Cuckold Point (M-5)	0.37
	Gut River (MC-6)	8	349,200 N 388,150 E	Bossue (M-10)	5.27
	Gut River #4 (MC-9)†				
St Elizabeth	Duff House (EC-11)	114	360,150 N 350,900 E	Rowe's Corner (M-3)	1.01
	Warminister (EC-15)	229	378,200 N 350,900 E	Bull Savannah (E-7) Montpelier (M-9)	8.11
	Red Bank (EC-16)*	373	376,550 N 329,850 E	Yardley Chase (E-9)	7.99
	Reynold Bent (EC-19)*	267	376,550 N 329,850 E	Yardley Chase E-9) Montpelier (M-9)	8.41
	Norman Bernard (EC-20)†				
	Eric McPherson (EC-21)†				
Westmoreland	Negril (WC-2)*	30	500,300 N 81,500 E	Negril (W-4)	0.64

*Seriously defaced, erased or removed.
†Location or coordinates unknown.

14  *Zemís*, Trees and Symbolic Landscapes: Three Taíno Carvings from Jamaica

NICHOLAS SAUNDERS
and
DORRICK GRAY

role of wooden "idols", *zemís*, which the Taíno appeared to worship, and which the Spanish regarded as evidence of pagan idolatry (Columbus 1969, 154). Wooden image-*zemís* have been found throughout the Greater Antilles, notably in the Dominican Republic, Haiti and Cuba (Fewkes 1907, 197–202; Lovén 1935, 598–602).

In 1792, three figures carved of a dark, polished wood were discovered in a cave in the Carpenter's Mountain in southern Jamaica (Anon. 1803, 1896; Joyce 1907, 402–7; Lester 1958). In 1992, three further wooden objects came to light, said to have been discovered in a cave in north-central Jamaica (Aarons 1994; Weintraub 1993).

This new discovery, a major find of Taíno wooden carvings, is the most important in Jamaica for two hundred years.[1] In studying these new images, we realized that they afforded an opportunity to re-examine the place of wooden *zemís* in Taíno religion, rather than simply "fit" the pieces into the accepted hierarchy of putative Taíno deities – which themselves are imperfectly known from a fragmentary and often ambiguous ethnohistorical record; they had a more complex symbolic importance. Here we consider these new discoveries as well as the generality of wooden *zemís* from the perspective of their material – wood, the trees from which the wood came and the conceptual association of the objects with the animated landscape of the Taíno world view.

The New Discoveries

Originally published in *Antiquity* 70, no. 270 (1996): 801–12.

In June 1992, the Jamaica National Heritage Trust heard that three Taíno wooden images had been discovered near the small village of Aboukir in the northern central highlands. The images, apparently discovered originally during the 1940s in a nearby cave, had subsequently been returned. They allegedly remained in the cave until 1972, when they were once again removed, this time by a Mr Clayton, and kept in his house for twenty years. These events, and the circumstances which led to the images finally coming to the attention of the Jamaica National Heritage Trust, appear to have been associated with *obeah*, Jamaican voodoo (Abrahams and Szwed 1983; Schuler 1979). The three objects, acquired by the Jamaica National Heritage Trust in September 1992, are currently (1994) on display in the National Gallery in Kingston. Each object is of a different type – an anthropomorphic figure, a bird and a small "utilitarian" spoon-like object with an anthropomorphic handle. On the basis of photographs, Arrom and Rouse (1992), seeing the aged and cracked appearance of the wood, judged them authentic.

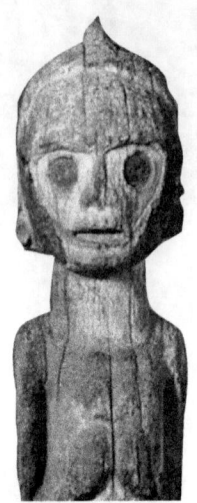

The anthropomorphic figure (Figures 14.1 and 14.2) is 168.4 cm high with a maximum width of 26 cm. The form of the bent legs suggests the presence of ligatures – a practice well known among the Taíno in general, and documented for the Jamaica Taíno by Columbus (1969, 196). It has prominent male genitals and thin arms with hands reclining on the chest. Arrom and Rouse (1992) consider these features characteristics of Taíno representations of *Baibrama*, the deity identified with the cultivation and consumption of cassava (Arrom 1989, 68–73), and not to be confused with *Yúcahu*, the supreme Taíno deity, whose name means "spirit of cassava" (ibid., 17–20). The eye sockets, ears and mouth probably originally held inlay, possibly shell, but conceivably gold or *guanine*, a copper-gold alloy.

Figure 14.1 Anthropomorphic figure from Aboukir (detail), possibly representing the Taíno deity Baibrama. Note traces of white around face and mouth and eye sockets, which probably originally held inlay.

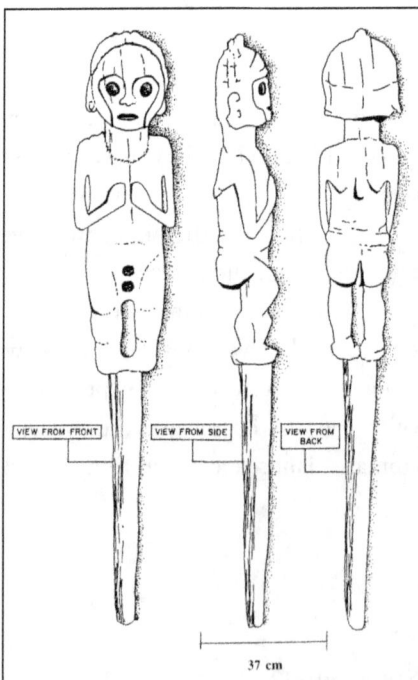

Figure 14.2 Anthropomorphic figure from Aboukir. Figure is 168.4 cm high, 28 cm maximum width. (JNHT [Archaeology Division], recorded 29.9.1992. Illustration by T. Lindsay.)

According to Arrom and Rouse (1992), the projection at the top of the figure may have supported a table or "canopy" (see below), and the pole upon which the figure is perched may have served as a support, replacing the circular base upon which such figures normally stand. Aarons (1994, 17) regards this figure, more speculatively, as the ceremonial "staff of office" of a paramount *cacique* (chief). According to

Lewis (1994, 1), the colour and texture of the wood, as well as the presence of insect boreholes and possibly trunk thorns, strongly suggests the *Ceiba* or silk cotton tree (*Ceiba pentandra*).

The bird figure (Figures 14.3 and 14.4) is 61 cm high with a maximum width of 28 cm. Thought by Arrom and Rouse (1992) to represent an aquatic species, possibly a pelican, it recalls a similar avian image in the British Museum (Figure 14.5) (Joyce 1907, 406, plate L1, Figure 2; Rouse 1992, 117, Figure 29f). However, a comparison of the two images shows possibly significant differences in style, structure and type of wood. Arrom and Rouse (1992) also note that the circular table or "canopy" protecting the back of the bird image is associated with the *cohoba* ceremony (see below). On the basis of colour and grain pattern, Lewis (1994, I) identifies three kinds of wood from which this figure might have been made – West Indian mahogany (*Swietenia mahogoni*), West Indian cedar (*Cedrela odorata*) and Santa Maria (*Calophylum calaba*).

The third and smallest object (Figures 14.6 and 14.7) appears to be half of a container used for ritual purposes (Arrom and Rouse 1992) – possibly a ladle or spoon. It is 15.9 cm high with a maximum width of 7.7 cm. The handle is

Figure 14.3 Bird figure from Aboukir (frontal view), with circular table, possibly used for snuffing hallucinogenic cohoba powder

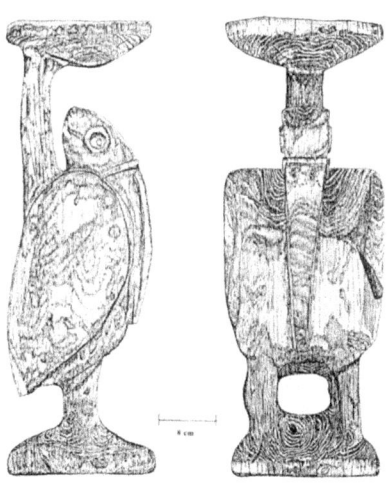

Figure 14.4 Bird figure from Aboukir. Height is 61 cm, maximum width 28 cm. (JNHT [Archaeology Division], recorded 1.10.1992. Illustration by B. Callum.)

Figure 14.5 Carved wooden *zemí* of a bird standing on the back of a turtle or tortoise, probably from Jamaica. Note eye socket for inlay, and damaged column upon which originally was a circular table, probably for cohoba snuffing. The figure is 66.5 cm high. (Reproduced by permission of the British Museum.)

Figure 14.6 Small ladle/spoon with anthropomorphic handle, from Aboukir. Note high polish and eye and mouth sockets, which originally had inlay.

in the shape of a "human" head, and the eyes, mouth and possibly ears may originally have been inlaid. Arrom and Rouse (1992), considering that the minimal details preclude an exact identification, tentatively suggest that it might be *Maquetaurie Guayaba*, the Taíno Lord of the Underworld (Arrom 1989, 54–55). Again on the basis of wood colour and grain, Lewis (1994, II) identified this object as being made probably from either *Hibiscus tiliaceus* or *H. elatus*.

The Context of Sacredness

Taíno wooden *zemís*, like any sacred object, exist within social and spatial contexts – overlapping spheres of symbolic and ritual activity. What conferred

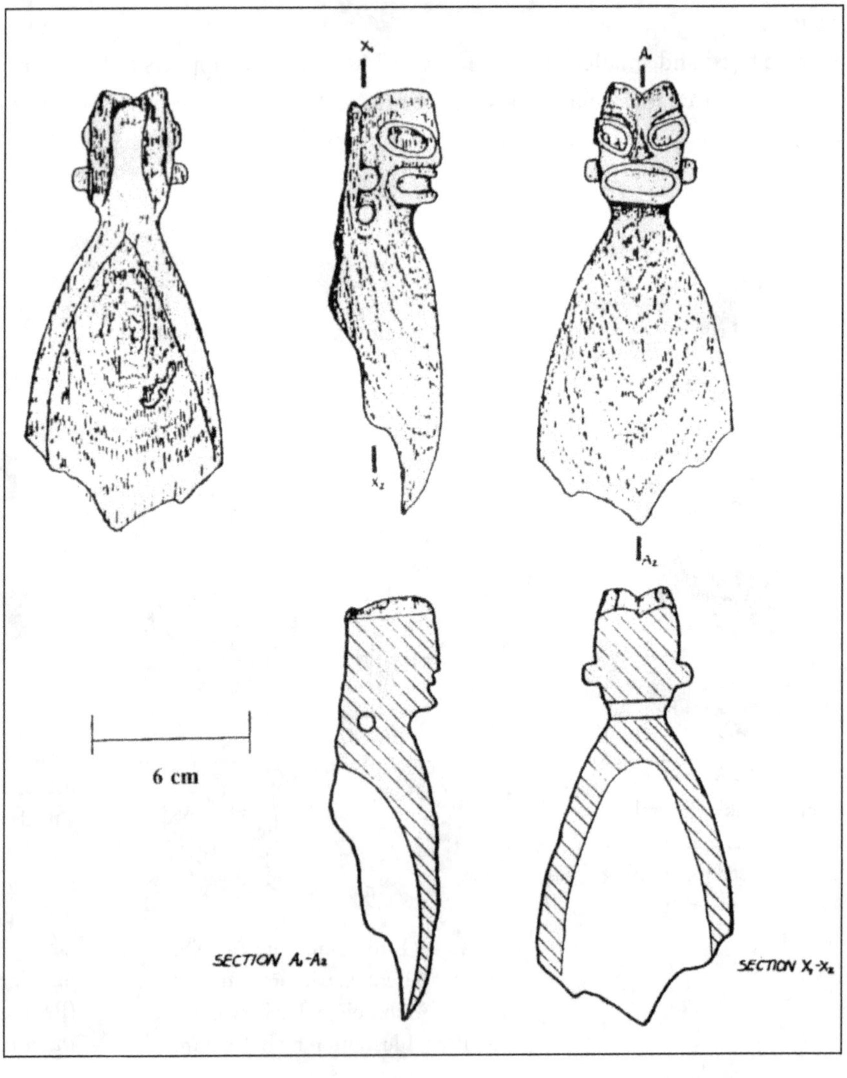

Figure 14.7 Small ladle/spoon with anthropomorphic handle, from Aboukir. Height is 15.9 cm, maximum width is 7.7 cm. (JNHT [Archaeology Division], recorded 1.10.1992. Illustration by B. Callum.)

their sacredness was a combination of form, material, production process, use and the ascription of specific cultural values to each of these. It is these values that we wish to explore, as they exemplify the way in which the Taíno conceptualized and classified their phenomenological universe, and situated themselves within it.

The shape of the Taíno world view reveals a distinctively Caribbean Amerindian way of creating and maintaining what Kus (1983, 278) has called a "meaningful universe". The spiritual significance of wooden *zemís*, native fauna and flora and the meteorological phenomena which enveloped them is a product of the architecture of Taíno symbolic reasoning and religious thought. The ethnographic, ethnohistorical and archaeological evidence show that the Taíno view of the natural world had much in common with those of lowland Amazon societies – particularly in recognizing as animate aspects of the physical world which Western science classifies as inanimate (for example, Eliade 1974, 47–48; Hallowell 1969, 54; Lévi-Strauss 1969, 184–85; Ruggles and Saunders 1993, 1–31). The richness of Amazonian ethnography, compared with Caribbean ethnohistory, is such that it can throw light on Taíno beliefs and broaden the scope of investigation into the nature of wooden *zemís* (and see Roe 1995).

Zemís and the Taíno Spirit World

The Taíno, like other Amerindian peoples of Central and South America, viewed the world as animated by spiritual forces and articulated by myth (Alegría 1986; López-Baralt 1985). Spirits resided in every feature of nature. The propitiation and manipulation of these omnipresent, powerful but ambivalent spirits made social life possible. In this sense, the Taíno world view was fundamentally shamanic; ethnohistorical sources show that shamans were active in their society, particularly in curing (D'Anghera 1970, 172–73; Lovén 1935, 575–78; Rouse 1948, 537–38).

While the Taíno shared characteristic traits of lowland Amazonian shamanism, one feature appears unique – the practice of *zemí* worship. According to Lovén (1935, 583), the origins of "*zemíism*" lay in ancestor worship, and Fewkes (1907, 54) finds the term *zemí* applied by the Taíno to anything that possessed "magic power".

Although *zemís* have been recognized as formal deities – such as Yúcahu, the supreme god (Arrom 1989, 17–30; Rouse 1992, 13, 118), and Atabey, his mother, goddess of human fertility (Arrom 1989, 31–36; Rouse 1992, 13) – they have also been regarded as spiritual forces residing in trees, rocks, caves and other features of the landscape. Apart from wooden images, the term *zemí* has been applied to artefacts of different forms and sizes made from stone, shell, pottery, cotton and human bones (Fewkes 1907, 53–54; Lovén 1935, 585–86, 591, 597 620; Rouse 1992, 13; Vega 1987).

Clearly, *zemí* is a widely used but analytically imprecise term. This is due partly to the relative poverty and ambiguity of the ethnohistorical record, and partly to the favoured ascription of the term to one kind of artefact – the distinctive "three-pointed stone" (for example, Fewkes 1907, 111–33; Lovén 1935, 638–43). This imprecision, and the corresponding practice of labelling many disparate items as *zemís*, may obscure meaningful Taíno discrimination between gods, spirits, ancestors, forces resident within the landscape, and the kinds of material (in this case varieties of wood) from which *zemís* were made. While *zemís* could have been perceived as ubiquitous links between the natural and supernatural worlds (Stevens-Arroyo 1988, 59), it is unclear to what extent any hierarchy of sacredness or spiritual power existed, although some *zemís* were more esteemed than others (ibid., 62). For the Taíno, *zemí* was spirit, not object.

The "social life" of *zemís* also is problematical. In Amazonia it was shamans who possessed toolkits of magical objects, including wooden images, to contact the spirit world (for example, Reichel-Dolmatoff 1961, 1975, 46). Among the Taíno, it appears, every person possessed at least one *zemí*, with some individuals owning possibly as many as ten (Rouse 1948, 535; 1992, 13). It is probable that owning certain types or categories of *zemís* was a privilege of the *caciques* (Columbus 1969, 192), a view inferred by Rouse (1948, 536), with reference to the chiefs' depending for their power and status on the superiority of their *zemís*.

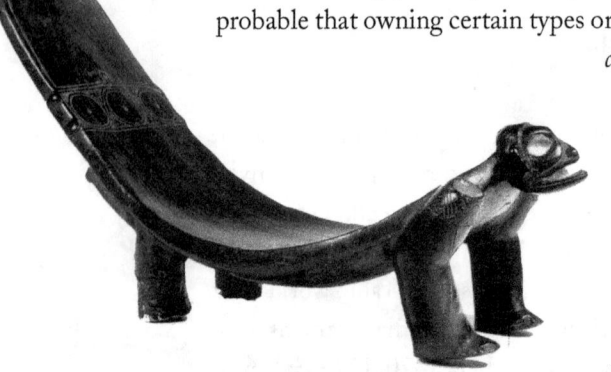

Supporting this view is the fact that representations of *zemís* (as spirits or "gods") occur as decoration on religious paraphernalia, including the elite *duho* stools (Figure 14.8) (Rouse 1992, 121).

Figure 14.8 Carved wooden *duho* stool, Dominican Republic. Note high polish, gold inlays on face and shoulders and engraved decoration. Figure is 22.2 cm high, 43.4 cm long. (Reproduced by permission of the British Museum.)

Another possibility is that an older tradition of lineage-based *zemí* ancestor images was developing into a situation where *caciques* were vying for status through the manipulation of their *zemís* – a case perhaps of incipient stratification, which may, in turn, have been leading to the appearance of formal deities.

Kept in niches or on tables within the dwellings, and sometimes in separate structures (Lovén 1935, 598), *zemís* could be inherited, traded, given away or even stolen (Rouse 1992, 13). The possible pre-eminence of wooden *zemís* over other kinds is suggested by references to a category of hollow "speaking *zemís*" which appeared to have had an oracular function. They were regarded by the Spanish as a method of hoodwinking the gullible by ventriloquy, with a shaman speaking through a tube (Bourne 1906, 312; Lovén 1935, 599–600). If wooden *zemís* were the most spiritually important, it is possible that some stone *zemís* imitated wooden originals (Lovén 1935, 603; Stevens-Arroyo 1988, 58).

As Wilson (1990, 88) notes, *zemís* were less a symbol of a *cacique's* power than his supernatural allies, to be venerated, respected and consulted. The role of the manipulation of wooden image-*zemís* in articulating shaman links between the physical world and the spirit realm is seen in the important *cohoba* ceremony.

By sniffing the hallucinogenic *cohoba* powder,[2] Taíno *caciques* and shamans (*bohitu*) communed with the spirit world (Bourne 1906, 327; D'Anghera 1970, 174) – particularly, it appears, with ancestor spirits resident within trees and wooden *zemís*, an association suggested by the arboreal nature of *cohoba*. It was snuffed through polished wood or cane tubes (Kerchache 1994, 85) from a round wooden table, an integral part of the class of wooden *zemí* figure (for example, Joyce 1907, 403; Lovén 1935, 599) to which the bird image from Jamaica belongs.[3] Most suggestive in this report is the description by Las Casas (Arrom 1989, 106) of a *cacique* taking *cohoba* while sitting on an elaborately carved wooden *duho* stool. It was the *cohoba* ceremony that Columbus observed in 1495 (1969, 192):

> In these houses are highly carved tables, round in shape like a chopping table, on which lies a special powder, which they place on the heads of their cemis with certain rites. They then sniff up this powder through a double-branched cane, which they place in their nostrils. This powder intoxicates them . . .

Trees and the Supernatural

Wooden *zemís*, *cohoba* and trees associate the physical and supernatural worlds of the Taíno in ways which are deeply rooted in wider Amerindian as well as specifically lowland Amazonian traditions of mythic thought (for example, Heyden 1993). For Amazonian societies, trees possess a complex, multilayered cosmological symbolism that links origin myths (for example, Métraux 1946, 369), the bestowal of cultural identity (for example, Descola 1994, 19) and ideas of shamanic access to the spirit world (for example, Karsten 1964, 198–204; Roe 1982, 118–19; Sullivan 1988, 60–61). The Amazonian Baranana, for example, believe that the paxiuba palm (*Iriartea exorrihiza*) has grown from the ashes of the culture hero's body and carried his soul heavenwards as it grew, thus becoming a mediator between earth and sky (Hugh-Jones 1979, 157–58). The Brazilian Kuikuru believe that trees were once people, in mythic time (Carneiro 1978, 214).

Analogous ideas are found among the Taíno of Hispaniola, of whom D'Anghera (1970, 168) records an origin myth in which men who failed to return to their caves before sunrise were turned into "myrobolane" trees.[4] The same author says that some *zemís* were made of wood "because it is amongst the trees and in the darkness of the night they have received the message of the gods" (1970, 173). For lowland South American Amerindians as for the Taíno, the depths of the forest were sacred zones, spatially distant from the "socialized" fields and village, and home to the largest trees; they were the places where spirits revealed themselves to humans.

According to Lovén (1935, 586–87), the Taíno of Hispaniola made wooden *zemís* only from trees occupied by the spirits of a dead *cacique*. Once carved, and no longer confined within the tree, the image-*zemí* was believed to be able to move about. In nineteenth-century Jamaica, Afro-Caribbean peoples believed that *Ceiba* trees assembled together at night (Rashford 1985, 51, and see below). These Caribbean beliefs parallel similar ones from northeastern South America concerning trees that move around at night (Roth 1887).

The way in which trees and wooden *zemís* articulate within the Taíno world view can be seen in an extraordinary quotation from Dr Chanca, Columbus's physician during his second voyage (Pané 1974, 41–42).

> When a native was passing by a tree which was moved more than others by the wind, the Indian in fear calls out, "Who are you?" The tree responds, "Call where a *behique* or priest and I will tell you who I am." When the priest or shaman had come to the tree . . . he performed certain prescribed ceremonies. . . . He would ask the tree, "What are you doing here? What do you wish of me? . . . Tell me if you wish me to cut you down and . . . whether I shall make you a house and a farm and perform ceremonies for a year." The tree answered these questions, and the man cut it down and made of it a statue or idol.

Here the tree advertises its presence by being moved by the wind more than other trees – interestingly, a structural characteristic of the *Ceiba* (Descola 1994, 50). Is there a symbolic association between the animating wind, Amazonian ideas of the shaman's magical blowing powers (Butt 1956; Hugh-Jones 1979, 90–93) and – more specific to the Caribbean – the dangerous hurricanes, which were deified by the Taíno as Guabancex, the "Lady of the Winds" (Arrom 1989, 46, 49–51; Bourne 1906, 333; Stevens-Arroyo 1988, 234–38)?

Another important correspondence between Amazonian and Caribbean expressions of arboreal symbolism concerns mortuary associations. The Kuikuru carve the memorial post to a dead chief from the *uengifi* tree, which is believed to be occupied by the chief spirit of the forest (Carneiro 1978, 214–15). Similarly, among the Irurí during the seventeenth century, the principal men, their wives and children were buried in great hollow tree trunks (Porro 1994, 88). Among the Warao of coastal Venezuela, trees are conceived as mythically important anthropomorphic spirits, and canoes made from their trunks can be used as coffins (Wilbert 1975, 169; 1977, 33, 36, 37, Figure 8).

There is analogous evidence for the Taíno. Not only were tree trunks recognized as *zemís*, but also some image-*zemís* carved from them functioned as coffins, containing the remains of dead *caciques* (Arrom 1989, Figure 42; Centro de estudios avanzados de Puerto Rico y el Caribe 1987, 54, illustrations; Fewkes 1907, 56–57; Kerchache 1994, 130–39; Lovén 1935, 585). In a probable burial cave in Jamaica, human bones were associated with a cedarwood canoe (Flower 1895, 607). To be buried in a wooden *zemí* was to be symbolically interred within a hollow tree, and thus to be assured of rebirth (Peter G. Roe, personal communication, 1994). When not disposed of in this way, a Taíno *cacique* might be buried sitting on his carved wooden *duho* stool (Fewkes 1907, 70; Scott 1985, 7, illustration), quite literally supported by the spirit of an ancestor who inhabited the wood.

Occasionally it is possible to be specific in terms of a particular tree. As Roe (personal communication, 1994) has shown, the silk cotton tree (*Ceiba pentandra*) is the principal "spirit tree" of the Amazonian Shipibo. The tallest tree in the forest canopy, its upper reaches form a ladder to enable the shaman to visit the celestial sphere, and its deep roots help him visit the underworld.

The *Ceiba* is also present in the Greater Antilles (Vázquez de Espinosa 1942, 330), where, for example, modern rural populations in Puerto Rico still revere it (Roe, personal communication, 1994). Given their regard for trees, it is possible that the Taíno also regarded the *Ceiba* as a spirit tree, perhaps the pre-eminent one – a view expressed by Nicholson (1983, 19). The continued spiritual importance of the *Ceiba* in Afro-Caribbean (especially Jamaica) culture as a "god tree" associated with snakes, obeah and ghosts is documented by Rashford (1985); it probably descends, at least in part, from the Taíno (Cundall 1894c, 65). The choice of *Ceiba* wood to carve the Jamaican figure of *Baibrama* clearly possesses levels of meaning which are difficult to assess solely by recourse to Caribbean ethnohistory.

The *Ceiba* has sharp, spiny thorns on its lower trunk (Standley 1920–1926, 791), and in lowland Amazonia these are analogous to the shaman's supernatural *yoto* missiles, sent to cause illness or death (Roe, personal communication, 1994). Similar beliefs about the nature of illness are evident for the Carib and Taíno (Fewkes 1907, 60–62) and suggest the possibility that for them also the *Ceiba* was a shaman's spirit tree. More generally for the Taíno, Europeans and Afro-Caribbean peoples, there are many beliefs concerning the spiritual and medicinal qualities of trees, their bark and leaves (for example, Cundall 1894c, 55–56; Rashford 1985, 52; Sloane 1725, 134; Vásquez de Espinosa

1942, 116, 330). The *Ceiba* itself is said to have emetic, diuretic and antispasmodic properties (Standley 1920–1926, 791). Fernández de Oviedo (1959, 8–9) reports that for the Taíno a decoction of wood from the *guayacán* tree (*Guaiacum officinale*) was a much-valued cure for syphilis (see also Crosby 1972, 154–55). Lovén (1935, 540) reports that the Taíno made their *zemís* from wood which they believed to possess strong curative properties – an observation supported by Lehmann's study of an elaborate *duho* stool from Haiti that was carved from *guayacán* wood (Lehmann 1951, 153n2).

Having established the spiritual importance of trees, it is appropriate to consider wood as a symbolically important material. Objects made of black, polished wood were regarded by the Taíno as markers of elite status (Helms 1986; Wilson 1986, 142–43). Chiefly *duhos*, canoes (Wilson 1986, 143–44) and ritual paraphernalia, such as *cohoba* sniffing tubes, were associated with Taíno *caciques* and shamans (Helms 1986, 27–29). Apart from the spirituality of trees per se, there was evidently also a cultural value placed on the shiny qualities of certain wooden artefacts, including their shell and metal inlays (see Figure 14.8) (Stevens-Arroyo 1988, 66). The idea that carving and polishing wooden objects enabled ancestral spirits or essences dwelling within to be revealed or liberated suggests complex and apparently pan-Amerindian notions of "sacred brilliance" associated with metals (Lechtman 1993, 269; Reichel-Dolmatoff 1988), precious and semi-precious stones (Reichel-Dolmatoff 1981) and mirrors (Saunders 1988).

The symbolism of trees and wooden artefacts featured also in the contacts between the Taíno and the Spanish. On first seeing Hispaniola and Jamaica, Columbus was amazed at the remarkable abundance and variety of trees (Columbus 1969, 155; Vásquez de Espinosa 1942, 118). He saw these forests sawn up into planks for caravels or raised as masts for the largest ships in Spain (Gerbi 1986, 18). Conversely, the Taíno saw the Spanish, their unfamiliar goods and large wooden ships with masts like trees, as *turey*, things which came from the sky, charged with supernatural powers (Chanca 1932, 64; and see Helms 1988, 187).

When Bartolomé Columbus visited the Taíno chiefdom of Xaraguá on Hispaniola, he was met by people whose first act was to offer him branches and palms (Las Casas 1992). Subsequently, the high-ranking Taíno woman Anacaona presented him with prestige items of black polished wood, including fourteen beautifully carved *duho* (D'Anghera 1970, 125). Despite Taíno beliefs in the spiritual and life-giving qualities of trees, the Spanish subsequently hanged Anacaona and burnt Taínos whom they suspended from specially constructed timber gibbets (Las Casas 1992, 16, illustration, 22; Walker 1992, 299, illustration).

Conclusion

Wooden *zemís*, among the most elaborate and distinctive of Taíno artefacts, have received little systematic analytical study (but see Helms 1988). Despite being amenable to radiocarbon dating, botanical identification, chemical analysis, adhering resin and the potential of analogous explanation, many remain undated, their material unidentified and their possible semantic "connections" with South America unexplored. They have been identified with a few major gods, regardless of wood type, age, stylistic variability and geographical/cultural location, in an approach that denies the informative role of diversity in throwing light on wider conceptual issues – on, for example, the significance of wood type and of the presence or absence of polishing and form.

Evidence from lowland South America as well as the Caribbean indicates that trees and wood possessed a rich symbolism for indigenous peoples. For the Taíno, trees contained spirits, and the *zemís* carved from them bestowed animated shape and elite status. The complex relationship between the physical and symbolic landscapes of the Taíno represents a unique opportunity to investigate a world view that was fundamentally Amerindian and also distinctively Caribbean.

Acknowledgements

We would like to thank the Jamaica National Heritage Trust; the Department of History, University of the West Indies, Mona, Jamaica; Leonard Clayton ("Chemist") of Aboukir, St Ann; Tony Aarons; the Museum of Mankind, London; and Patrick

Lewis of the University of the West Indies Herbarium, Mona, Jamaica. We are particularly grateful to Peter G. Roe for his insightful comments on an earlier version of this chapter.

Notes

1. There has been some confusion about the number and location of Taíno wooden objects from Jamaica. To the three pieces from Carpenter's Mountain can be added the figure of a bird on the back of a turtle or tortoise, in the British Museum (Joyce 1907, 406, plate L1, figure 2), an anthropomorphic seated figure, currently in the Museum of Primitive Art New York (Arrom 1985, figures 43 and 44), and a *duho* found by C.B. Lewis at the site of Cambridge Hill (Howard 1956, 56). Aarons (1994, 15) reports a wooden "doll" figure, 31 cm high, found in a shallow cave in front of the gate at the New Seville Great House Estate, which disappeared some fifty years ago. Including the three new discoveries, possibly ten wooden Jamaican Taíno objects/*zemís* are known. A small anthropomorphic figure in the British Museum (Register no. Am St 332) may also be from Jamaica. Although labelled by Arrom (1989, figure 48) as coming from Haiti or Dominican Republic, its British Museum record shows no definite provenance, and it is stylistically similar to the figure from Carpenter's Mountain.
2. After much confusion concerning botanical identification, it is now recognized that *cohoba* was hallucinogenic snuff made from the ground-up seeds of *Anadenanthera peregrina* (Naxon 1993, 178; Wilbert 1987, 17–18), a mimosa-like tree closely related to *A. colubrine*, the source of the sacred *huilca* snuff used in western South America (Gollán and Gordillo 1994; Wessén 1967).
3. The association of avian-image *zemís* and hallucinogenic *cohoba* may relate to complex Taíno beliefs concerning shamanic flight and spirit trees, for which there exist South American parallels. Warao shamans launch supernatural attacks accompanied by an effigy of their avian master (Wilbert 1985, 154), and the Cubeo possess bird images representing patrons of mourning rituals and said to be under the effects of the hallucinogen *Banisteriopsis coapi* (Goldman 1979, 249).
4. This term is sometimes recognized as the *Ceiba*, and sometimes as a generic term for several tree varieties which had medicinal qualities.

Aarons, G.A. 1983a. Archaeological sites in the Hellshire area. *Jamaica Journal* 16, no. 1: 76–87.

———. 1983b. Sevilla la Nueva: Microcosm of Spain in Jamaica, part 1. *Jamaica Journal* 16, no. 4: 37–46.

———. 1984. Sevilla la Nueva: Microcosm of Spain in Jamaica, part 2. *Jamaica Journal*

References

17, no. 1: 28–37.

———. 1994. Taínos of Jamaica: The Aboukir zemis. *Jamaica Journal* 25, no. 2: 11–17.

Abbott, R.T. 1954. *American Seashells*. New York: D. Van Nostrand Company Inc.

Abrahams, R.D., and J.F. Szwed. 1983. *After Africa*. New Haven: Yale University Press.

Adams, C.D. 1971. *The Blue Mahoe and Other Bush: An Introduction to the Plant Life of Jamaica*. Kingston: Sangster's Book Stores, and Singapore: McGraw-Hill Far Eastern Publishers.

———. 1972. *Flowering Plants of Jamaica*. Kingston: University of the West Indies.

Agorsah, E.K. 1992. Jamaica and Caribbean archaeology. *Archaeology Jamaica*, n.s., 6: 1–14.

———. 1993. An objective chronological scheme for Caribbean history and archaeology. *Social and Economic Studies* 21: 119–47.

———. ed. 1994. *Maroon Heritage: Archaeological, Ethnographic and Historical Perspectives*. Kingston: Canoe Press.

Alegría, R.E. 1981. *El uso de la terminología etno-histórica para designar las culturas aborigines de las Antillas*. Cuadernos Prehispánicas. Valladolid: Seminaro de Historia de América, University de Valladolid.

———. 1986. *Apuntes en torno a la mitología de los Indios Taínos de las Antillas Mayores y sus origenes Suramericanos*. San Juan: Centro de Estudios Avanzados de Puerto Rico y El Caribe, Museo del Hombre Dominicano.

Alexander, J. 1969. The indirect evidence of domestication. In *The Domestication and Exploitation of Plants and Animals*, ed. Peter Ucko and G.W. Dimbleby. London: Gerald Duckworth.

Allgood, J.L. 2000. Faunal analysis of the Green Castle Estate assemblage. Unpublished report.

Allsworth-Jones, P., G. Lalor, G. Lechler, S.F. Mitchell, E. Rodriques, and M. Vutchkov. 2001. The Taino settlement of the Kingston area. *Proceedings of the Eighteenth International Congress for Caribbean Archaeology, Grenada, 1999*: 115–27.

Allsworth-Jones, P., and K. Wesler. 1999. Excavations at Green Castle Estate (STM25) St Mary Parish. Unpublished annual report.

———. 2000. Excavations at Green Castle Estate (STM25) St Mary Parish. Unpublished annual report.

———. 2001. Excavations at Green Castle Estate (STM25) St Mary Parish. Unpublished annual report.

Anonymous. 1803. Appendix, 11 April 1799. *Archaeologia* 14: 269, pl. 46.

———. 1896. Jamaican wooden images in the British Museum. *Journal of the Institute of Jamaica* 2, no. 3: 303–4.

Arrom, J.J. 1989. *Mitologia y artes prehispanicas de las Antillas*. México: Siglo Veintiuno.

Arrom, J.J., and I. Rouse. 1992. Comments on the three woodcarvings from St Anne's, Jamaica. Letter on file at Jamaica National Heritage Trust.

Asprey, G.F., and R.G. Robbins. 1953. The vegetation of Jamaica. *Ecology Monographs* 23, no. 4: 359–412.

Atkinson, L. 2002. Jamaican cave art: An overview. Paper presented at the Archaeological Society of Jamaica symposium Current Research in Jamaican Archaeology, Kingston, April 25.

———. 2003. Jamaican Redware revisited. Paper presented at the Archaeological Society of Jamaica symposium Zemis, Yabbas and Pewter: The Diversity of Jamaican Archaeology, Kingston, 3 April.

Bennett, J.P. 1989. *Arawak/English Dictionary*. Georgetown: Walter Roth Museum of Anthropology.

Blake, E. 1895. The Norbrook kitchen midden. *American Antiquarian Society*, n.s., no. 9: 283.

Bourne, E.G. 1906. Columbus, Ramon Pane and the beginning of American anthropology. *Proceedings of the American Antiquarian Society*, n.s., no. 17: 310–48.

Bretting, P. 1983a. Jamaica's flowering plants: the five endemic genera. *Jamaica Journal* 16, no. 1: 20–23.

———. 1983b. Jamaica's flowering plants: the five endemic genera. *Jamaica Journal* 16, no. 2: 49.

Bullen, R.P. 1974. Certain petroglyphs of the Antilles. *Proceedings of the Fifth International Congress for the Study of Pre-Columbian Cultures of the Lesser Antilles, Antigua, 1973*: 94–109.

Bullen, R.P., and A.K. Bullen. 1974. Inferences from Cultural Diffusion to Tower Hill, Jamaica, and Cupercoy Bay, St Martin. *Proceedings of the Fifth International Congress for the Study of Pre-Columbian Cultures of the Lesser Antilles, Antigua, 1973:* 48–60.

Butt, A.J. 1956. Ritual blowing. *Man* 56: 49–55.

Carey, M.W. 1975. The rock iguana, *Cyclura pinguis*, on Anegada, British Virgin Islands, with notes on *Cyclura ricordi* and *Cyclura cornuta* on Hispaniola. *Bulletin Florida State Museum Biological Science* 19, no. 4: 191.

Carneiro, R. 1978. The knowledge and use of rain forest trees by the Kuikuru Indians of central Brazil. In *The Nature and Status of Ethnobotany*, ed. R. Ford. Ann Arbor, Michigan: Museum of Anthropology, University of Michigan.

Carr, A.F. 1952. *Handbook of Turtles of the United States, Canada, and Baja California*. New York: Cornell University Press.

Centro de Estudios Avanzados de Puerto Rico y El Caribe. 1987. *Exposician de Esculturas de los Indios Tainos*. San Juan: Centro de Estudios Avanzados de Puerto Rico y El Caribe.

Chace, F.A., Jr., and H.H. Hobbs, Jr. 1969. Freshwater and terrestrial decapod crustaceans of the West Indies with special reference to Dominica. Bredin-Archbold Smithsonian Biological Survey of Dominica. *Smithsonian Institution Bulletin* 292: 123–24, 194–202.

Chanca, D.A. 1932. Letter to the city of Sevilla. London: Hakluyt Society.

Clarke, C. 1974. *Jamaica in Maps*. London: Hodder & Stoughton.

Claypole, W.A. 1973. The settlement of the Liguanea Plain between 1655 and 1673.

Jamaican Historical Review 10: 7–15.

Collins and Longman Atlas for Jamaica and the Western Caribbean. 1978. Hong Kong: Collins and Longman: 10–15.

Columbus, C. 1969. *The Four Voyages of Christopher Columbus*. London: Penguin Books.

Cotter, C.S. 1970. Sevilla la Nueva: The story of excavation. *Jamaica Journal* 4, no. 2: 15–22.

———. n.d. Field notes of excavations at Sevilla la Nueva 1953–1968.

Crosby, A.W. 1972. *The Columbian Exchange*. Westport: Greenwood Press.

Cundall, F. 1894a. Pre-Columbian Jamaica. *Journal of the Institute of Jamaica* 2, no. 1: 62.

———. 1894b. The Aborigines of Jamaica. *Journal of the Institute of Jamaica* 2, no. 1.

———. 1894c. The story of the life of Columbus and the discovery of Jamaica. *Journal of the Institute of Jamaica* 2, no. 1: 1–79.

———. 1895. Discovery of aboriginal Indian remains in Port Royal Mountains. *Journal of the Institute of Jamaica* 2, no. 2: 188.

———. 1939. *A Record of Investigations into the Subject of Arawak Remains in Jamaica*. Kingston: Institute of Jamaica.

Cundall, F., and J.L. Pietersz. 1919. *Jamaica under the Spaniards*. Kingston: Institute of Jamaica.

D'Anghera, P.M. 1970. *De Orbe Novo: The Eight Decades of Peter Martyr D'Anghera*. New York: Burt Franklin. (Orig. pub. 1912.)

Davis, D.D. 1988. Calibration of the ceramic period chronology for Antigua, West Indies. *Southeastern Archaeology*, no. 7: 52–60.

Deagan, K. 1978. Material assemblage of sixteenth-century Spanish Florida. *Historical Archaeology* 12: 25–50.

———. 1983. *Spanish St Augustine: The Archaeology of a Colonial Creole Community*. New York: Academic Press.

———. 1988. The archaeology of the Spanish contact period in the Caribbean. *Journal of World Prehistory* 2, no. 2: 187–233.

De Booy, T. 1913. Certain kitchen middens in Jamaica. *American Anthropologist* 15: 425–34. Reprinted in *Contributions from the Heye Museum*, no. 3, 1916.

De Wolf, M. 1953. Excavations in Jamaica. *American Antiquity* 18, no. 3: 230–38.

Descola, P. 1994. *In the Society of Nature*. Cambridge: Cambridge University Press.

Draper, G., and W.T. Horsfield. 1973. Blue schist metamorphism in Jamaica. Transactions of Second Congreso Latino-Americano de Geologia, Caracas, Venezuela.

Duerden, J.E. 1895. Discovery of aboriginal remains in Jamaica (letter). *Nature* 52: 173–74.

———. 1897. Aboriginal Indian remains in Jamaica. *Journal of the Institute of Jamaica* 2, no. 4: 1–51.

Eliade, M. 1974. *Shamanism: Archaic Techniques of Ecstasy*. Princeton: Princeton University Press.

Emerson, W.K., and M.K. Jacobson. 1976. *American Museum of Natural History: Guide to Shells*. New York: Alfred Knopf.

Esteva-Fabregat, C. 1995. *Mestizaje in Ibero-America*. Trans. by John Wheat. Tucson:

University of Arizona Press.

Ewan, C.R. 1991. *From Spaniards to Creole*. Tuscaloosa: University of Alabama Press.

Faerron, J. 1985. The Tainos of Hispaniola. Part 1. *Archaeology Jamaica* 85, nos. 1–2: 1–4.

Fernández de Oviedo, G. 1959. *Natural History of the West Indies*. Trans. and ed. S.A. Stoudemaire. University of North Carolina Studies in the Romance Languages and Literature, No. 32. Chapel Hill: University of North Carolina Press.

Fewkes, J.W. 1907. *The Aborigines of Puerto Rico and Neighbouring Islands*. American Bureau of Ethnology Annual Report, no. 25. Washington, DC: American Bureau of Ethnology.

———. 1922. *A Prehistoric Island Culture of the Americas*. American Bureau of Ethnology Annual Report, no. 34. Washington, DC: American Bureau of Ethnology,: 35–281.

Flower, W.H. 1895. On recently discovered remains of the aboriginal inhabitants of Jamaica. *Nature* 52: 607–8.

Frink, D.S. 1994. The oxidizable carbon ratio (OCR): A proposed solution to some of the problems encountered with radiocarbon data. *North American Archaeologist* 15, no. 1: 17–29.

Gerbi, A. 1986. *Nature in the New World: From Columbus to Oviedo*. Pittsburgh: University of Pittsburgh Press.

Goggin, J.M. 1968. *Spanish Maiolica in the New World*. Yale University Publications in Anthropology, no. 72. New Haven: Yale University Press.

Gollán, J.A.P., and I. Gordillo. 1994. Vilca/Uturuncu: Hacia una arqueología del uso alucinógenos en las sociedades prehispánicas de los Andes del Sur. *Cuicuilco* 1, no. 1: 99–140.

Green, G.W. 1977. Structure and stratigraphy of the Wagwater Belt, Kingston, Jamaica. *Overseas Geology and Mineral Resources* 48: 1–21.

Gupta, A., and R. Ahmad. 2000. Urban steeplands in the tropics: An environment of accelerated erosion. *Geojournal* 84, no. 1.

Hall, E.R. 1981. *Mammals of North America*. New York: John Wiley & Sons.

Hallowell, A.I. 1969. Ojibwa ontology, behavior, and world view. In *Primitive Views of the World*, ed. S. Diamond. New York: Columbia University Press.

Harris, P.O. 1991. A Paleo-Indian stemmed point from Trinidad, West Indies. *Proceedings of the Fourteenth Congress of the International Association of Caribbean Archaeologists*, ed. A. Cummins and P. King. Bridgetown: Barbados Museum and Historical Society: 73–93.

Hastorf, C.A., and V.S. Propper, eds. 1988. *Current Paleoethnobotany: Analytical Methods and Cultural Interpretation of Archaeological Plant Remains*. Chicago and London: University of Chicago Press.

Helms, M.W. 1986. Art styles and interaction spheres in Central America and the Caribbean: Polished black wood in the Greater Antilles. *Journal of Latin American Lore* 12, no. 1: 25–43.

———. 1988. *Ulysses' Sail: An Ethnographic Odyssey of Power, Knowledge and Geographical Distance*. Princeton: Princeton University Press.

Hendry, M.D. 1978. Historical evidence of shoreline evolution for the Palisadoes, Kingston, Jamaica. *Journal of the Geological Society of Jamaica* 17: 39–48.

Hennessy, A. 1993. The nature of the conquest and the conquistadors. In *The Meetings of*

Two Worlds: Europe and the Americas 1492–1650, ed. Warwick Bray. Oxford: Oxford University Press: 5–36.

Heyden. D. 1993. El árbol en el mito y el símbolo. *Estudios de Cultura Náhuatl* 23: 201–19.

Highway 2000 Supplement. 2002. Development Bank of Jamaica. *Daily Gleaner*, 24 April.

Hill, V.G. 1978. Distribution and potential: Clays in Jamaica. *Jamaica Journal* 12: 64–75.

Hoese, H.D., and R.H. Moore. 1977. *Fishes of the Gulf of Mexico.* Texas: Texas A & M University Press.

Howard, R.R. 1950. The archaeology of Jamaica and its position in relation to circum-Caribbean culture. PhD diss., Yale University.

———. 1956. The archaeology of Jamaica: A preliminary survey. *American Antiquity* 22, no. 1: 45–59.

———. 1965. New perspectives on Jamaican archaeology. *American Antiquity* 31: 250–55.

Hughes, I.G., ed. 1973. The mineral resources of Jamaica. Geology Survey Department, Mines and Geology Division, Kingston. Bulletin no. 8: 1–79.

Hugh-Jones, S. 1979. *The Palm and the Pleiades.* Cambridge: Cambridge University Press.

Humfrey, M. 1975. *Seashells of the West Indies. A Guide to the Marine Molluscs of the Caribbean.* New York: William Collins Sons.

Iverson, J.B. 1979. Behavior and ecology of the rock iguana *Cyclura carinata*. *Bulletin of the Florida State Museum of Biological Sciences* 24, no. 3: 175.

Jane, C., trans. and ed. 1988. *The Four Voyages of Columbus.* New York: Dover.

Johnson, K.F. 1976. Supplement on Cinnamon Hill: Faunal analysis. *Archaeology Jamaica* 76, no. 1: 9–18.

Johnson, T.H. 1988. *Biodiversity and Conservation in the Caribbean: Profiles of Selected Islands.* ICBP Monograph No. 1. Cambridge: International Council for Bird Preservation.

Joyce, T.A. 1907. Prehistoric antiquities from the Antilles in the British Museum. *Journal of the Royal Anthropological Institute* 37: 402–19.

Karsten, R. 1964. Studies in the religion of the South American Indians east of the Andes. *Commentations Humanarum Litterarum* 29, no. 1.

Kaye, Q. 1999. Intoxicant use in the prehistoric Caribbean with particular reference to spouted inhaling bowls. *Papers from the Institute of Archaeology* 10: 55–75.

Keegan, W.F. 1992. *The People Who Discovered Columbus: The Prehistory of the Bahamas.* Gainesville: University Press of Florida.

———. 2000. West Indian archaeology 3: Ceramic age. *Journal of Archaeological Research* 8: 135–67.

———. 2002. Archaeology at Paradise Park, Westmoreland. *Archaeology Jamaica*, n.s., no. 14: 2–6.

———. 2003. Islands of chaos. In *The Late Ceramic Age in the Eastern Caribbean*, ed. C. Hofman and A. Delpuech. Oxford: BAR International Series.

Kenward, H.K., A.R. Hall, and A.K.G. Jones. 1980. A tested set of techniques for the extraction of plant and animal macrofossils from waterlogged archaeological deposits. *Science and Archaeology* 42: 3–15.

Kenward, H.K., and F. Large. 1998. Recording the preservational conditions of archaeological insect assemblages. *Environmental Archaeology* 2. Oxford: Oxbow Books: 49–60.

Kerchache, J, ed. 1994. *L'art des sculpteurs Tainos chefs d'oeuvre des Grandes Antilles Précolombiennes*. Paris: Paris- Musées.

Khudoley, K.M., and A.A. Meyerhoff. 1971. *Palaeogeography and geological history of the Greater Antilles*. Geological Society of America Memoir 129.

Kus, S.M. 1983. The social representation of space: Dimensioning the cosmological and the quotidian. In *Archaeological Hammers and Theories*, ed. J.A. Moore and A.S. Keene, 278–300. New York: Academic Press.

Lalor, G.C. 1995. *A Geochemical Atlas of Jamaica*. Kingston: Canoe Press.

Las Casas, B. 1992. *A Short Account of the Destruction of the Indies*. London: (Harmondsworth) Penguin. (Orig. pub. 1951.)

Lechler, G.P. 2000. Chancery Hall, St, Andrew: A recently discovered Taino site on the outskirts of Kingston. *Archaeology Jamaica*, n.s., no. 12.

Lechtman, H. 1993. Technologies of power: The Andean case. In *Configurations of Power*, ed. J.S. Henderson and P.J. Netherly, 244–80. Ithaca: Cornell University Press.

Lee, J.W. 1966. Current activity. *Archaeology Jamaica* 66, no. 6: 1.

———. 1967a. Current activity. *Archaeology Jamaica* 67, no. 7: 1.

———. 1967b. Current activity. *Archaeology Jamaica* 67, no. 12: 1.

———. 1970a. Current activity. *Archaeology Jamaica* 70, no. 4: 2.

———. 1970b. The Coleraine site (Y-19) St Mary. *Archaeology Jamaica* 70, no. 1: 2.

———. 1970c. Iter Boreale (Y-14) St Mary. *Archaeology Jamaica* 70 no. 3: 1–2.

———. 1971. Site survey. *Archaeology Jamaica* 71, no. 2: 2.

———. 1972a. Site survey. *Archaeology Jamaica* 72, no. 2: 2.

———. 1972b. Naggo Head. *Archaeology Jamaica* 72, no. 4: 1.

———. 1974. Petroglyphs and pictographs. *Archaeology Jamaica* 74, no. 4.

———. 1976a. Jamaican Redware. *Archaeology Jamaica* 76, no. 2: 1–5.

———. 1976b. Society activities. *Archaeology Jamaica* 76, no. 3: 1.

———. 1978a. Fish Net Sinkers. *Archaeology Jamaica* 78, no. 1: 1–5.

———. 1978b. Site survey. *Archaeology Jamaica* 78, no. 2: 5.

———. 1978c. The Jamaican Redware culture. Paper presented at Simposio sobre Problemas de la Arqueologia Antillana, Ponce, Puerto Rico, 1978.

———. 1980a. Arawak burens. *Archaeology Jamaica* 80, no. 2: 1–11.

———. 1980b. Jamaican Redware. *Proceedings of the Eighth International Congress for the Study of Pre-Columbian Cultures of the Lesser Antilles, St Kitts, 1979*: 597–609.

———. 1982. The Mountain River cave (SC-1), St Catherine, Jamaica. *Archaeology Jamaica* 82, no. 2: 10–13.

———. 1983a. Site survey. *Archaeology Jamaica* 83, no. 1: 9.

———. 1983b. Adornos, Jamaica and Caribbean – Figure 2d. *Archaeology Jamaica* 83, no. 2.

———. 1984. Field trips. *Archaeology Jamaica* 84, no. 4: 41.

———. 1985a. Activities. *Archaeology Jamaica* 85, nos. 1–2: 5.

———. 1985b. Activities. *Archaeology Jamaica* 85, nos. 3–4: 5.

———. 1991. Dr James W. Lee's articles and papers published in *Archaeology Jamaica*. *Archaeology Jamaica*, n.s., no. 3: 11–12.

Lehmann, H. 1951. Un 'duho' de la civilisation Taino au Musée de l'homme. *Journal de la société des Américanistes*, n.s., 40: 153–61, plates 1–3.

Lester, S. 1958. Jamaican treasures in London. *The West Indian Review* 4, no. 30.

Lévi-Strauss, C. 1969. *The Savage Mind*. London: Weidenfeld & Nicolson.

Lewis, P. 1994. Probable tree identities of Taino sculptures. Letter to Dorrick Gray, Jamaica National Heritage Trust, 22 June 1994. University of the West Indies Herbarium, Mona, Jamaica.

Long, E. 1774. *History of Jamaica*. London: T. Lowndes.

Longley, G. C. 1914. Kitchen middens of Jamaica. *American Museum Journal* 14: 296–98.

López-Baralt, M. 1985. *El Mito Taíno: Raiz y Proyección en la Amazonia Continental*, rev. ed. Río Piedras: Ediciones Huracan.

Lovén, S. 1932. *Stone Dart Points from the District of Old Harbour, Jamaica*. Göteborg: Erlanders Boktryckerie Aktiebolag, 1932.

———. 1935. *Origins of the Tainan Culture, West Indies*. Göteborg: Erlanders Boktryckerie Aktiebolag, 1935.

MacCormack, R.C. 1898. Indian remains in Vere, Jamaica. *Journal of the Institute of Jamaica* 2, no. 5: 744–48.

Matley, C.A. 1951. *Geology and Physiography of the Kingston District, Jamaica*. London: Crown Agents of the Colonies.

McDonald, C. 1993. Report on visit to Chancery Hall. JNHT Files.

McEwan, B.G. 1982. Faunal remains from Sevilla Nueva, Jamaica. Unpublished report. Gainesville, Florida: Florida State Museum.

———. 1995. Spanish precedents and domestic life in Puerto Real: The archaeology of two hispanic homesites. In *Puerto Real: The Archaeology of a Sixteenth-Century Spanish Town in Hispaniola*, ed. Kathleen Deagan, 195–230. Gainesville: University Press of Florida.

McKusick, M. 1959. The distribution of ceramic styles in the Lesser Antilles, West Indies. PhD diss., Yale University.

McManamon, F. 2000. Archaeological messages and messengers. *Public Archaeology* 1. no. 1.

———. 1977a. Part 3: Bellevue site, K-13 – analysis of mollusc shells. *Archaeology Jamaica* 77, no. 1: 8–9.

———. 1977b. The Bellevue site, K-13 – analysis of mollusc shell. *Archaeology Jamaica* 77, no. 3: 1–9.

———. 1980. The Rodney's House site: A preliminary report on the April 1979 excavation. *Archaeology Jamaica* 80, no. 4: 1–16.

Medhurst, C.W., and H. Clarke. 1976a. The Bellevue site. *Archaeology Jamaica* 76, no. 3: 3–23.

———. 1976b. The Bellevue site. *Archaeology Jamaica* 76, no. 4: 12–40.

Métraux, A. 1946. Indians of the Gran Chaco. In *The Handbook of South American Indians: The Marginal Tribes*, ed. J.H. Steward. Washington, DC: Smithsonian Institution.

Ministry of Agriculture. 1987. Jamaica: Country Environmental Profile. Government of Jamaica. Natural Resources Conservation Division and Ralph M. Field, Assoc., Inc.

Morbán Laucer, F. 1982. Interpretation of Jamaican pictographs. *Archaeology Jamaica* 82, no. 2: 13.

Morison, S.E. 1974. *The European Discovery of America: The Southern Voyages 1492–1616*. New York: Oxford University Press.

Moure, R.D., and M. Rivero de la Calle. 1996. *Art and Archaeology of Pre-Columbian Cuba*. Pittsburgh: University of Pittsburgh Press.

National Gallery of Jamaica. 1994. *Arawak Vibrations: Homage to the Jamaican Taino*. Kingston: National Gallery of Jamaica and the Jamaica National Heritage Trust.

Natural Resources Conservation Authority/National Environmental Planning Agency. 2001. *Towards a National Strategy and Action Plan on Biological Diversity in Jamaica*. Green paper no. 3/01. Jamaica: Ministry of the Land and Environment.

Naxon, R.M. 1993. *The Nature of Shamanism: Substance and Function of a Religious Metaphor*. Albany: State University of New York Press.

Nicholson, D.V. 1983. *The Story of the Arawaks in Antigua and Barbuda*. Antigua: Antigua Archaeology Society and Linden Press.

Old Harbour Bypass, North Coast Highway Project and Highway 2000 Projects. www.mtw.gov.jm/projects.

Oliver, J.R. 1989. The archaeological, linguistic, and ethnohistorical evidence for the expansion of Arawak into northwestern Venezuela and northeastern Colombia. PhD diss., University of Illinois, Urbana.

Oliver, W. 1983. Looking for conies. *Jamaica Journal* 16, no. 2.

Osborne, S.J., and J.W. Lee. 1976. Preliminary report on the Cinnamon Hill site (J-10). *Archaeology Jamaica* 76, no. 1: 1–7.

———. 1977. Skeletal material from Cinnamon Hill site (J-10). *Archaeology Jamaica* 77, no. 2: 1–2.

Osgood, C. 1942. The Ciboney culture of Cayo Redondo, Cuba. Yale University Publications in Anthropology. New Haven: Yale University Press.

Padron, F.M. 1952. *Jamaica Española*. Seville: Consejo Superior de Investigaciones Cientificas.

Pané, R. 1974. *Relacíon Acerca de las Antigüedades de los Indios*, 41–42. Mexico City: Siglo Vientiuno. Quoted in Stevens-Arroyo 1988, 59.

Parry, J.H., and P.M Sherlock. 1971. *Short History of the West Indies*. New York: St Martin's Press.

Paynter, R. 2000. Historical archaeology and the post-Columbian world of North America. *Journal of Archaeological Research* 8, no. 3: 169–217.

Pérez-Mallaína, P. 1998. *Spain's Men of the Sea: Daily Life on the Indies Fleets in the Sixteenth Century*, trans. Carla Rahn Phillips. Baltimore: Johns Hopkins University Press.

Perrins, W.A.T. 1981. The White Marl Arawak village site. *Archaeology Jamaica* 81, no. 2: 1–4.

Pollard, V. 1983. Frederic G. Cassidy dictionary-marker. *Jamaica Journal* 16, no. 2: 11–17.

Porro, A. 1994. Social organization and political power in the Amazonian Floodplain: The ethnohistorical sources. In *Amazonian Indians from Prehistory to Present*, ed. A.C. Roosevelt, 79–94. Tucson: University of Arizona Press.

Porter, A.R.D. 1990. *Jamaica: A Geological Portrait*. Kingston: Institute of Jamaica Publications.

Prior, J., and J. Tuohy. 1987. Fuel for Africa's fires. *New Scientist* 115: 48–51.

Proctor, G., and A. Oberli. 2002. The vascular flora of Long Mountain. Paper presented at the Long Mountain Symposium, University of the West Indies, January.

Raffaele, H., J. Wiley, O. Garrido, A. Keith, and J. Raffaele. 1998. *A Guide to the Birds of the West Indies*. Princeton: Princeton University Press.

Rainey, F.G. 1940. Porto Rican archaeology: Scientific survey of Porto Rico and the Virgin Islands. *New York Academy of Sciences* 18, no. 1.

———. 1941. Excavations in the Ft. Liberté Region, Haiti. Yale University Publications in Anthropology. New Haven: Yale University Press.

Randall, R.E. 1968. *Caribbean Reef Fishes*. Hong Kong: T.F.H. Publications.

Rashford, J. 1985. The cotton tree and the spiritual realm in Jamaica. *Jamaica Journal* 18, no. 1: 49–57.

———. 1991. Arawak, Spanish and African contributions to Jamaica's settlement vegetation. *Jamaica Journal* 24, no. 3: 17–23.

———. 1998. Human influence on the vegetation of Jamaica. In *A Reader in Caribbean Geography*, ed. David Barker, Carol Newby and Mike Morrissey, 37–43. Kingston: Ian Randle, 1998.

Reichard, A. 1904. Archaeological discoveries in Jamaica. *Globus* 86.

Reichel-Dolmatoff, G. 1961. Anthropomorphic figurines from Colombia, their magic and art. In *Essays in Pre-Columbian Art and Archaeology*, ed. S.K. Lothrop et al., 229–41. Cambridge: Harvard University Press.

———. 1975. *The Shaman and the Jaguar: A Study of Narcotic Drugs among the Indians of Colombia*. Philadelphia: Temple University Press.

———. 1981. Things of beauty replete with meaning: Metals and crystal in Colombian Indian cosmology. In *Sweat of the Sun, Tears of the Moon: Gold and Emerald Treasures in Colombia*, 17–33. Los Angeles: Terra Magazine Publications/Natural History Museum Alliance of Los Angeles County.

———. 1988. *Orfebrería y Chamanismo: Un Estudio Iconográfico del Museo del Oro*. Medellín: Compañía Litográfico Nacional.

Renfrew, C., and P. Bahn. 2000. *Archaeology: Theories, Methods, and Practice*. New York: Thames & Hudson.

Roe, P.G. 1982. *The Cosmic Zygote: Cosmology in the Amazon Basin*. New Brunswick, NJ: Rutgers University Press.

———. 1995. Myth–material cultural semiotics: prehistoric and ethnographic Guiana-Antilles. Paper presented at the ninety-fourth annual meeting of the American Anthropological Association, Washington, DC.

Roobol, M.J., and J.W. Lee. 1976. Petrography and source of some Arawak rock artefacts from Jamaica. *Proceedings of the Sixth International Congress for the Study of Pre-Columbian Culture of the Lesser Antilles, Guadeloupe, 1975*: 304–13.

Roobol, M.J., H. Petitjean Roget, and A.L. Smith. 1976. Mt. Pelée and the island population of Martinique. *Proceedings of the Sixth International Congress for the Study of Pre-Columbian Culture of the Lesser Antilles, Guadeloupe, 1975*: 46–53.

Roth, H.L. 1887. The aborigines of Hispaniola. *Journal of the Royal Anthropological Institute of Great Britain and Ireland* 16: 247–86.

Rouse, I. 1939. *Prehistory in Haiti: A Study in Method*. Yale University Publications in

Anthropology no. 21. New Haven: Yale University Press.

———. 1941. *Culture of the Ft. Liberté Region, Haiti*. Yale University Publications in Anthropology no. 24. New Haven: Yale University Press.

———. 1942. *Archaeology of the Mariabon Hills, Cuba*. Yale University Publications in Anthropology no. 26. New Haven: Yale University Press.

———. 1948. The Arawak. In *Handbook of South American Indians*, ed. J. H. Steward, 507–46. Vol. 4, Bulletin of the Bureau of American Ethnology, no. 142. Washington, DC.

———. 1951. Areas and periods of culture in the Greater Antilles. *Southwestern Journal of Anthropology* 7, no. 3: 248–65.

———. 1952. *Porto Rican Prehistory. Introduction: Excavations in the West and North*. Scientific Survey of Porto Rico and the Virgin Islands, no. 18. New York: New York Academy of Sciences: 307–460.

———. 1964. Prehistory of the West Indies. *Science* 144, no. 3618: 499–513.

———. 1972. *Introduction to Prehistory: A Systematic Approach*. New York: McGraw-Hill.

———. 1986. *Migrations in Prehistory: Inferring Population Movements from Cultural Remains*. New Haven: Yale University Press.

———. 1987. Whom did Columbus discover in the West Indies? In *On the Trail of Columbus*, ed. C.A. Hoffman. *American Archaeologist* (Ridgefield) 6, no. 2: 83–87.

———. 1992. *The Tainos: Rise and Decline of the People Who Greeted Columbus*. New Haven: Yale University Press.

———. 1996. History of archaeology in the Caribbean area. In *The History of Archaeology: An Encyclopaedia*, ed. T. Murray. New York: Garland Publishing.

Rouse, I., and L. Allaire. 1978. Caribbean. In *Chronologies in New World Archaeology*, ed. R. E. Taylor and C. Meighan, 431–81. New York: Academic Press.

Ruggles, C.L.N., and N.J. Saunders. 1993. The study of cultural astronomy. In *Astronomies and Cultures*, ed. C.L.N. Ruggles and N.J. Saunders, 1–31. Niwot: University Press of Colorado.

Sakai, S. 1996. Notes on the contemporary classification of Dermaptera and recent references on Dermaptera II. In *Taxonomy of the Dermaptera Proceedings of the Twentieth International Congress of Entomology*, ed. S. Sakai, 1–10. Tokyo: Seiroku Sakai.

Santos, A.L. 2001. Green Castle burials: Anthropological report. Unpublished report.

Sauer, C.O. 1966. *The Early Spanish Main*. Berkeley: University of California Press.

Saunders, N.J. 1988. Chatoyer: Anthropological reflections or archaeological mirrors. In *Recent Studies in Pre-Columbian Archaeology* 1, ed. N.J. Saunders and O. de Montemollin, 1–40. Oxford: British Archaeological Reports International Series 421.

Saunders, N.J., and D. Gray. 1996. Zemis, trees, and symbolic landscapes: Three Taino carvings from Jamaica. *Antiquity* 70: 270.

Scarre, C. ed. 1999. *The Times Archaeology of the World*. London: Times Books.

Scott, J.F. 1985. *The Art of the Taino from the Dominican Republic*. Gainesville: University Gallery, College of Fine Arts, University of Florida.

Scudder, S. 1992. Early Arawak subsistence strategies: The Rodney site of Jamaica. *Archaeology Jamaica*, n.s., no. 6: 28–43.

Seifriz, W. 1943. Plant life of Cuba. *Ecology Monographs* 13: 375–426.

Seigel, P.E. 1996. An interview with Irving Rouse. *Current Anthropology* 37: 671–89.

Senior, O. 1985. *A–Z on Jamaican Heritage*. Kingston: Heinemann.

Sherlock, P.M. 1939. *The Aborigines of Jamaica.* Kingston: Institute of Jamaica.

Silverberg, J., R.L. Vanderwal and E.S. Wing. 1972. *The White Marl Site in Jamaica.* Report of the 1964 Robert R. Howard Excavations. Milwaukee: Department of Anthropology, University of Wisconsin.

Sloane, H. 1707. *A Voyage to the Islands Madera, Barbados, Nieves, S. Christophers, and Jamaica.* 2 vols. London: B.M. for the author.

Standley, P.C. 1920–26. *Trees and Shrubs of Mexico.* Washington, DC: Smithsonian Press.

Stevens-Arroyo, A.M. 1988. *Cave of the Jagua: The Mythological World of the Tainos.* Albuquerque: University of New Mexico Press.

Sullivan, L.E. 1988. *Icanchu's Drum.* London: Macmillan.

Thomas, D.H. 1979. *Archaeology.* New York: Holt, Rinehart & Winston.

Tyndale-Biscoe, J.S. 1962. The Jamaica Arawak. *Jamaican Historical Review* 3, no. 3: 1–9.

Ucko, P., and G.W. Dimbleby. 1969. *The Domestication and Exploitation of Plants and Animals.* London: Gerald Duckworth.

Vanderwal, R.L. 1968a. The prehistory of Jamaica: A ceramic study. MA thesis, University of Wisconsin–Milwaukee.

———. 1968b. Problems of Jamaican pre-history. *Jamaica Journal* 2, no. 3.

Vega, B. 1987. Descubrimiento de la actual localización único *zemí* del algodón antillano aún existente. In *Santos, Shamans, y Zemies*, 1–16. Santo Domingo: Fundación Cultural Dominicana.

Veloz Maggiolo, M. 1997. The daily life of the Taíno people. In *Taíno: Pre-Columbian Art and Culture from the Caribbean*, ed. F. Bercht, E. Brodsky, J.A. Farmer and D. Taylor, 34–45. New York: Monacelli Press.

Veloz Maggiolo, M., and E.J. Ortega. 1996. Punta Cana y el origin de la agricultura en la isla de Santo Domingo. In *Ponencias del Primer Semimario de Arqueologia del Caribe*, ed. Marcio Veloz Maggiolo and Angel Caba Fuentes. República Dominicana: Museo Arqueológico Regional Altos de Chavón.

Walker, D.J.R. 1992. *Columbus and the Golden World of the Island Arawaks: The Story of the First Americans and their Caribbean Environment.* Kingston: Ian Randle.

Walker, E.D. 1975. *Mammals of the World*, 3rd ed. Baltimore: Johns Hopkins University Press.

Wallace, V. 1992. The socio-cultural life of Arawak Indians of Jamaica: An archaeological evaluation. *Archaeology Jamaica*, n.s., no. 6: 73–96.

Warmke, G.L., and R.T. Abbott. 1961. *Caribbean Seashells.* Pennsylvania: Livingston Publishing.

Watson, K. 1988. Amerindian cave art: Mountain River Cave, St Catherine. *Jamaica Journal* 21, no. 1: 13–20.

Watters, D.R. 1997. Maritime trade in the prehistoric Eastern Caribbean. In *The Indigenous People of the Caribbean*, ed. S.M. Wilson, 88–99. Gainesville: University Press of Florida.

Watters, D.R., and I. Rouse. 1989. Environmental diversity and maritime adaptations in the Caribbean area. In *Early Ceramic Population Lifeways and Adaptive Strategies in the Caribbean*, ed. P.E. Siegel, 129–44. Oxford: BAR International Series 506.

Weintraub, B. 1993. Geographica. *National Geographic Magazine* (September).

Wesler, K.W. 2001. *Excavations at Wickliffe Mounds.* Tuscaloosa: University of Alabama Press.

Weyl, R. 1966. *Geologie der Antillen*. Gebruder Borntraeger. Berlin-Nicolasse.

Wheeler, A., and A.K.G. Jones. 1989. *Fishes*. Cambridge Manuals in Archaeology. Cambridge: Cambridge University Press.

Wilbert, J. 1975. Eschatology in a participatory universe. In *Death and the Afterlife in Columbian America*, ed. E.P. Benson, 163–90. Washington, DC: Dumbarton Oaks.

———. 1977. Navigators of the winter sun. In *The Sea in the Pre-Columbian World*, 16–46. Washington, DC: Dumbarton Oaks.

———. 1985. The house of the swallow-tailed kite. Warao myth: The art of thinking in images. In *Animated Myths and Metaphors in South America*, ed. G. Urton, 145–82. Salt Lake City: University of Utah Press.

———. 1987. *Tobacco and Shamanism in South America*. New Haven: Yale University Press.

Williams, A.B. 1984. *Shrimps, Lobsters, and Crabs of the Atlantic Coast of the Eastern United States, Maine to Florida*. Washington, DC: Smithsonian Press.

Willis, R. 1976. The archaeology of sixteenth-century Nueva Cadiz. MA thesis, University of Florida.

Wilman, J.C. 1978. Rodney's House (S-5) St Catherine. *Archaeology Jamaica* 78, no. 3: 1–10.

———. 1979. Rodney's House: A postscript. *Archaeology Jamaica* 79, no. 4: 2–3.

———. 1983. Arawak site: Upton (A-43). *Archaeology Jamaica* 83, no. 3.

———. 1984. Arawak site: Upton (A-43) Part II. *Archaeology Jamaica* 84, no. 2: 2–3.

———. 1992. An archaeological investigation of the Upton site (A-43) St Ann, Jamaica. *Archaeology Jamaica*, n.s., no. 6: 17–27.

Wilson, S.M. 1986. The conquest of the Caribbean chiefdoms: Socio-political change on prehispanic Hispaniola. PhD diss., University of Chicago. Ann Arbor: University Microfilms, 1986.

———. 1990. *Hispaniola: Caribbean Chiefdoms in the Age of Columbus*. Tuscaloosa: University of Alabama Press.

———, ed. 1997a. *The Indigenous People of the Caribbean*. Gainesville: University Press of Florida.

———. 1997b. The Caribbean before European conquest: A chronology. In *Taíno: Pre-Columbian Art and Culture from the Caribbean*, ed. F. Bercht, E. Brodsky, J.A. Farmer and D. Taylor, 15–17. New York: Monacelli Press.

Wing, E.S. 1972. The White Marl Site in Jamaica. Report of the 1964 Robert R. Howard Excavation, 18–35. University of Wisconsin–Milwaukee: Department of Anthropology.

———. 1977. Use of animals by the people inhabiting the Bellevue site. *Archaeology Jamaica* 77, no. 1: 2–7.

———. 1991. Animal exploitation in prehistoric Barbados. In *Proceedings of the Fourteenth Congress of the International Association for Caribbean Archaeology, Barbados, 1989:* 360–67.

———. 1994. Manatee in Arawak diet. *Archaeology Jamaica*, n.s., 8: 4.

Wing, E.S., and A.B. Brown. 1979. *Paleonutrition*. New York: Academic Press.

Wing, E.S., and C.W. Medhurst. 1977. The Bellevue site (K-13). *Archaeology Jamaica* 77, no. 1: 2–9.

Wood, P.A. 1976. The evolution of drainage in the Kingston area. *Journal of the Geological Society of Jamaica* 15: 1–6.

Woodward, R. 1988. The Charles Cotter collection: A study of the ceramic and faunal remains from Sevilla la Nueva. MA thesis, Texas A & M University.

Wright, I. 1921. The early history of Jamaica 1511–1536. *English Historical Review* 36: 70–95.

Yeager, T.J. 1989. Encomienda or slavery? The Spanish Crown's choice of labour organization in sixteenth-century Spanish America. *Journal of Economic History* 50: 842–59.

Supplemental Biliography

Aarons, G.A. 1988. The Mountain River cave. *Jamaica Journal* 21, no. 3: 21.

Alegría, R.E. 1985. Christopher Columbus and the treasure of the Taino Indians of Hispaniola. *Jamaica Journal* 18, no. 1: 2–11.

Armstrong, D. 1990. *The Old Village and the Great House*. Chicago: University of Illinois Press and University of Chicago Press.

Atkinson, L. 1998. The Tainos: The aborigines of Jamaica – A research text. Unpublished manuscript.

———. 2003. The distribution of the Taino cave art sites in Jamaica. *Proceedings of the Nineteenth International Congress for Caribbean Archaeology, Aruba, 2001*: 300–312.

Auld, M. 2000. Tainos of Jamaica: The myth of extinction. *United Confederation of Taino People Newsletter*, 4 April. www.indigenouspeople.org/natlit/uctp/UCTP_ Newsletter_ April_04.html

Bercht, F., E. Brodsky, J. A. Farmer and D. Taylor, eds. 1997. *Taíno: Pre-Columbian Art and Culture from the Caribbean*. New York: The Monacelli Press, 1997.

Black, C.V. 1957. Historical notes on the food plants of Jamaica. *The Farmers' Food Manual: A Recipe Book for the West Indies*. Kingston: Jamaica Agricultural Society and Glasgow: Robert Maclehoses: 335–40.

Braunholtz, H.J. 1970. *Sir Hans Sloane and Ethnography*. London: Shenval Press.

Browne, P. 1756. *The Civil and Natural History of Jamaica*. London: Institute of Jamaica.

Campbell, S. 1974. Bush teas a cure all: Corollary to folklore and food habits. *Jamaica Journal* 8, no. 2 and 3: 60–65.

Carnegie, J. 1979. The Institute of Jamaica: A century of culture. *Americas* 31: 11–12.

Cotter, C.S. 1954. A comment on the Windsor site, Jamaica. *American Antiquity* 20: 2.

Cundall, F. 1934. *The Aborigines of Jamaica*. Kingston: Institute of Jamaica.

Dadea, R. 1981. Porcacchi Map text translation. *Archaeology Jamaica* 81, no. 4.

Dams, L. 1980. *Prehistoric Art*. Vol. 4, *Lexicon Universal Encyclopaedia*. New York: Lexicon Publications, 1980.

Dehring, P., and J.K. Southerland. The Bellevue Estate archaeological field season May–June 1991. *Archaeology Jamaica*, n.s., 4: 27–30.

Downer, A., and R. Sutton. 1990. *Birds of Jamaica: A Photographic Field Guide*. Cambridge: Cambridge University Press.

Ebanks, R. 1997. *Heritage Resource Survey of the North Coast Highway Development Project: Segment One – Negril to Montego Bay*. JNHT files.

Edwards, A. 2001. The road to nowhere. *Daily Gleaner*, 28 February.

Environmental Solutions Limited. 1997. Environmental impact assessment: Beaches Whitehouse Resort, Westmoreland – Final report. Prepared for Mortimer and Associates.

Eyre, A. 1996. The tropical rainforests of Jamaica. *Jamaica Journal* 26, no. 1: 26–37.

Faerron, J. 1985. The Tainos of Hispaniola (Part 2). *Archaeology Jamaica* 85, nos. 3–4: 1–6.

Farr, T.H. 1984. Land animals of Jamaica: Origins and endemism. *Jamaica Journal* 17, no. 1: 38–48.

Fincham, A.G. 1997. *Jamaica Underground: The Caves, Sinkholes, and Underground Rivers of the Island*, 2nd ed. Kingston: The Press, University of the West Indies.

Fincham, A.G., and A.M. Fincham. 1998. The Potoo Hole pictographs: A preliminary report on a new Amerindian cave site in Clarendon, Jamaica. *Jamaica Journal* 26, no. 3: 2–6.

Gleaner Company. 1985. *The Gleaner Geography and History of Jamaica*, 22nd ed. Kingston: Gleaner Company.

Government of Jamaica. 1998. *Cultural Heritage*. Technical Report 7, Multisectoral preinvestment programme: South Coast sustainable development study. Sir William Halcrow and Partners.

Handler, J. 1977. The "Bird Man": A Jamaican Arawak wooden "idol". *Jamaica Journal* 11, nos. 3–4: 25.

Ingram, K. 1975. *Manuscripts Relating to Commonwealth Caribbean Countries in United States and Canadian Repositories*. Belgium: Caribbean Universities Press/Bowker Publishing.

Joyce, T.A. 1916. *Central American and West Indian Archaeology*. London: Philip Lee Warner.

Krieger, H.W. 1931. Aboriginal Indian pottery of the Dominican Republic. *US National Museum Bulletin* 156.

Lee, J.W. 1981. Field trip to St Elizabeth petroglyphs. *Archaeology Jamaica* 81, no. 1.

Lewis, C.B. 1967. History and the Institute. *Jamaica Journal* 1, no. 1: 4.

Mattson, P.H., and L. Glover. 1960. Stratigraphic distribution of detrital quartz in the pre-Oligocene rocks of south-central Puerto Rico. United States Geological Survey Professional Paper 400, B: 367–68.

Nicholas, G. 1980. Caves. *Lexicon Universal Encyclopaedia*. New York: Lexicon Publications.

Rashford, J. 1982. Roots and fruits: Social class and intercropping in Jamaica. PhD diss., City University of New York.

Reichel-Dolmatoff, G. 1971. *Amazonian Cosmos: The Sexual and Religious Symbolism of the Tukano Indians*. Chicago: University of Chicago Press.

Rosenberg, M. 2000. History in a rich soil. http://abcnews.go.com/sections/travel/DailyNews/jamaica000706.htm 1

Rouse, I. 1982. Ceramic and religious development in the Greater Antilles. *Journal of New World Archaeology* 5, no. 2: 45–55.

Sangster, A.W. 2001. Highway 2000. *Daily Gleaner,* 29 January.

Seifriz, W. 1972. *The White Marl Site in Jamaica*. Report of the 1964 Robert R. Howard Excavation. Milwaukee: Department of Anthropology, University of Wisconsin.

Smith, G.C. 1995. Indians and Africans at Puerto Real. In *Puerto Real: The Archaeology of a Sixteenth-Century Spanish Town in Hispaniola*, ed. Kathleen Deagan, 335–74. Gainesville: University Press of Florida.

Stokes, B. 2002. Settlement patterns and the placement of Jamaican Taino chiefdoms in a Greater Antilles context: Theory and practical method. Paper presented at the Archaeological Society of Jamaica symposium Current Research in Jamaican Archaeology, Kingston, Jamaica, 25 April.

Thompson, D.A., P.K. Bretting and M. Humphreys, eds. 1986. *Forests of Jamaica*. Kingston: Jamaican Society of Scientists and Technologists.

Tyndale-Biscoe, J.S. 1954. Arawak specimens from some middens of Jamaica. *Bulletin of the Jamaica Historical Society* 5, no. 10.

Vanderwal, R.L. 1967. Summer Excavation Programme. *Archaeology Jamaica* 67, no. 8: 2–3.

Ven der Veen, M., and N.R.J. Fieller. 1982. Sampling seeds. *Journal of Archaeological Science* 9, no. 3: 287–98.

Walters, S. 1994. Site visitation report: Chancery Hall (Phase II) St Andrew. JNHT files.

———. 1996. Chancery Hall Phase II report. JNHT files.

———. 1998. Beaches Whitehouse Resort report. JNHT files.

Wassén, S.H. 1967. Anthropological survey of the use of South American snuffs. In *Ethnopharmacologic Search for Psychoactive Drugs*, 233–89. Washington, DC: US Government Printing Office. Public Health Service Publication 1645.

Wilman, J.C. 1981. Additional comments by J.C. Wilman. *Archaeology Jamaica* 81, no. 1: 1–2.

Woodley, J.D. 1968. A history of the Jamaican fauna. *Jamaica Journal* 2, no. 3: 14–20.

Wright, R.M., and W.R. Dickinson. 1972. Provenance of Eocene volcanic sandstones in east Jamaica: A preliminary note. *Caribbean Journal of Science* 12: 107–13.

Lesley-Gail Atkinson is Archaeologist, Archaeology Division, Jamaica National Heritage Trust, Jamaica.

Philip Allsworth-Jones is Senior Lecturer, Department of History and Archaeology, University of the West Indies, Mona, Jamaica.

Contributors

Anthony Gouldwell is a technician with the Environmental Laboratories, School of Archaeology and Ancient History University of Leicester, United Kingdom.

Dorrick Gray is Deputy Technical Director of Archaeology, Archaeology Division, Jamaica National Heritage Trust, Jamaica.

William F. Keegan is Associate Curator of Anthropology and Associate Professor of Anthropology, Florida Museum of Natural History, Department of Anthropology, University of Florida, United States.

Gerald C. Lalor is Director General, International Centre for Environmental and Nuclear Sciences, University of the West Indies, Mona, Jamaica.

George Lechler is Technical Director, Explosive Sales and Services, Jamaica.

James W. Lee is a geologist and the founder and former president of the Archaeological Society of Jamaica, now based in Vancouver, British Columbia, Canada.

Wendy A. Lee is an environmental educator with the St Ann Environment Protection Agency, Jamaica.

Simon F. Mitchell is Lecturer, Department of Geography and Geology, University of the West Indies, Mona, Jamaica.

Andrea Richards is Assistant Archaeologist, Archaeology Division of the Jamaica National Heritage Trust, Jamaica.

Norma Rodney-Harrack is a potter and Lecturer, Edna Manley College of the Visual and Performing Arts, Jamaica.

Esther Z. Rodrigues is Inventory and Database Officer, Jamaica Bauxite Institute, Jamaica.

M. John Roobol, is a consultant geologist, New Saudi Geological Survey, Jeddah, Saudi Arabia.

Nicholas J. Saunders is Lecturer, Institute of Archaeology, University College of London, United Kingdom.

Sylvia Scudder is Senior Biologist and Collections Manager, University of Florida Museum of Natural History Department of Anthropology, University of Florida, United States.

Mitko Vutchkov is Senior Research Fellow, International Centre on Nuclear Sciences, University of the West Indies, Jamaica.

Selvenious Walters is Senior Archaeologist, Archaeology Division, Jamaica National Heritage Trust, Jamaica.

Jane Webster is Lecturer, School of Archaeology and Ancient History, University of Leicester, United Kingdom.

Kit Wesler is Professor, Murray State University, Kentucky, United States.

Robyn Woodward is a PhD candidate, Simon Fraser University, Burnaby, British Columbia, Canada.

Robert Young is Senior Lecturer, School of Archaeology and Ancient History, University of Leicester, United Kingdom.

www.ingramcontent.com/pod-product-compliance
Lightning Source LLC
Chambersburg PA
CBHW080733300426
44114CB00019B/2573